THE CAMBRIDGE COMPANION TO MANGA AND ANIME

In recent years, manga and anime have attracted increasing scholarly interest beyond the realm of Japanese studies. This Companion takes a unique approach, committed to exploring both the similarities and differences between these two distinct but interrelated media forms. Firmly based in Japanese sources, it offers a lively and accessible introduction, exploring the local contexts of manga and anime production, distribution, and reception in Japan, as well as their global impact. Chapters examine common characteristics such as visuals, voice, serial narrative, and characters, while also highlighting distinct challenges and histories. Thus, the volume provides both a basis for further research in this burgeoning field and a source of inspiration for those new to the topic.

Jaqueline Berndt is a professor in Japanese culture at Stockholm University. She previously taught comics theory at Kyoto Seika University, Japan. Her main academic work is in manga studies and anime research, approached from the perspective of media aesthetics. She has also directed exhibitions on manga in art-historical contexts.

A complete list of books in the series is at the back of the book.

T0372479

THE CAMBRIDGE
COMPANION TO
MANGA AND ANIME

EDITED BY
JAQUELINE BERNDT
Stockholm University

CAMBRIDGE
UNIVERSITY PRESS

Shaftesbury Road, Cambridge CB2 8EA, United Kingdom

One Liberty Plaza, 20th Floor, New York, NY 10006, USA

477 Williamstown Road, Port Melbourne, VIC 3207, Australia

314–321, 3rd Floor, Plot 3, Splendor Forum, Jasola District Centre,
New Delhi – 110025, India

103 Penang Road, #05–06/07, Visioncrest Commercial, Singapore 238467

Cambridge University Press is part of Cambridge University Press & Assessment,
a department of the University of Cambridge.

We share the University's mission to contribute to society through the pursuit of
education, learning and research at the highest international levels of excellence.

www.cambridge.org
Information on this title: www.cambridge.org/9781316518793

DOI: 10.1017/9781009003438

First published 2024

A catalogue record for this publication is available from the British Library

Library of Congress Cataloging-in-Publication Data
NAMES: Berndt, Jaqueline, 1963– editor.
TITLE: The Cambridge companion to manga and anime / edited by Jaqueline
Berndt, Stockholms Universitet.
DESCRIPTION: Cambridge, United Kingdom ; New York, NY : Cambridge
University Press, 2024. | Includes bibliographical references and index.
IDENTIFIERS: LCCN 2024007247 | ISBN 9781316518793 (hardback) |
ISBN 9781009003438 (ebook)
SUBJECTS: LCSH: Manga (Comic books) – History and criticism. | Animated
films – Japan – History and criticism. | Animated television
programs – Japan – History and criticism. | LCGFT: Essays.
CLASSIFICATION: LCC PN6790.J3 C36 2024 | DDC 741.5/952–dc23/eng/20240515
LC record available at https://lccn.loc.gov/2024007247

ISBN 978-1-316-51879-3 Hardback
ISBN 978-1-009-00998-0 Paperback

CONTENTS

CONTENTS

CONTENTS

FIGURES

CONTRIBUTORS

JAQUELINE BERNDT is a professor in Japanese culture at Stockholm University, Sweden. Prior to that, she taught comics theory at Kyoto Seika University, Japan. Her main academic work is in manga studies and anime research, approached from the perspective of media aesthetics. She has also directed exhibitions on manga in art-historical contexts.

SELEN ÇALIK BEDIR is an assistant professor at Beykoz University, Istanbul, and the head of its Animation Department. Her research interests include audience engagement with popular narratives and transmedial narrative tendencies changing over time. She focuses especially on narration in anime and manga in comparison to video games under postdigital conditions.

BLANCHE DELABORDE is a manga translator, a French language instructor at Fukuoka University, and an independent researcher. Their research investigates narration in Japanese manga and European comics, particularly the materiality of writing in graphic narratives and the representation of the mind. Their PhD thesis (National Institute for Oriental Languages and Civilizations, Paris, 2019) focused on onomatopoeia in manga.

PATRICK W. GALBRAITH is an associate professor in the School of International Communication at Senshu University in Tokyo. His recent publications include *Otaku and the Struggle for Imagination in Japan* (2019), *Erotic Comics in Japan: An Introduction to Eromanga* (2020), and *The Ethics of Affect: Lines and Life in a Tokyo Neighborhood* (2021).

SHEUO HUI GAN is a lecturer at the Puttnam School of Film and Animation, LASALLE, University of the Arts, Singapore. Holding a PhD in human and environmental studies from Kyoto University (2008), she has published widely in English and Japanese. Her current book project is on Japanese animation directors.

BRYAN HIKARI HARTZHEIM is an associate professor of new media at Waseda University, Japan, specializing in anime, manga, and digital games. He is the coeditor of *The Franchising Era: Managing Media in the Digital Economy* (2019) and the author of *Hideo Kojima: Progressive Game Design from Metal Gear to Death Stranding* (2023).

MINORI ISHIDA is a professor in the Faculty of Economic Sciences at Niigata University, Japan, specialized in media aesthetics. She has published widely on voice and gender in anime, including *Anime to seiyū no mediashi* (*A Media History of Anime and Its Voice Actors*, 2020).

DALMA KÁLOVICS is an assistant professor at Kwansei Gakuin University, Japan. She approaches manga from a media-historical perspective with a special focus on materiality and publication formats in their relation to the visual structure of comics from 1960s children's magazines, rental books, and newspapers to current webtoons.

JOON YANG KIM is an associate professor in interdisciplinary Japanese studies at Niigata University, Japan, and associate editor for *animation: an interdisciplinary journal*. His recent interests include the film vectors and ideologized kinesthetics of animation, as well as anime's archived intermediate materials and their potential remediation with the effect of hypermediacy.

BON WON KOO is an assistant professor in the Manga Faculty at Kyoto Seika University. She teaches the praxis and theory of drawing manga. Her research interests are manga expression and the reading process, as well as the manga market and production process in and outside Japan.

OLGA KOPYLOVA is an assistant professor at the Graduate School of Arts and Letters, Tohoku University, Japan. Her research is informed by comparative media studies and adaptation theory, addressing issues of visual style, material connections between media forms, and the labor of creative workers involved in the production of transmedia franchises in Japan.

DARIO LOLLI is an assistant professor in Japanese and visual culture at Durham University. A media scholar by training, his in-progress monograph investigates the ecologies of affect, creativity, and value established by anime franchises against the backdrop of global licensing. His work has been published in journals such as *Convergence, Media, Culture & Society*, and *Mechademia*.

KŌICHI MORIMOTO is a professor emeritus at the Graduate School of Arts and Letters at Tohoku University, Sendai, Japan. In addition to teaching literary theory in a broad sense, he has conducted various studies on fictional narratives, including manga, and has published widely in Japanese on narrative experience.

RENATO RIVERA RUSCA is a lecturer at Seijo University, Rikkyo University, Meiji University, and Okayama University, Japan. His teaching and research focus on

Japanese popular-culture production and consumption, in particular, animation, about which he has published numerous articles in English and Japanese. He is also involved in international coproductions of animated content.

DEBORAH SHAMOON is an associate professor in the Department of Japanese Studies at the National University of Singapore. She is the author of *Passionate Friendship: The Aesthetics of Girls' Culture in Japan* (2012), which traces the development of shōjo manga. Her next book will be on visual analysis of manga.

RONALD STEWART is a professor at Daito Bunka University, Japan. A member of the Japan Society for Studies in Cartoons and Comics since 2003, his research focuses primarily on manga history and Japanese cartoon humor. He coauthored the wide-ranging introduction *Manga: A Critical Guide* (2023, with Shige (CJ) Suzuki).

STEVIE SUAN is an associate professor at Hosei University's Faculty of Global and Interdisciplinary Studies, Tokyo. Engaging with performance theory and media theory, he explores the media form of anime and its aesthetics. This is the topic of his book *Anime's Identity: Performativity and Form beyond Japan* (2021).

AKIKO SUGAWA-SHIMADA is a professor at Yokohama National University, Japan. She has contributed chapters to *Japanese Animation: East Asian Perspectives* (2013), *Shōjo across Media* (2019), *Contents Tourism and Pop Culture Fandom* (2020), and *Idology in Transcultural Perspective* (2021), and coedited the *Mechademia* issue on "2.5D Culture" (2023).

LUKAS R.A. WILDE is an associate professor in the Department of Art and Media Studies, Norwegian University of Science and Technology (NTNU), Trondheim. His research topics include comics/manga studies, transmedia narratology, generative AI-imagery, and pictorial semiotics. He is Vice President of the German Society for Comics Studies (ComFor).

ACKNOWLEDGMENTS

The Companion to Manga and Anime is the result of companionship with colleagues who have been professionally engaged in the academic study of manga and/or anime and who share, at least in part, my interest in approaching manga and anime from the perspective of media aesthetics, materialities, and a broad understanding of forms. Together we have done our best to meet the challenge posed by the Companion format, namely, to present up-to-date scholarship in an accessible way. I would like to express my heartfelt thanks to all authors for their commitment, collaboration, and patience. My gratitude extends to Amy Reigle Newland, who provided valuable support not only with her outstanding expertise in copyediting but also with astute "outsider" questions that helped me to address the blind spots of an "insider." I would further like to acknowledge the assistance that I have received from Bethany Thomas and her team at Cambridge University Press. I am truly grateful to Professor Laura Moretti for setting this whole project in motion, and I am looking forward to the new companionships it may induce.

NOTES ON JAPANESE NAMES, TERMS, AND TITLES

The romanization of Japanese words follows the modified Hepburn system. Extended vowels are marked by a macron, except for certain proper names (like Kodansha) and widely known place names (like Kyoto). The indication of newspapers follows the company's preferred spelling (for example, *Tokyo Shimbun* instead of *Tokyo Shinbun*). Anglicisms in globally renowned magazine titles, such as *Shōnen Jump*, are given in the English spelling, but not in romanized work titles (*Kidō senshi Gandamu* not *Kidō senshi Gundam*, *Shinseiki Evangerion* not *Evangelion*). The animation studio Tōei Dōga is indicated with a macron, even in the abbreviation Tōei, but without a macron in the English name that has been in use since 1998, Toei Animation. Japanese names are indicated in the Western order, first name preceding surname, except for a few older cases that include pen names (Toba Sōjō, Santō Kyōden, Kitazawa Rakuten, Tagawa Suihō). The ending -s that marks the plural form in English is omitted in the case of Japanese words. Japanese terms are italicized, with the exception of "manga," "anime," and other words that have already entered the English lexicon. Italics are, however, used for combinations such as *shōjo manga* and *story-manga*. Translated genre names like girls comics, ladies comics, boys love, and so on, are given without apostrophes in order to highlight their status as proper names. The capitalization of Japanese words is avoided, for example, in terms like "light novel," and also in the romanized indication of Japanese books and article titles, except for proper nouns. In the field of manga studies, titles of magazines are italicized, and titles of serials in such magazines are indicated in quotation marks ("..."), whereas the same work titles appear in italics if referring to book editions. In order to avoid confusion, work titles are italicized uniformly in this Companion.

CHRONOLOGY

1814–78	Publication of the copybook series *Hokusai Manga* (fifteen volumes).
1862	Charles Wirgman launches the illustrated journal *Japan Punch*, which leads to the emergence of cartoonesque "Punch Pictures" (*ponchi-e*).
1899	The *Frolicking Animals* scrolls (*Chōjū [jinbutsu] giga*) are designated a National Treasure.
1902	Kitazawa Rakuten starts a weekly comics page, "Current-Affairs Manga" (*Jiji Manga*), in the newspaper *Jiji Shinpō*.
1914	The all-female Takarazuka Revue is founded.
1923–40	Japanese translation of US cartoonist George McManus' *Bringing Up Father* serialized in Japanese newspapers.
1925	Launch of radio broadcasting in Japan.
1931–41	Children's manga *Norakuro* by Tagawa Suihō serialized in the magazine *Shōnen Kurabu*.
1938	The Japanese government publishes new guidelines for children's publications, condemning comics as vulgar.
1941	The four-level multiplane camera starts to be employed in Japanese animated film.
1945	Release of *Momotaro: Sacred Sailors* (*Momotarō: umi no shinpei*, 74 min., dir. Mitsuyo Seio, Shochiku), the first feature-length animated movie produced in Japan.
1946–48	Picture story (*emonogatari*) *Puchar in Wonderland* (*Fushigina kuni no Puchā*) by Fukujirō Yokoi serialized in magazine *Shōnen Club*.

1946–74   Serialization of the *yonkoma* comic strip *Sazae-san* in the daily newspaper *Asahi Shimbun*.

1947   Osamu Tezuka publishes *The New Treasure Island* (*Shintakarajima*), allegedly the founding instance of postwar *story-manga*.

1950   Disney's *Snow White and the Seven Dwarfs* (1937) finally screened in Japan.

1950s–70s   Postwar heyday of graphic narratives exclusively published for rental stores (*kashihon'ya*).

1952–68   Manga *Astro Boy* (*Tetsuwan Atomu*) by Osamu Tezuka serialized in the magazine *Shōnen*.

1953   Beginning of TV broadcasting in Japan.

1955   Launch of the girls manga magazines *Ribon* and *Nakayoshi*.

1956   Establishment of animation studio Tōei Dōga (renamed Toei Animation in 1998).

1957   Yoshihiro Tatsumi coins the term *gekiga* to distinguish graphic narratives for adults from "manga" as children's media.

1959   Mainstream publishers launch weekly manga magazines targeted at boys, *Weekly Shōnen Magazine* and *Weekly Shōnen Sunday*.

1961–73   Tezuka runs his own studio, Mushi Production.

1962   Dubbing Controversy (*Atereko Ronsō*) pertaining to voice acting.

1963   Launch of weekly manga magazines for girls, *Weekly Margaret* and *Shōjo Friend*.

1963–66   Airing of the first weekly TV anime series, *Astro Boy*, inducing the first "anime boom." Beginning of anime-typical *afureko* ("after recording").

1964–2002   Monthly manga magazine *Garo*, the epitome of Japanese alternative comics.

1966   Opening of the first manga museum, located in Saitama and dedicated to cartoonist Kitazawa Rakuten (1876–1955).

1967	The print run of *Weekly Shōnen Magazine* exceeds one million copies, followed by *Weekly Margaret* in 1969.
1968	Launch of *Big Comic*, the first manga magazine to target (male) adults.
1968	Launch of the boys manga magazine *Shōnen Jump*.
1968	Collected trade paperbacks of manga (*tankōbon*) emerge, establishing the successful magazine-to-paperback publishing system.
1974	Airing of the first TV anime based on location hunting in Europe and subsequently inducing "contents tourism," *Heidi, Girl of the Alps* (*Arupusu no shōjo Haiji*, dir. Isao Takahata, Zuiyō Eizō).
1975	First Comic Market (*Komike*, Comiket) held in Tokyo, by now the largest spot-sales event for material published outside the official commercial channels (*dōjinshi*) and a venue for secondary productions, or derivative works (*niji sōsaku*).
1977	The animated movie *Space Battleship Yamato* (*Uchū senkan Yamato*, dir. Toshio Masuda) incites the second "anime boom."
1978	Launch of specialist anime magazine *Animage* (Tokuma Publ.).
1978	The Hiroshima manga *Barefoot Gen* (*Hadashi no Gen*, 1973–87) by Keiji Nakazawa begins to be published in English translation (by Project Gen and Leonard Rifas' EduComics).
1979	Airing of the TV anime series *Mobile Suit Gundam* (dir. Yoshiyuki Tomino, Nippon Sunrise) as the first instance of a later franchise.
1980	Launch of the Gundam Plastic Model by toy-maker Bandai.
1980	The launch of *Be Love* magazine marks the beginning of the ladies comics as a genre.
1981	Launch of the monthly *Manga Time* as a specialist magazine for *yonkoma* comic strips.
1982–90	Serialization of the youth manga *Akira* by Katsuhiro Ōtomo (in *Young Magazine*). Release of the animated movie in 1988 (Tokyo Movie Shinsha).

1982–93	Commercial magazine *Anime Parody Comics* (renamed *Ani-Paro Comics*) promotes transformative works by fans.
1983	Publication of the first substantial introduction to Japanese comics in English, *Manga! Manga! The World of Japanese Comics* by Frederik L. Schodt (Kodansha International).
1983	First OVA (original video animation), a direct-to-video format in between the TV series and the theatrical feature film. Shift from VHS to DVD in the mid-1990s.
1983	First use of 3D computer animation in the anime *Golgo 13: The Professional* (dir. Osamu Dezaki, Tokyo Movie Shinsha).
1984	Animated movie *Nausicäa of the Valley of the Wind* (*Kaze no tani no Naushika*, dir. Hayao Miyazaki, Topcraft).
1984–95	Serialization of *Dragon Ball* by Akira Toriyama in *Weekly Shōnen Jump*.
1984–2020	Biennial *Hiroshima Animation Film Festival*, dedicated to international, noncorporate, animated short films.
1985	Establishment of Studio Ghibli by Hayao Miyazaki, Toshio Suzuki, and Isao Takahata.
1985	Launch of monthly magazine *Gekkan Newtype* (Kadokawa).
1985	Opening of the Machiko Hasegawa Art Museum in Tokyo.
1990	Large-scale Osamu Tezuka retrospective at the National Museum of Modern Art, Tokyo.
1991	Release of the first substantial monograph on manga in French, *L'univers des mangas: Une introduction à la bande dessinée Japonaise* by Thierry Groensteen (Paris: Tournai).
1991	Beginning of Naoko Takeuchi's girls manga that eventually led to the franchise *Pretty Guardian Sailor Moon*. First TV anime series by Toei Animation, 1992–97.
1993	*The Irresponsible Captain Tylor* (*Musekinin kanchō Tairā*, dir. Kōichi Mashimo, Tatsunoko Productions) becomes the first TV anime series to be funded by a production committee.
1993	First comprehensive introduction in English, *Anime! A Beginner's Guide to Japanese Animation* by Helen McCarthy (London: Titan).

1994	Opening of the Osamu Tezuka Memorial Museum in Takarazuka.
1995	Commercial peak of printed manga magazines with *Weekly Shōnen Jump* circulating more than 6 million copies.
1995	Release of the animated movie *Ghost in the Shell* (*Kōkaku kidōtai*, dir. Mamoru Oshii, Production I.G).
1995–96	The TV anime series *Neon Genesis Evangelion* (*Shinseiki Evangelrion*, dir. Hideaki Anno, Gainax), funded by an extensive production committee, becomes a nationwide phenomenon and incites the third "anime boom."
1996	Late-night anime broadcasting is pioneered by *Those Who Hunt Elves* (*Erufu o mamoru monotachi*, dir. Kazuyoshi Katayama, Group TAC).
1996	Beginning of the *Pokémon* franchise with role-playing game and trading cards as well as Game Boy titles. Anime productions by OLM, Inc. since 1997.
1997	Release of the Studio Ghibli movie *Princess Mononoke* (*Mononokehime*, dir. Hayao Miyazaki).
1997	Beginning of the franchise *One Piece* with the manga by Eiichirō Oda in *Weekly Shōnen Jump*.
1999	Establishment of internet platform 2-Channel, which becomes vital for fan-cultural communication in Japanese.
1999	Establishment of the Japan Society for Animation Studies.
2001	Opening of the Museo d'Arte Ghibli/Mitaka no Mori Ghibli Museum.
2001	Founding of the Japan Society for Studies in Cartoons and Comics (*Nihon Manga Gakkai*).
2005	Trade book paperback sales eventually overtake those of manga magazines.
2006	Launch of video-sharing service Nico Nico Douga by Dwango.
2006	Opening of the Kyoto International Manga Museum, based on a public–private partnership between Kyoto City, Kyoto Seika University, and a civic association.

2006 First issue of *Mechademia: An Annual Forum for Anime, Manga, and the Fan Arts* (University of Minnesota Press). Since 2018, *Mechademia: Second Arc.*

2006 Kyoto Seika University establishes Japan's first university department for training comics artists, the Faculty of Manga, which is followed by a graduate school in 2010.

2007 Arrival of Vocaloid software.

2007 YouTube service begins in Japan, becoming an important site for fan videos.

2010 Controversial revision of the Tokyo Metropolitan Ordinance Regarding the Healthy Development of Youths (*Seishōnen kenzen kyōiku ikusei jōrei*). Protest by renowned manga artists.

2011 First appearance of Korean webtoons in Japanese through a now defunct Naver app, *Muryō manga: Webtoon/Online Free Comics: Webtoons*. (Naver registered the webtoon trademark in Japan in 2021.)

2013 Launch of webtoon provider in Japan. Beginning of webtoon series *ReLIFE* by Yayoiso (until 2018).

2014 Launch of online manga magazine *Shōnen Jump+* (Shueisha).

2015 Launch of the Japanese subsite of the Korean webtoon portal Lezhin.

2014 *Knights of Sidonia* (*Shidonia no kishi*, dir. Kōbun Shizuno, Polygon Pictures) streamed as the first Netflix Original Anime.

2016 Japanese translations of Korean webtoons provided by Naver's XOY and Kakao Japan's Piccoma.

2016 Debut of anime-styled online entertainer Kizuna Ai under the name "virtual YouTuber," or VTuber.

2018 Launch of online manga magazine *Hana Yume Ai*, in place of the suspended print magazine *Bessatsu Hana to Yume* (Hakusensha).

2019 Fortieth anniversary of the anime series *Mobile Suit Gundam*.

2019 Digital comics top overall print manga sales.

2020   Fourth "anime boom," driven by *Attack on Titan* (*Shingeki no kyojin*, 2013–22), *Jujutsu Kaisen* (2020–), and *Demon Slayer: Kimetsu no Yaiba* (2019–22). The latter's *Infinity Train* (*Mugen ressha*) becomes the highest-grossing movie of all time in Japan and Taiwan.

2022   Launch of international animation festival Hiroshima Animation Season.

2022   Opening of Ghibli Park in Nagakute, Aichi Prefecture.

2023   Launch of the Niigata International Animation Festival.

JAQUELINE BERNDT

Introduction
Two Media Forms in Correlation

Manga and anime are no novelties anymore, neither as terms nor as media forms and subcultures. Information is globally available on multiple channels, and expertise far exceeds the academic sphere. Under these conditions, a guidebook to the field may quickly fall short of expectations, especially if it tries to cover the whole range of manga and anime and the broadest possible spectrum of critical approaches. This volume does not aim at completeness or didactic authority; it rather seeks to be a companion for dialogue on the study of manga and anime, addressing itself to both newly interested and highly experienced readers.

In contrast to similar publications, this book conjoins manga and anime as distinct while interrelated media forms. Their companionship may be obvious from the perspective of non-Japanese fan cultures, or research fields that are invested in Japanese popular culture, franchising, and classroom pedagogy. But as comics and animations, manga and anime do also diverge, and not all types of manga and anime interconnect easily. To do justice to both the commonalities and the differences between the two media forms, this Companion is divided into thematic sections that, in principle, consist of two chapters, one taking the perspective of manga studies and the other one taking the standpoint of anime research. Some chapters consider both media forms equally. Here, I will introduce the types of manga and anime addressed in this Companion and how they are approached before outlining the individual contributions in the order of their appearance, as well as their interrelations.

"Manga" and "Anime"

"Manga" is often translated as Japanese comics, just as "anime" is frequently defined as Japanese animation. But the wide range of animations created in contemporary Japan does not pass as "anime" abroad, and the entire spectrum of Japanese comics is not necessarily recognized as "manga." Against this backdrop, *The Cambridge Companion to Manga and Anime* limits its scope to comics and animations that are recognized as manga and anime on a global scale, which are also the types that interconnect easily. Narrowing this further, the main emphasis of this volume is on entertaining fiction and, most specifically, serial narratives. Finally, this Companion prioritizes the professional and official, that is, corporate productions published in specialized venues and formats: not American-modeled "comic books" but magazines, trade paperbacks (*tankōbon*), and webtoons in the case of manga; TV series and related franchise movies of drawing-based animation in the case of anime. Comic strips and manga-styled illustrations in fashion magazines and advertising, or anime-like animations in commercials and video games are not included. Fan productions are not singled out either, but they receive credit in numerous chapters.

The Japanese word "manga" has seen a wide semantic variety since it first circulated in the early nineteenth century. In written form, it consists of two Sino-Japanese logographic characters (unless phonetic syllables replace these): The latter, "ga," designates pictures and, more precisely, line drawings; the first, "man," is often assumed to mean "funny" but has not maintained that meaning continuously throughout history – at times, it was understood in a quantitative sense ("manifold"), and at other times in a qualitative one ("capricious," "humorous"). As discussed in more detail in my own chapter in this volume, "manga" has been used to label formats – caricatures, comic strips, and extended graphic narratives – as well as drawing styles, for example, simple line drawing in contrast to detailed depiction. From the late 1950s onward, "manga" was understood as the childish opposite of less playful graphic narratives for young adults named *gekiga* (literally, dramatic pictures) before the two strands coalesced in the 1970s to form the genre of *seinen* (youth) *manga*. Additionally, "manga" has been associated with magazine serials since the 1960s. Several major magazines, however, have used the Japanized word *komikku* in their title, for example, *Big Comic* and *Shōjo Comic*, and the collected book editions following magazine serialization have come to trade under the name of *komikkusu* (i.e., comics). Given this variety, it can be misleading when translations from Japanese indiscriminately render "manga" as manga.

The term "anime," an abbreviation of the English loanword *animēshon*, gained momentum in the late 1970s when young adults began to get enthusiastic about science fiction rendered in cel-animation (that is, the audiovisual animation of drawings or paintings applied to transparent sheets of celluloid, or cels for short). There have been other names for cel-animation than anime, for example, *dōga* (literally, motion pictures) and *manga eiga* (manga film). "Anime" is the most widely used term now, and it may designate many different things simply out of linguistic convenience. This Companion, however, acknowledges the distinctions that exist in the Japanese setting. Both anime audiences and art institutions have been inclined to separate TV series and franchise movies from feature-length works by renowned directors such as Satoshi Kon and Mamoru Oshii. Hayao Miyazaki has famously rejected the anime label for his animated films. Independently created "Art Animation," which is screened mainly at specialist festivals, also distances itself from "anime" – suffice to recall the short films by Taku Furukawa (who is briefly mentioned in Renato Rivera Rusca's chapter) or Kōji Yamamura. Similar to "anime," this volume prioritizes what has been embraced as "manga proper." In Japan, the word "manga" is used to signify all kinds of comics, but consumers and critics have given preference to narratives that begin as magazine-based serials or are released by established manga publishing houses as distinct from instructional comics (*gakushū manga*) or highly individual graphic novels in translation.

Both "manga" and "anime" imply Japaneseness. This Companion complies insofar that it confines itself to Japanese productions. But the underlying motivation is not to emphasize nationally specific concepts at the cost of transnational flows or to generate knowledge about Japanese culture utilizing manga and anime. Instead of manga/anime studies serving Japanese studies, here, the latter's expertise serves the exploration of manga and anime as locally situated transcultural media forms. The contributions in this Companion are based on primary Japanese-language sources as well as intimate knowledge of public, subcultural, and academic discourses. But in equal measure, they draw on globally shared, mainly English-language scholarship in comics studies and animation studies. These new research fields facilitate the focus on manga and anime's media specificity, while familiarity with the particularities of the Japanese environment helps balance media specificity and convergence.

Correlating Manga and Anime

The perception of manga and anime abroad has been fundamentally informed by transmediality. But as evident from the paragraphs above, where certain aspects had to be exemplified for manga and anime individually, media specificity cannot easily be dismissed in this context. Thus, our Companion correlates, rather than conflates, manga and anime as two media forms that have more in common with each other than with the literary novel or modern cinema to which they are so often compared. Both are based more on drawing than photographic capture, and both show a strong inclination to refrain from explicit sociopolitical representation in favor of fantastic settings and unpredictable narrative outcomes. Their peculiarity has been conceptualized as "manga/anime-typical realism" (*manga-anime-teki riarizumu*).[1] This concept refers to the reality-effect that competent users experience in apparently escapist, doubly "flat" storyworlds because – and not despite – of an abundance of tropes and codes. As such manga/anime-typical realism differs from the realism of paintings and novels of the Western tradition, in particular, the scientific accuracy of the central perspective, and the biologically plausible narrative with mortal characters who cannot resurge in a gamic fashion.[2]

Notably, the compound "manga/anime-typical realism" puts manga in front instead of following the alphabetical order, and our Companion is titled in the same way. This relates to both the precedence of manga as an umbrella term in Japanese public discourse today and a historical fact. Since the start of the TV anime adaptation of Osamu Tezuka's manga *Astro Boy* (*Tetsuwan Atomu*) in 1963, printed graphic serials had been the point of departure for transmedia developments; only recently do they cede ground to video games and light novels (i.e., dialog-heavy popular fiction accompanied by mangaesque illustrations). Placing manga first is justified not only with regard to the media forms' evolution but also the central role of graphic style, as Olga Kopylova's chapter makes clear. Nevertheless, popular and scholarly discourse outside of Japan has favored anime over manga which stands to reason with respect to contemporary economic and subcultural concerns.

In aesthetic terms, manga and, in its wake, anime, are multimodal forms of storytelling based on simple line drawing and mostly immobile images. Their static visuals may appear dynamic by virtue of the drawings' linework, the layout of the manga pages, or the way in which anime scenes are edited. Often, the audience is invited to supplement what does not become explicit – for example, when action in anime can only be heard but not seen, when abrupt changes in register happen but are left unsubstantiated, or when key moments of a manga narrative are to be inferred from the space between panels, also known as the gutter. Omissions and allusions are possible because the audience is used to them, and they operate as gateways for audience participation in return.

The familiarity with established motifs extends to narratives. Manga and anime as foregrounded in this volume are firmly committed to genre fiction. In the Japanese setting, and again starting with manga, the primary genre categories have been demographic, that is, age and gender-specific: *shōnen* (boys) and *shōjo* (girls), *seinen* ([male] youth) and *josei* (women). These demographic categories predominate in our Companion, while thematic genres are also considered, especially in the chapter by Deborah Shamoon. The preference for demographics has distinguished the domestic Japanese scene from foreign markets. On a transcultural scale, fans and scholars agree that manga and anime are to be understood as media forms rather than genres, be that a genre of Japanese literature and cinema or a subclass of comics and animation.

A general characteristic that can be observed on multiple levels in both media forms is the inclination to escape either/or positions, first of all, in pertaining to national-cultural in-betweenness: Manga and anime intertwine Japanese particularities with transnational traits. The combination of the exotic with the familiar in their stories and styles proved inspiring in postwar Japan, and it has facilitated global dissemination since the late 1990s. A second trademark of both manga and anime is characters with fluid identities. Adult characters may assume an underage appearance, and female-looking characters may turn out to be male. Queer narratives enjoy a striking presence, represented in the main by the thematic genres of girls love (*yuri*) and boys love (abroad also used synonymously with *yaoi* and *shōnen'ai*).[3] The transcending of divides applies furthermore to audiences. Outside of Japan, manga is often perceived as a youth culture that fills the gap between comics for children and adults. Yet, in Japan, manga has not only targeted actual teenagers; it has also accommodated children curious about adult subjects and grown-ups nurturing their inner child. Since the 1990s fluid notions of identity have gained ground worldwide, and manga's global dissemination clearly relates to that trend, but ambiguity has also caused problems, especially concerning representations of sexuality. Patrick W. Galbraith demonstrates in his chapter the importance of considering context. What may look improper to a gaze that isolates individual images often becomes reasonable if engaging in the narrative in which it is embedded; and what appears highly minor or niche outside of Japan presents itself as a massive subculture within the country. There, manga and anime have served both professionals and amateurs as means of imaginative agency – and not necessarily confined to the domain of specialized fandoms.

It would, however, be misleading to assume that the bypassing of binaries as such makes manga and anime distinct. What calls for critical attention is the specific form that the bypassing takes. Anime, for example, is typically perceived as a variant of minimal or "limited animation" (due to the employment of fewer than twelve cuts for twenty-four seconds of film), with the immobility of the visuals being compensated by sound and editing. Yet closer inspection reveals the significant role of a certain ratio dynamism, that is, the juxtaposition of almost motionless extended cuts with sequences of concise cuts in high-speed editing.[4] Furthermore, limited animation is conjoined with full animation at key points and increasingly so in the digital age. Equally common is the assemblage of flat or two-dimensional character imagery with three-dimensional (and in recent years often computer-generated) backgrounds – an aspect touched upon in the chapters by Olga Kopylova and Selen Çalık Bedir. Finally, anime's indifference toward firm binaries applies to how its characters perform: not exclusively in a figurative (i.e., codified) over embodied (i.e., individualist) acting manner. In actuality, alternations and combinations of "figurative" and "embodied" (or individualist) acting abound, as Stevie Suan expounds in his chapter.

Media and Forms

This Companion promotes consideration of a broad scope of forms that are relevant to both manga and anime. Attention to form "as a producer of meaning, as a vehicle for spectacle, as generative of a strangely intimate experience of reading, and as an enriching engagement with aesthetics," according to Bukatman,[5] is interrelated with the analysis of materialities and technologies, practices and institutions. The form-conscious approach that prevails here is, first of all, a consequence of the central position ceded to audiences – less as social groups than as persons who perceive manga and anime and their concrete instantiations in specific settings, and who exercise agency through the choices they make according to taste, degree of exposure, and length of engagement. As distinct from older types of restrictive formalism, this Companion seeks to extend the focus on textual properties and stylistic devices to readers', or viewers', familiarity with recurring conventions, their orientation at sharing with others, and their affective interaction with the texts; in other words, to forms of mediation, communication, and commodification. It is in this regard that economic forces, cultural identities, and power relations are taken into account.

Producers, too, make an appearance, ranging from artists to editors and studio operators. The chapters by Bon Won Koo, Bryan Hikari Hartzheim, and Minori Ishida, in particular, introduce them as actors who calibrate a whole range of creative, corporate, and communicative requirements. An author-centered approach would not be viable in any case, given that manga and anime are corporate and highly networked media forms. In due consideration of that, the chapters of this Companion proceed from the crucial textual form components – visuals, voices, and storytelling – to the immediate context provided by genres and from there to studio production, publication formats, and licensing practices to ultimately arrive at usages within and without fandom.

History

Our Companion approaches manga and anime historically but without a specific chapter to outline their evolution in chronological order. History chapters are an essential part of similar publications.[6] Usually, they determine a point of destination in view of which canonical works and authors are lined up to form a progressive narrative. Several such points are available for manga and anime. Economically, manga peaked in the mid-1990s, when the magazine *Weekly Shōnen Jump* reached its highest print run with approximately 6 million copies, and the TV anime series *Neon Genesis Evangelion*, aimed at a geek, or *otaku*, audience, unexpectedly appealed to adult viewers across the nation. Semiotically, the evolution of the manga medium has been measured against the degree to which text and image intertwine, or more specifically, the full-fledged emergence of "audiovisual comics."[7] Manga historiography also highlights the shift in predominance from humorous shorts to serious extended narratives, as mentioned in Ronald Stewart's chapter.

The mainstream narrative of anime history focuses on drawing-based or cel-animation. Therein, it juxtaposes the smooth movements of Miyazaki's full lineage of animation with the more static visuals characteristic of Tezuka's approach.[8] Biographical accounts of Miyazaki, for example, tend to salute his departure from manga-based TV series that employ "limited" techniques, suggesting that full animation in the format of feature films represented a higher developmental level of the media form. But the limited animation style has not perished despite new technologies, a topic addressed in the chapters by Kopylova and Çalık Bedir. Progress tends to be identified also with respect to industrialization (the transition from artisanal workshops to big studios), viewer demographics (the shift from children to adults), and, closely related, fandoms (for example, regarding the rise of self-curated platforms). The chapter by Akiko Sugawa-Shimada delineates the latter's evolution in line with the so-called anime booms that prevail in Japanese popular discourse.[9]

A typical narrative of manga history takes the course from Tezuka's alleged invention of enthralling *story-manga* for children in the late 1940s through the more realist *gekiga* narratives for young adults in the 1960s and 1970s to contemporary *seinen manga* as an increasingly universal genre no longer exclusively targeted at young men. In this narrative, the masculine genres, beginning with *shōnen manga* (boys comics), usually form the unmarked standard from which comics for girls and women (*shōjo manga*, *josei manga*) are supposed to derivate, even if hailed for an aesthetic and narrative "revolution" that unleashed the thematic genre of boys love in

7

the late 1970s, among other things. In recent years, the gendered genre categories have ceased to represent the initially targeted audience segments. Girls have come to read boys manga and men to consume media content aimed at women. Similarly, a clear divide between mainstream commercial magazines (such as *Shōnen Jump*) and alternative periodicals (such as the former *Garo*) is challenging to find. The postwar divide into "major" and "minor" positions, as they were called in Japan, is one of the multiple strands of manga history that would call for attention.

Against this backdrop, a separate history chapter did not seem to be as helpful as letting facets of the media forms' histories surface in an interspersed manner. Many contributors provide historical insight in accordance with their specific subject: Sheuo Hui Gan with respect to the multiplane camera, Ishida in regard to voice acting, and Hartzheim related to Studio Gainax; Blanche Delaborde concerning onomatopoeia, Stewart in terms of newspaper comic strips and humor, and Koo in connection with manga magazine editing and the rise of professional *mangaka* (manga artists). In addition to the contribution by Dalma Kálovics, the two concluding chapters by Galbraith and Sugawa-Shimada provide large-scale overviews following a chronological axis. They bring full circle what the first section of this Companion sets out to do in its approach to times past: revisiting the popular references to traditions and illuminating aspects of history that often go unnoticed in contemporary manga and anime discourse.

The Individual Contributions

Part I of this Companion explores claimed origins and overlooked traditions and is the only part consisting of three chapters. Chapter 1 raises the question of how to attend to the much-invoked "roots" of *story-manga*, namely, medieval picture scrolls (*emaki*) and the nineteenth-century *Hokusai Manga* copybooks. Besides these art-historical references, entertaining graphic narratives from around 1800 (*kibyōshi*) are briefly addressed. Instead of tracing possible continuities from past to present, the chapter takes the opposite vector, using contemporary *story-manga* as the touchstone for retrospection. The primary focus is on the manga-typical experience of graphic narratives: reading as an embodied act afforded by specific forms and materials. Consequently, visual movement takes center stage – on the one hand, as guided by monochrome line drawing, sequenced images, and panel sequences, and on the other hand, as dependent on the reader alternating their frame of vision in interaction with handheld artifacts. But the chapter relates manga-likeness also to particularities of use, especially the fact that contemporary manga invites sharing and motivates redrawing.

Chapter 2 by Ronald Stewart highlights comic strips, a format that is underrepresented in contemporary manga studies although it has played a vital role throughout the twentieth century. In Japan, newspaper-based comic strips comprise, in principle, four vertically arranged panels (*yon-koma*). Allowing for less variation in the frames compared to horizontal strips, this format is usually equated with the four rhetorical steps of classical Chinese poetry: setting, evolvement, twist, and wrap-up (*ki-shō-ten-ketsu*). Stewart analyzes two examples of "laughs in four panels" and reveals potential discrepancies in interpreting stages 3 and 4 of *ki-shō-ten-ketsu*. Thus, he establishes that the concept is neither helpful in explaining humor nor unique to Japanese comic strips, which in any case have not always consisted of four panels throughout history. A more contemporary challenge to humor studies, the methodological foundation of this chapter, may be posed by the cartoonish characters, or *chara*, that are introduced in Chapter 10.

Chapter 3 by Joon Yang Kim introduces an understudied period and an often-overlooked ideological type of media ecology through the lens of the world-famous character Astro Boy (*Tetsuwan Atomu*), interrelating the little robot with the children of wartime Japan. It demonstrates how a vast web of state policies, magazines, toys, and graphic narratives prepared youngsters for the empire's warfare by promoting scientific rather than manga/anime-typical realism. It maintains that the eventual "weaponization" of children resonated with postwar audiences through Astro Boy. In terms of media history, Kim's discussion suggests seeing manga and anime characters in the light of Japan's modern imperialism rather than premodern aesthetics. It also reminds us that the two media forms began as children's culture, which became obscured when they shed their childish reputation from the 1970s onward. Finally, the chapter raises awareness for the fact that *story-manga* began already in the 1930s, that is, before Tezuka's postwar debut.

Part II attends to visuals, or more precisely, drawing, and the related interdependence of manga and anime. Both media forms rest on hand-drawn lines for relating palpable movement that is not necessarily tied to narrative or visual representation. This observation provides the starting point for Olga Kopylova's media-comparative discussion of graphic style in anime and manga. Considering aesthetic, technological, and industrial aspects, the chapter shows how the inherent dynamism of the hand-drawn line and the visible actions of the animated figure combine in a way that blurs the distinction between still and moving images. Indifference toward binaries extends to the assemblage of 2D figures with intricate 3D backgrounds, characters in default style and in distortion, and the above-mentioned ratio dynamism. The embrace of such disparities, which itself has been subject to historical change, opens possibilities for reconciling today's 3D computer-generated (CG) imagery with the hand-drawn 2D aesthetics typical of anime, a timely issue that is tackled narratologically in Chapter 9.

Chapter 5 by Sheuo Hui Gan also emphasizes the importance of manga-based drawing for the implication of movement in anime's visual storytelling. What the previous chapter called prefigurative quality is conceptualized here as emotion. Gan argues that anime's preference for affecting audiences emotionally hampered Disney's multiplane camera from prevailing. Historically, the multiplane camera remained the "other" of anime and with it the mimicking of live-action film in animation, up to and including digitally generated 3D space. But instead of replacing an allegedly underdeveloped type of animation (the "limited" one) with an allegedly more advanced type (the "full animation"), cel-animation in Japan gave rise to assemblages of cinema-derived and drawing-derived techniques, encompassing but not necessarily prioritizing the aesthetics of the multiplane camera.

Part III focuses on sound, or more specifically, voice, yet not the vibrant and stylized voices anime is known for. Which voices manga readers "hear" is not at stake either, although many of them certainly associate voice actors with whom they are familiar through anime adaptations. Blanche Delaborde's chapter "Hearing Manga" inspects the highly conventional visual and linguistic devices used to relate sound effects on printed pages: mimetic words, or mimetics for short. Contemporary manga stands out by a tremendous quantity and variety of mimetics. Once a marker of childishness due to their facilitation of exaggerated expression and affective impact, mimetics became more widely appreciated when they changed from representing actual sounds to indicating feelings and moods in the 1970s. The chapter raises awareness of the graphic role of mimetics as part of the page design, but it also considers linguistic aspects such as the creative use of reading aids attached to Sino-Japanese characters, or the historically changing connotations of the two Japanese syllabaries.

In "Voice Acting for Anime," Minori Ishida analyzes punctuation marks in recording scripts and compares them with the ultimately audible voice performance to establish that the dubbing of anime does not exclude acting. To that end, punctuation marks are scrutinized with respect to how they help to intertwine the visual and the vocal. This is especially vital in anime productions, where the visuals take precedence over the audio track. Animated films for theatrical release have employed prescoring which affords lip-syncing, that is, the harmonization of mouth movements and spoken dialogue. However, "after recording" (*afureko*) became the norm for TV series from *Astro Boy* onward, involving a discrepancy between the visible and the audible. The chapter illuminates the rising role of anime-specific voice actors and calls to acknowledge their particular contribution to constructing anime characters within a strictly predetermined framework.

Part IV provides two approaches to media-specific storytelling. Kōichi Morimoto's chapter begins with a definition of reading in a general sense, namely, as the narrative experience of a storyworld rather than an external reality. Manga itself is understood as a graphic narrative that falls into episodes, or installments, which ultimately align with a progressive plot. Similar to Ishida's notion of creativity in strictly conditioned settings, this chapter conceives reading manga as primarily compliant with a given frame. The reader "synchronizes" imaginatively with the characters by following the guidance of the artist-author (and that of the invisible editor). Morimoto introduces three phases of reading: the microscopic phase, where the focus is on the single panel; the mesoscopic phase, where the visible range is the double-page spread, and the macroscopic one, where the pages at hand are interpreted with regard to what has already happened and what is probably still to come. It is made clear that mainstream manga privileges the first two phases due to magazine-based serialization.

Another aspect related to serialization is highlighted by Selen Çalık Bedir. Her chapter departs from the observation that anime's employment of 2D limited animation goes hand in hand with narrative unpredictability. Instead of providing a logical chain of irreversible events, typical anime narratives lead to incalculable outcomes, as characters' actions are substantiated by feelings. 3D computer-generated animation, however, relies on the opposite, that is, calculation. While digital techniques help to make the production of anime less time-consuming and labor-intensive, they also undermine the typically exaggerated and discontinuous storytelling of handmade anime. As such, a concept like 3D anime seems paradoxical. The chapter explores how anime narratives become compatible with 3D aesthetics, eventually arriving at the answer: "through ceaseless labor" by characters and fans.

Part V focuses on characters. In Chapter 10, Lukas R.A. Wilde introduces the Japanese term *kyara*, an abbreviated form of "character" and therefore rendered as "chara" in English. This term allows the conceptualization of one element that manga and anime are recognized for in recent years: cartoonish figures who incite affective responses inside and outside of narratives and invite users to enter parasocial relationships. While independence from narratives sets them free to move across media, these figures are still fundamentally connected to manga and anime not only by connotation but also by line drawing and stylized acting. Wilde analyzes instants where anime characters turn into nonnarrative charas by stepping out into the paratexts. Considering narratological, media-theoretical, and fan-studies concerns, charas are conceptualized as facilitators of networks and participation.

Stevie Suan's chapter investigates how anime characters act. Animation is essentially defined by visible movement and characters' movements in particular. Suan establishes that the latter can indicate notions of selfhood – an individualized one where interiority determines external expression and thus appears embodied, and a networked one where external others become an integral part of the self by means of stylized, or figurative, forms. This is illustrated through the example of *Yūri!!! on Ice* (2016), which interrelates the two modes of acting with gender as performance and with the essential paradox of both figure skating and anime: how to stand out individually when prescribed conventional moves have to be mastered. What proves crucial in conclusion is the assemblage of the two modes of acting, on ice as well as in anime. Competition can be won with an emotionally convincing performance even if it is technically flawed (which echoes the narrative incalculability discussed by Çalık Bedir).

Thus, the two chapters in this section take different approaches. While Wilde highlights nonnarrative instantiations of characters, Suan relates characters' visible movements to what the story may tell us, last but not least about anime itself. Nevertheless, the two chapters meet at one point: the figurative acting mode. Marked by eyes overflowing with emotion, upper cheeks blushing, and nonmedical nosebleeds that point to manga/anime-typical realism, this mode could also be called chara mode because its recurring elements serve as nodal points in networks of connections.

Part VI comprises two explorations of genre. It begins with Deborah Shamoon's chapter that introduces genres of *story-manga* determined by demographics and themes. Here, "genre" is employed as an analytical tool to gain insight into the management of target audiences and their expectations. For most of the twentieth century, Japanese genre fiction has been divided by gender. Genre-defining features such as action narratives for boys, where teams of companions strive for "friendship, effort, victory" (to cite the famous motto of *Shōnen Jump*), and stories of intimate relationships for girls, where feelings and moods come to the fore, trace back to Japan's prewar media ecology. Yet the degree to which these traditions entered manga's postwar genres was not the same in the feminine and the masculine domains. In the course of her historical overview, Shamoon also touches on the changing meaning of "manga" from the 1950s onward, continuing where the first chapter of this volume leaves off.

Shamoon considers thematic genres such as sports manga, boys love, and *isekai* (literally, otherworld, as the protagonist is to act in an "other," often video-gamic fictional world). In contrast, Bryan Hikari Hartzheim fore-grounds a genre that has helped anime to cross borders in the first place: science fiction. He argues that the crucial role of sci-fi in Japan harks back to the industrial, institutional, and communal networks that preceded the for-mation of anime fandoms from the 1970s onward, and he demonstrates this by looking at "Gainax before Gainax." The famous Gainax Studio started out from a licensing store and a film production company, Daicon Film, relied heavily on an already existing fan-cultural infrastructure, and suc-cessfully repurposed fan-cultural institutions within its industrial scheme. Here, the sci-fi genre operated not only as a set of textual traits but more so as an organizing principle for exploiting character images and allowing fans to control them. By way of its analytical focus on one studio, the chapter reveals how closely interrelated industry and fandom have been. It also illu-minates particularities of the anime industry, which eventually hamper an indiscriminate application of American-modeled film studies tools.

Part VII is dedicated to forms of production. Instead of attempting an encyclopedic overview, it highlights two divergent cases: magazine edi-tors and their importance for manga artists on the one hand, and on the other, anime studios outside of Tokyo and their ties to local municipalities. According to Bon Won Koo, manga's contemporary sociocultural power originates from its economic potency, the industry's capability to sell cap-tivating and commercially successful stories. This is rooted in specific pub-lication formats with precedence having changed from magazines to trade paperback editions and, more recently, webtoons (i.e., vertically scrolled, or swiped, graphic narratives read on small screens). Manga's potency has been sustained by editors-in-charge, an occupational category that devel-oped together with the specifically Japanese business model. Koo's chapter introduces the multiple roles that editors at manga magazines have taken on, and also brings their manga artists into focus regarding paths to a pro-fessional debut, economic conditions, and differences between print and digital publications.

Production committees, a vast web of major and subcontracted studios mainly located in Tokyo, and a multitude of poorly paid freelancers are well-known characteristics of the anime industry. But as Renato Rivera Rusca observes in his chapter, digitization and the gradual shift away from pencil-on-paper materials to be physically delivered have increased possi-bilities to move production out of Tokyo's metropolitan area. His chapter analyzes regional studios regarding their economic conditions, as well as the support they are offered by municipal revitalization programs. While most newly established studios work as subcontractors without any licens-ing revenue, there are also some public initiatives to facilitate the formation of independent creative bases. In contrast, anime tourism is compared with fans' "pilgrimages" to locations featuring in popular anime, and the related interindustry collaboration.

Part VIII examines forms of distribution. In her chapter, Dalma Kálovics revisits manga's material history since the immediate postwar period to figure out the specific affordances of the magazine in comparison to other analog and digital formats. As a result, it becomes clear that formats of publication and republication require as much attention as genres and target audiences, especially in the digital age. Recent webtoons, for example, are subjected to far-reaching changes in page layouts upon remediation just like the rental comics of the 1960s in which *gekiga* flourished, although print editions differ between Japan and the birthplace of these digital comics, the Republic of Korea. As a whole, this chapter makes a strong case for attention to manga's materiality as effectuating the aesthetic forms of the texts themselves as well as their consumption.

Just as the distribution of manga has traditionally been understood as magazine-centered, the distribution of anime has been tied to TV broadcasting and movie theaters. Dario Lolli's chapter advances a broader notion of the latter and exemplifies this by *Mobile Suit Gundam*, an anime-induced multimedia franchise developed by a media corporation and initially targeted to dedicated fans. Its fortieth anniversary was the occasion for a campaign that involved various, but not necessarily anime-related, brands to disseminate anime also off-screen – through canned coffee, immersive architecture, and urban space – in order to reach a wider audience, in particular, older demographics with a high disposable income. The chapter conceptualizes anime as a media form that has the capacity to generate strong feelings and affective attachments, to bring characters as well as storyworlds to life, and thus to animate commodities beyond the traditional sphere of merchandising. Eventually, this reads like a case of media specificity facilitating transmediality.

Part IX highlights forms of use. It deliberately sidesteps "consumption" or "reception" in order to avoid the impression of passiveness. The larger manga and anime became as industries, the more opportunities to develop imaginative and creative agency were available to their readers and viewers. This agency takes center stage in both chapters with a special emphasis on freedom of expression and fan-cultural activities. Whereas negative aspects have often been foregrounded outside of Japan (and in circles that lack familiarity with the two media forms), this part identifies the possibilities that participants have exhausted in the domestic setting.

Patrick W. Galbraith begins his chapter with patterns of use that were afforded by printed manga magazines and their serial narratives. He brings forward the intimacy of communication that this publication format enabled as well as its capability to induce the formation of proto-virtual taste communities, based on which artists, readers, and editors have pushed the boundaries of both sexual representation and copyright. Freedom to "play gender and sexuality" has been vital for the exceptional scale of production and readership that manga exhibits today. This was facilitated by a tacit agreement between the corporate and the alternative domains before the age of online circulation and global licensing of intellectual property. The chapter calls for going beyond the rising "erotic barrier" by means of grounded analysis and public discussion.

The final chapter by Akiko Sugawa-Shimada zooms in on the agency of specific users, namely, fans and their venues of communication. It traces four "anime booms" that have contributed to the extension of the media form's audience, ranging from fan-club magazines that the studios themselves released, to fan-driven associations and spot-sales events for material published outside the official channels (dōjinshi), including cosplay, anime-induced "contents tourism," and more recently, fansubbed videos uploaded without authorization, as well as 2.5D musicals. In short, the chapter surveys how fans' "prousing" (i.e., using as producing, or creating) has grown over the years, and it shows how closely this has been interconnected with going beyond anime as a specific media form.

As outlined above, the individual chapters of this Companion approach manga and anime in various ways. What they share is the focus on *how* the two media forms operate. The respective attention to mediality and mediations applies to many aspects: semiotic properties and stylistic devices, technologies and publication formats, practices, institutions, and crucial actors. Illuminating a broad range of forms, this Companion seeks to intertwine the experience of manga and anime with closely related reflections on networks, communality, participation, identity performance, and the endeavor to find a balance between media specificity and transmediality.

Notes

1. The term *manga-anime-teki riarizumu* has been translated also as "manga/anime-esque realism," and "manga/anime-like realism," but the semantic distance implied in the latter two gets easily lost in translation.
2. Eiji Ōtsuka, *Kyarakutā shōsetsu no tsukurikata* (Tokyo: Kodansha, 2003), 24. An English-language summary of Ōtsuka's still untranslated discussion is provided by Marc Steinberg, "Realism in the Animation Media Environment: Animation Theory from Japan." In *Animating Film Theory*, edited by Karen Beckman (Durham: Duke University Press, 2014), 287–300.

3. Boys love is a Japanese Anglicism (*boīzu rabu*), abbreviated to BL, that gained ground from the 1990s onward as the name for the commercially viable variant of male-male romance narratives by heterosexual women for, in principle, heterosexual women. The fan-cultural, more sexually accentuated variant is called *yaoi* (shorthand for what translates as *no climax, no punch line, no meaning*), while *shōnen'ai* (literally, boy-boy love) was the initial designation, which in Japanese is associated with the 1970s.
4. Introduced by José Andrés Santiago Iglesias, "Not Just Immobile: Moving Drawings and Visual Synecdoches in Neon Genesis Evangelion." In *Anime Studies: Media-Specific Approaches to Neon Genesis Evangelion*, edited by José Andrés Santiago Iglesia and Ana Soler Baena (Stockholm: Stockholm University Press, 2021), 19–48. Open Access.
5. Scott Bukatman, "Form." In *Keywords for Comics Studies,* edited by Ramzi Fawaz, Deborah Whaley, and Shelley Streeby (New York: New York University Press, 2021), 105.
6. Typical examples include *The Routledge Companion to Comics*, edited by Frank Bramlett, Roy T. Cook, Aaron Meskin (2017); Shige (CJ) Suzuki & Ronald Stewart, *Manga: A Critical Guide* (New York: Bloomsbury Academic, 2022).
7. Eike Exner, *Comics and the Origins of Manga: A Revisionist History* (New Brunswick: Rutgers University Press, 2022).
8. See the translated extract from a Japanese monograph by Nobuyuki Tsugata, "A Bipolar Approach to Understanding the History of Japanese Animation." In *Japanese Animation: East Asian Perspectives*, edited by Masao Yokota and Tse-yue G. Hu (Jackson: University Press of Mississippi, 2013), 25–33.
9. For a discourse-analytical approach to these "anime booms," see Zoltan Kacsuk, "The Making of an Epoch-Making Anime: Understanding the Landmark Status of Neon Genesis Evangelion in Otaku Culture." In *Anime Studies: Media-Specific Approaches to Neon Genesis Evangelion*, edited by José Andrés Santiago Iglesia and Ana Soler Baena (Stockholm: Stockholm University Press, 2021), 227–31. Open Access.

PART I

Claimed Origins and Overlooked Traditions

I

JAQUELINE BERNDT

Premodern Roots of *Story-Manga*?

Comics discourse abounds with recourses to presumed origins, and not without reason: Age-old traditions have proven effective for both subcultural and state actors. Advocates of comics have referred to authoritative fine art for legitimization, while established public institutions are now utilizing comics to attract younger audiences. In Japan and other Asian settings, the identification of culturally distinctive ancient roots has been motivated not only by intra-societal hierarchies but also by geopolitical power gaps. Thus, twentieth-century manga discourse referenced Japanese art appreciated in Europe and North America – early-modern woodblock prints (*ukiyo-e*) and medieval handscrolls (*emaki*), in particular. Manga researchers, however, have grown cautious about such origin claims. Pointing to the noticeable stylistic, narrative, and material differences from alleged progenitors, they have argued for understanding manga as a fundamentally modern media form – in terms of both the technologies and institutions implemented since the late nineteenth century, and of the effective role played by contemporaneous Western models. Today, specialists in manga (and anime) studies no longer seek art-historical connections; attempts to do so tend to meet suspicion of either restrictive formalism or nationalist intent.[1]

Manga and anime are often lumped together, but anime has not received nearly as much attention as manga in relation to traditional art. There have been references to historic painting styles in animated feature films of the 1950s produced by the studio Tōei Dōga when they aimed to become the "Disney of the East," and decades later also in anime series such as *Samurai Champloo* (2004) and *Mononoke* (2007). TV anime's imagery has occasionally been associated with the art-historical tradition of providing blanks, or "negative space," to be filled imaginatively. Yet, in technological terms, anime could not easily hide its modernity, based as it was on film. In the early days, until the 1960s, anime was frequently called by the name *dōga*, a composite of "movement" (*dō*) and "drawing" (*ga*) – literally, "motion pictures," so to speak. From an art-historical perspective, this name may easily appear tautological, as traditional paintings are not necessarily still. Illuminated handscrolls, for example, relate to movement in at least two regards: representation (avowedly, with noble characters "animated" less than commoners) and appreciation mode (via unrolling). But this mobility has been overshadowed by the modern technology of film, which introduced segregation – between drawings as the stronghold of stillness and the moving-image domain. Instead of such divides, this chapter foregrounds correlations between the two poles, while giving more space to manga.

As the next sections will specify, critics have focused primarily on three things when analyzing mangalikeness in forms of visual and narrative art: the semiotic properties of the work itself, its sociocultural status, and the involved actors. Starting with an emphasis on whimsical drawings in the 1920s, the focus changed to the interplay of text and image. In the 1980s and 1990s, visual storytelling based on sequenced images and frames, or panels, was given priority. In relation to that, attention concentrated on equivalents of motion lines, speech balloons, and onomatopoeia – so-called transdiegetic devices that are visible, in principle, only to the reader.[2] Over time, such formal features have been upstaged in favor of sociocultural and contextual aspects, stretching from religious studies seeking traces of animism in anime to cultural studies concerned with creators, mediators, and audiences.[3] More recently, perceptual aspects have also attracted interest: reading as providing not only cognitive but also sensory and affective enjoyment, facilitated by a self-determined pace of appreciation in intimate settings.

The association of aesthetic and cultural "origins" has been highly selective and rested on changes in the notion of manga itself. Manga was easily brought in line with art-historical traditions of drawing when caricatures and short comic strips for adults prevailed. But once the graphic narrative, or story-manga, gained momentum during the 1960s, references shifted from premodern domestic painting to modern cinema,[4] and back again to early-modern graphic fiction (kibyōshi, or more broadly, kusazōshi). Since around 2000, the centrality of story-manga, too, has been challenged – on the one hand, by transmedially migrating characters and consumers' indifference to their origination from specific narratives; on the other hand, by an increased awareness that reading is embodied and meaning-making affected by the materiality of the objects at hand.

This chapter revisits the most-cited progenitors of manga (and, in part, anime). Tracing core features, it acknowledges the historical contingency of "manga." The issues that will come to the fore are: first, that the assumption of continuity does not match the actual course of history; second, that manga cannot be ahistorically homogenized; and third, that the radical break with the premodern past stipulated by critical researchers does not necessarily hold in view of experiencing visual narratives, especially under postdigital conditions. I will propose to go beyond the established oppositions of traditional versus modern, domestic versus foreign, still versus moving images, and – in the case of manga – also watching versus reading. The emphasis is not on deconstructing origin claims and foregrounding divergences but rather on demonstrating that correlations of today's manga with aesthetic traditions may be highly instructive depending on *how* they are performed, that is, which type of manga is compared to which art form from the past against which set of contemporary concerns.

Scrolls: Indeterminate Frames

The identification of manga's "origins" was initially focused on monochrome line drawing (*hakubyō*), funny animals, and comics-specific transdiegetic devices. In this regard, the *Frolicking Animals* scrolls (*Chōjū [jinbutsu] giga*, twelfth century) have been the undisputed progenitor for a long time, especially the first out of a set of four, which features only animals.[5] Unfolding in the Japanese reading direction from right to left, this scroll is populated by scenes of more or less anthropomorphized monkeys, rabbits, frogs, and the like, engaged in swimming, wrestling, or picnicking. In one scene, wavy lines escape the mouth of a monkey monk seated in front of a frog Buddha statue as he recites a sutra, apparently for a deceased one. In another scene, a frog emanates similar lines while ruthlessly kicking off a rabbit, obviously jubilant about his victory in a match. These lines have been regarded as antecedents of speech balloons, although they merely indicate sound.[6]

The *Frolicking Animals* present movements in time, but the connections between the scenes are not substantiated by a recognizable narrative. No verbal text is attached, and a matching literary source has not been found either among the surviving tales. One answer to the mystery is to treat the *Frolicking Animals* as a collection of non-narrative drawings, and lighthearted ones at that. This stance traces back to the mid-eighteenth century when the scrolls were rediscovered. Back then, the term *Toba-e* (Toba pictures) was coined, alluding to their purported creator, the Buddhist abbot Toba Sōjō (1053–1140). Yet, even if the scrolls do not have an identifiable plot and characters to follow, their fragmentary scenes evoke a story, as recent research suggests – the story of excessive forces that must be restrained to preserve the social order.[7] The brutality of a frog biting a rabbit's ear, the fear of two mice hiding from cats in courtly attire, and the appearance of a feral snake at the end of the first scroll all bespeak that the idyllic world is fragile. Viewed in the light of their historical context, the scrolls are not funny at all.

Both the *Frolicking Animals* and postwar manga address volatile social orders, although in opposite ways: The first were aimed at reinforcing state power (in particular, imperial sovereignty as the pacifier of the unsettling forces); the latter has been inclined to escape or subvert state authority, especially from the postwar period onwards. Consider animal characters in serials such as *Kimba, the White Lion* (*Janguru taitei*, 1950–54) by Osamu Tezuka and *Beastars* (2016–20) by Paru Itagaki. The audience of the *Frolicking Animals* was a small aristocratic community that could do without fully represented narratives because its members shared the same knowledge (for example, of the Chinese classics). Their ability to understand allusions and to play with characters may evoke practices of contemporary fan communities, which points to the issue of usage as an aspect of correlations between past and present. But scrolls were precious hand-drawn items, limited in accessibility as much as in operability – they were not easy to browse, even if intended to be actually opened (which was not always the case, although the repulped paper of the *Frolicking Animals* suggests a purpose other than devotion).

Studio Ghibli director Isao Takahata called medieval scrolls "animation of the 12th century."[8] Intrigued by pictorial techniques to convey movement in time, he highlighted, for example, a device that resembles speed lines. In the *Miraculous Tales of Mount Shigi* (*Shigisan engi emaki*), such lines support the impression that a whole warehouse full of rice is magically lifted off the ground by the alms bowl of monk Myōren, the legendary founder of a temple on Mount Shigi. Elsewhere, a guardian deity, sent by the monk to help the ailing emperor in his stead, rushes into the scene on cloud-like curly lines. This device looks comics-like indeed, but it does not show up often among the approximately three dozen remaining narrative handscrolls, and it has not been continuously passed down to modern Japan either: The last premodern motion lines appeared in the *Miraculous Tales of the Ishiyama Temple* (*Ishiyamadera engi emaki*), the last "sound lines" in the *Tale of Fukutomi* (*Fukutomi zōshi*), both from around 1400.[9]

Since the 1980s, Japanese critics have prioritized neither the blending of image and text nor transdiegetic devices but the panel (*koma*), that is, the bordered drawing that arguably articulates a discrete point in time and forms the basic unit of (not necessarily grid-like) page layouts. Imported from abroad and echoing the analytical work of the camera, it was taken as another testament to manga's modernity. But the breakdown of a surface into sequential images had not been entirely new to Japanese artists when they first encountered French, British, and American newspaper strips in the late nineteenth century – they just had not been fond of this technique. After all, a prescribed path to follow did not leave the viewer much room to playfully construct pictorial sequences by themselves. Furthermore, paneling was laden with religious and didactic connotations, as in the case of hanging scrolls that featured scenes from the life of a famous monk. Priests used them to aid oral instruction.[10]

As distinct from those hanging scrolls, the narrative handscrolls did not employ panels. When they were unrolled by hand, mist or clouds indicated the end of one scene and the beginning of another, remotely reminiscent of the cinematic dissolve. In the twelfth-century *Tale of Great Minister Ban* (*Bandainagon ekotoba*), which relates to a historical arson event in the imperial capital, flames and dark smoke divide and connect the opening scenes. In the narrative, the noble culprit manages to blame his political rival, but after a while, the truth comes to light through a quarrel between two boys. The scroll pictures how one boy gets pushed away by the other's father, a retainer of the culprit, after which the victim's mother loses her temper and shouts out the truth to insult the abuser. In a now-famous experiment, director Takahata "comicalized" this sequence by breaking it down into panels.[11] Arranged on a double-page spread in a way that privileged the progressive transition from panel to panel at the expense of the interplay between panel and page, the "indeterminacy of the frame" that is typical of both premodern scrolls and modern manga narratives was suspended.[12] Consisting of still and mute images and engendering a visual flow across interstices, both manga and scrolls lean on their recipients to determine the frame of vision through their embodied gaze – approaching the artifact from various angles, changing their posture, as well as their focus, zooming in and zooming out. Filmic shots, by contrast, predetermine the field of vision.

From the perspective of the material conditions that inform the reading experience, previously overlooked commonalities come to light. Both painted narrative handscrolls and printed *story-manga* rest on a still surface, mostly paper. They are handheld devices and reveal their narrative section by section while abiding mainly by a horizontal vector of progression. Not only the visual framing but also the pacing and orientation are up to the recipient (to some degree). Considering this type of mediality, the two share more with each other than with movies or digital comics that provide a visual track not to be strayed from. Webtoons, as the most popular variant of the latter, present a continuous vertical flow of visual elements that undermines the indeterminacy of the frame.

Hokusai Manga: Sharing Images

According to director Isao Takahata, the evolution of graphic storytelling that allegedly culminated in postwar *story-manga* progressed from medieval scrolls via early-modern illustrated fiction and mid-twentieth century "paper theater" (*kamishibai*). Takahata also included magic-lantern plays of the nineteenth century in that evolution, but not the famous *Hokusai Manga*, which popular belief regards as the origin of modern Japanese comics. Fifteen stitched-bound copybook volumes with sketches by the acclaimed woodblock artist and painter Hokusai (1760–1849) were released under that name between 1814 and 1878. The *Hokusai Manga* volumes, which were exceptionally popular, comprised four thousand woodblock-printed and basically monochrome drawings that were not linked by a narrative and not all intended to be humorous.[13]

"Manga" was a new word at the time, but it was not coined by Hokusai.[14] The word appeared in the title of a dozen other books during his lifetime. It signified primarily an extensive catalog of samples, a particular quantity arising from an indiscriminate, while not necessarily random, attitude. Hokusai himself defined manga in the preface to the first volume as "brush gone wild." This, however, applied more to the artist's mindset than the images' execution. Stylistically, they range from *ukiyo-e*, the art of the commoners, to older, more exalted Japanese schools and even the Chinese and European painting traditions. The motifs stretch from natural phenomena to manufactured objects, from the material to the spiritual world, from everyday life to Japanese classic poetry and Chinese literature. Saints and heroes appear, as well as commoners working, bathing, sleeping, or performing contortions. Nothing is too trivial to be depicted.

Popular attention to exaggerated facial and bodily expressions has led to the modern assumption that "manga" is synonymous with funny pictures eliciting laughs. Humor certainly helped to make the realm of art and literature accessible to commoners. But today's manga readers may not recognize the humor of the past, especially if it is rendered in a restrained rather than cartoonesque style. Hokusai's take on the well-known legend *The Dream of Kantan* is a good example. An ordinary man sees himself becoming the emperor when taking a short nap on a magic pillow in the Chinese village Handan (Japanese: Kantan). Volume 12 of the *Hokusai Manga* features the dreamer on a page that assembles several disconnected figures. A thought balloon attached to the left side of his head evokes the story pictorially. But the picture shows a wooden latrine instead of a palace and eight small men who carry two buckets each. Thus, the dream of social advancement takes the form of unlimited disposal of night soil and thereby dung.

The *Hokusai Manga* allude to various narratives that were familiar to contemporaries, but they do not engage in visual storytelling. Many pages archivally picture multiple things of the same category without any humorous or narrative orientation. Paneling, if employed at all, does not convey the passage of time but lists places like the Edo sights in Volume 8. Balloons or motion lines are rarely used. Apart from the monochrome line drawing, which affords print, the *Hokusai Manga* do not have much in common with the *story-manga* of today. Commonalities, however, are a matter of perspective. If focusing not on visual storytelling or typical designs but on usage, a significant similarity comes to the fore: Both the *Hokusai Manga* and contemporary Japanese manga owe much of their attraction to cultural circulation to being revisited, copied, and shared. Consequently, the *Hokusai Manga* are best correlated with manga manuals or how-to-draw-manga guides, which have facilitated participatory culture in Japan and abroad. Simply put, one core characteristic that unites "manga" across the centuries is the consumer-turned-creator.

During Japan's modernization, this pragmatic aspect took a backseat in favor of manga as a form of visual art, and so did the element of storytelling. With the advent of modern newspapers, Hokusai's (and others') umbrella term was narrowed down to a specific quality; it acquired the meaning of satirical and comical picture. This trend departed from the Sunday supplement of the newspaper *Jiji Shinpō*, where a "Current-Affairs Manga" section (*Jiji Manga*) was launched in 1902. Kitazawa Rakuten, who was in charge of that section and about to become the first professional cartoonist of modern Japan, appropriated Hokusai's term "manga," but not out of traditionalism. Instead, he aimed at modernity through pithy pictures that would not be "vulgar, too wordy, incapable of direct expression, and in sum, plain old-fashioned."[15] His aversion was directed at contemporaneous drawings, so-called Punch Pictures (*ponchi-e*). They were full of pictorial and verbal allegories that required reference to a shared pool of knowledge so that their enjoyment intertwined reading, watching, and talking. In contrast, the new American-modeled "manga" promoted individual viewing over communal reading and expressive images over narrative embedding. No wonder Rakuten partly copied the *Frolicking Animals* scrolls.[16] Technologically, his separation of the visual and the verbal was facilitated by the type-printing press, which required two distinct operations for integrating text and image on the same page, unlike the previous woodblock technique. Eventually, Rakuten contributed to institutionalizing manga as a subgenre of visual art dissociated from literature, including the entertaining illustrated fiction of the immediate past.[17]

Kibyōshi: Graphic Narratives

Kibyōshi, or yellow-cover books, were a genre of popular illustrated fiction for adult readers that flourished in the late eighteenth century. Edo, the capital, was their center of production and often also the setting for the narrative. A representative example is *Playboy, Roasted à la Edo* (*Edo umare uwaki no kabayaki*, 1785), authored and illustrated by Santō Kyōden.[18] On thirty pages (or fifteen folios), it tells the story of a wealthy, albeit not very attractive young man who enthuses fictional playboys so much that he eventually sets out to mimic them in reality. He gets help from two dubious assistants, even staging a topical love affair with a hired courtesan. This is supposed to culminate in a faked love-double suicide, but the intricate scheme fails. A bogus robbery organized by the protagonist's father stops the couple and is followed by their arranged wedding. Pointedly referencing contemporaneous urban culture, extended graphic narratives like this blended visual and verbal tracks in a way that evoked "comicity," or comicness, in the early twenty-first century.[19] In addition to their image-text the use of parody, exaggeration, and self-reflexivity, their seriality, and the close interrelation with other art forms of the time, especially the *kabuki* play, are today cited as evidence of the *kibyōshi* presenting "the first major comic book industry of the world."[20]

The *kibyōshi* booklets, printed in monochrome and offering entertaining narratives to readers across classes and genders, approximate contemporary *story-manga* to a much higher degree than the narrative picture scrolls or the non-narrative *Hokusai Manga*. But their reader is not guided by panel layouts, speech balloons, or transdiegetic devices; a predominantly visual flow based on sequenced images does not ensue.[21] The pages of *Playboy, Roasted à la Edo*, for example – slightly more than 50 percent of which form spreads – usually feature only one scene surrounded by a significant amount of unframed text in running script. Both pictorial and written components guide the reader visually forward toward the left, where the page turn awaits. But this progressive orientation is intertwined with a centripetal one that draws the reader's attention back to the scene and its details. The characters who inhabit the scene appear mostly in full-body size as if seen acting on a stage; the action itself, however, is not sequentially related. Like physical activities, feelings are primarily related through words in the text chunks, sometimes visually facilitated by body posture and gesturing hands rather than facial expressions and eyes. In the main, pictorial focalization and subjective perspective are missing, and so is empathy on the reader's part. The pictures, as well as the narrative, invite observation or even ridicule. As such, *Playboy, Roasted à la Edo* hardly reads like a manga. But then, which type of manga would be correspondent?

As a whole, the modern notion of manga is predominated by narratives that privilege not scenes but sequences, accelerate the possible pace of reading through variations in panel form and content, and involve the reader affectively using close-ups, jump-cuts, time-lapse, and the like. In light of this, Japanese criticism has labeled manga "cinematic." On closer inspection, however, it becomes apparent that the "cinematic" notion of manga is limited to certain genres: It prioritizes the media form's masculine genres – plot-driven serials targeted to boys and young men – at the expense of graphic narratives for girls and women, where the interplay of panel and page may easily override panel-to-panel transitions, especially when subtle changes in interpersonal relations take center stage. The presumption of a "cinematic" standard is limited also historically. Prewar children's magazines published many graphic narratives that looked "theatrical," with panels remaining largely uniform and characters presented primarily in full-body size from a more or less steady angle. While the most famous serial was *Norakuro* (1931–41) by Tagawa Suihō, the "theatrical" approach continued in the postwar period and surfaced even in Tezuka's early narratives. Against this backdrop, it stands to reason to correlate *kibyōshi* not with comics as such but more specifically with "non-cinematic" comics, just as the *Hokusai Manga* are best compared not to modern graphic narratives but to comics manuals.

Irrespective of whether *kibyōshi* actually affected modern manga artists and readers, their consideration sheds light on historical diversity. "Illustrated novels" (*sashi-e shōsetsu*) and "picture stories" (*emonogatari*) are particularly relevant in this regard, especially insofar as their venue was the commercial magazines for children. From the 1930s to the 1950s, children's magazines serialized illustrated novels and picture stories next to a third category called manga. This type of manga consisted primarily of short horizontal comic strips lining up regularly sized panels with "non-cinematic" black-and-white line drawings inside. In contrast, the illustrated novel featured only one or two images per spread. Its illustrations were shaped in a non-rectangular way and not demarcated by lines from the vertically typed surrounding text. While faintly reminiscent of *kibyōshi* with respect to the page compositions, their finely detailed imagery marks them as modern, that is, different from the domestic tradition. At the same time, the low degree of text-image integration, as well as the lack of visual vectorization, disconnects them from contemporary manga, including realist narratives for grown-ups (*seinen manga*).

Picture stories, however, were different, even if sharing with the illustrated fiction the fundamental separation of images and text. The serial *Puchar in Wonderland* (*Fushigina kuni no Puchā*) by Fukujirō Yokoi, published in the same monthly magazine as *Norakuro* from 1946 to 1948, is an instructive example (Fig. 1.1).

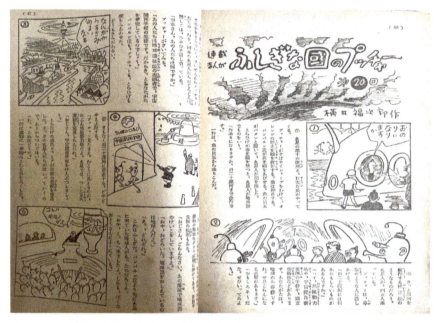

Figure 1.1 Fukujirō Yokoi, *Puchar in Wonderland*, in *Shōnen Club*, March 1948, pp. 46–47. Collection of Kyoto Seika University International Manga Research Center/Kyoto International Manga Museum.

Typical pages feature pairs of a text block and a panel in three tiers. The panels are regularly sized and have ruled frames, but their position alternates between right and left. The reading direction is indicated by numbers. Mostly attached to both the panels and the text sections, numbers guide the viewer from image to text to text to image and from tier to tier. In addition to their simple line drawings, the panels occasionally contain sound effects, pictorial runes, and speech balloons. But even if the same dialog line reappears in the text section, verbal and visual tracks are not necessarily redundant. Rather, they provide different perspectives, swinging back and forth between past and present tense, inviting observation and immersion in alternation. What appears as a clear-cut separation between the visual and the verbal modalities at first glance is actually an intricate collaboration between the two. This collaboration leans on the reader's "animating" gaze, which is visually guided by the page layout and its drawn as well as written elements. Magazine-based picture stories approximate today's manga insofar as they present framed images and text chunks in sequence. In view of the visual flow thus engendered, it cannot easily be assumed that the picture stories occupied a preliminary stage in the evolution of *story-manga*, as has been the case in Japanese manga historiography. Precisely this comes to the fore through their comparison with *kibyōshi*.

Coda

As demonstrated above, the identification of "comicitous" or "mangaesque" traits in narrative and non-narrative art of the past is not a matter of "either/ or" but of perspective and degree. It depends on the considered histori- cal period, the types of modern graphic narrative used in the comparison, and the aesthetic and cultural issues at stake. Foregrounding the reader's experience and potential agency, this chapter looked at textual and mate- rial affordances stretching from the basic elements of visual storytelling, including written text, to media-specific formats. It also considered usage, ranging from cognitive and sensory to communicative and participatory dimensions of experiencing graphic narratives. Yet, most importantly, cor- relating medieval *emaki*, early modern *kibyōshi*, and the famous *Hokusai Manga* with modern *story-manga* helped to realize conceptual heterogene- ity: first, "manga" as a form of visual art based on line drawing, but also visual narrative materialized through sequenced images and facilitated by transdiegetic devices; second, "manga" as designating fiction with a strong storyline, but also non-fiction narratives and non-narrative manuals; third, *story-manga* as not necessarily "cinematic" but also "theatrical" graphic narratives; and fourth, manga as defined by textual properties but also (sub) cultural practices of use. Pairs of options like these do easily turn into oppo- sites whenever their immediate narrative, medial, and visual contexts stay unconsidered, not to mention historical examination regarding frequency and continuity of production and access. In order to come to terms with more recent changes affecting the aesthetic and cultural contours of manga and anime, or their media specificity, "either/or" approaches are obviously less expedient than attention to historical contingency, not only with respect to discourses but also aesthetic experience.

Notes

1. Shige (CJ) Suzuki and Ronald Stewart, *Manga: A Critical Guide* (Bloomsbury Academic, 2022), 12–13.
2. For the term "transdiegetic," see Eike Exner, *Comics and the Origins of Manga: A Revisionist History* (New Brunswick, NJ: Rutgers University Press, 2022), 61–62.
3. For example, Eriko Ogihara-Schuck, *Miyazaki's Animism Abroad: The Reception of Japanese Religious Themes by American and German Audiences* (Jefferson, NC: McFarland & Co., 2014).
4. In addition to Exner, see Kentarō Miwa, *Manga to eiga* (Tokyo: NTT Shuppan, 2014).
5. Literally, *Caricatures of Birds, Animals, and Humans*, with the meaning of cari- cature reappearing in "frolicking." Hereafter, *Frolicking Animals*.

6. Critically examined by Yōko Yamamoto, "'Otona-genai mono' ga hattatsu suru toki: sōjikei toshite no emaki to manga," *Bijutsu Forum*, 21, no. 24 (2011): 25.

7. For the interpretation of the scrolls see Daisuke Itō, *Chōjū Giga o yomu* (Nagoya: Nagoya daigaku shuppankai, 2021).

8. Isao Takahata, *Jūni seiki no animeishon: Kokuhō emakimono ni miru eigateki, animeteki naru mono* (Tokyo: Tokuma shoten, 1999); Takahata, "12th-Century Moving Pictures," *Japan Quarterly*, 48, no. 3 (2001): 31–41.

9. Yamamoto, "'Otona-genai mono'," 24.

10. Yōko Yamamoto, "Manga izen no Nihon kaiga no jikan to kūkan hyōgen: Manga no koma to no taihi ni oite," *Meisei daigaku kenkyū kiyō*, no. 12 (2004): 125.

11. Panelling of the Scene "The Kid's Quarrel" of *Bandainagon ekotoba*, in Takahata, *Jūni seiki no animeishon*, 86; reproduced, for example, in Jaqueline Berndt, "Manga Flows: Reading the Paneled Spread against Handscroll and Webtoon." In *Love, Fight, Feast: The Multifaceted World of Japanese Narrative Art*, edited by Khanh Trinh (Zürich: Scheidegger & Spiess, 2021), 50.

12. Concept coined by Gō Itō in his monograph *Tezuka izu deddo: Hirakareta manga hyōgenron e* (Tokyo: NTT Publishing, 2005).

13. See Jaqueline Berndt, "Pictures that Come to Life: The Hokusai Manga." In *Hokusai*, edited by Wayne Crothers (Melbourne: National Gallery of Victoria, 2017), 21–27.

14. *Seasonal Passersby* (*Shiki no yukikai*, 1798) by Santō Kyōden & Kitao Shigemasa, according to Adam L. Kern, *Manga from the Floating World: Comicbook Culture and the Kibyōshi of Edo Japan* (Cambridge, MA: Harvard University Press, 2006), xxvi.

15. Ronald Stewart, "Manga as Schism: Kitazawa Rakuten's Resistance to 'Old-Fashioned' Japan." In *Manga's Cultural Crossroads*, edited by Jaqueline Berndt and Bettina Kümmerling-Meibauer (New York: Routledge, 2013), 34.

16. Displayed in the *The City Exhibition Manga* (British Museum, 2019) but not reproduced in the catalog. Rakuten was Kitazawa's artist name, which can be used on its own according to Japanese custom.

17. Hirohito Miyamoto, "The Formation of an Impure Genre: On the Origins of Manga," translated by Jennifer Prough, *Review of Japanese Culture and Society*, no. 14 (2002): 44.

18. Translated by Adam L. Kern, in *Manga from the Floating World*, 339–426.

19. For the neologism see Colin Beineke, "On Comicity," *Inks*, 1, no. 2 (2017): 226–253.

20. Adam L. Kern, "Manga," In *Keywords for Comics Studies*, edited by Ramzi Fawaz, Deborah Whaley, and Shelley Streeby (New York: New York University Press, 2021), 150.

21. See Chris Gavaler, *The Comics Form: The Art of Sequenced Images* (London: Bloomsbury Academic, 2022).

2

RONALD STEWART

Newspaper Comic Strips
Laughs in Four Panels

Humorous comic strips are given scant attention in most writing on manga, yet they have been vital to the art form and its evolution. Historically, newspapers were the major locus, and laughter was the main objective of manga as it developed during the first half of the twentieth century. With the rise to prominence of so-called *story-manga*, humor took a back seat to narrative. This resulted in the postwar emergence of some types of manga entirely devoid of humor, as seen, for instance, in darker themed comics for slightly older audiences (*gekiga*), that distinguished themselves from the then still strong connotations of manga as children's humorous reading material. From the 1970s onward, Japanese manga studies have focused primarily on entertaining graphic narratives serialized in specialist magazines, a type of manga that was initially targeted at children. Consequently, just like manga's historical correlation with foreign comics and contemporary art, the significant role of single-panel cartoons (*hitokoma manga*) and four-panel (comic) strips (*yonkoma manga*, also *4-koma*) fell into critical oblivion.[1] This is despite the importance of, in particular, the latter which has been routinely practiced, and referenced, by *story-manga* creators with respect to narrative structure; and which, in contrast to political cartoons, remains popular today – enjoyed as one type of "manga" appearing not only in their traditional home, newspapers, but also in major manga magazines, in manga book editions, and on social media.

The *yonkoma* format retains a strong connotation of humor for Japanese readers. Yet humor alone does not distinguish it from other variants of manga. Humor actually has a strong presence in long-form story-manga as well. This is evident, for example, in the running gag in Hiromu Arakawa's *Full Metal Alchemist* (*Hagane no renkinjutsushi*, 2001–10) about the height of the protagonist Ed, who is thrown into a rage whenever he is called short and who temporarily turns into a comical character by assuming a *chibi* (hyper-simplified or cartoonish) shape, thereby reducing him to pure hyperbolic emotion. Even the quite serious *Golden Kamuy* (2014–22) by Satoru

Noda introduces moments of surprise, at times almost childish, comic relief to offer a break from the tension built in this intense, often realistically violent, narrative. These contrast with the gentle situational humor of Kaori Tsurutani's *BL Metamorphosis* (*Metamorufōze no engawa*, 2017–20) that arises from an unlikely friendship between a girl and an elderly woman and their transgressions of social expectations in pursuit of their shared interest: boys love (BL) manga. But none of these examples belong to one of the established humor subgenres in graphic narratives, which include love comedy, gag manga, and essay manga, nor to the two defined by form – single-panel cartoons and *yonkoma* strips. The focus in this chapter is on the latter, particularly those appearing in newspapers, overviewing their past and present before exploring their narrative structure and humor.

Most Japanese newspapers contain some form of manga but *yonkoma* strips are the most commonly encountered and the most widely read. These are followed by political cartoons, and also single-panel gag cartoons, essay manga, and comics reportage.[2] The comparatively large circulation of Japanese newspapers allows these manga to be read by a broad and substantial segment of the population of various age groups. Like elsewhere in the world, Japanese newspapers have experienced a precipitous fall in readership as people have turned steadily to internet sites and social media for news over the last two decades. Although the market – comprising national, regional, and so-called sports newspapers – has witnessed an almost 40 percent drop in readership since the beginning of the twenty-first century, total circulation still exceeds 33 million and equates to roughly one newspaper for every two households. Despite the reduction in numbers, such figures can only be the envy of newspaper industries in other countries. Japan's two biggest national newspapers, *Yomiuri Shimbun* and *Asahi Shimbun*, have circulations of around seven and five million, respectively, and most of Japan's roughly forty regional papers have circulations ranging from between 150,000 and 400,000.[3] Almost all of these papers carry at least one daily *yonkoma* (four-panel) strip intended to deliver a daily dose of humor to their readers, and while this form has become synonymous with newspapers in Japan, it is also found in magazines and increasingly on the internet.

Yonkoma Manga

Today, almost without fail, *yonkoma manga* appear in a vertical format and look like four identically sized building blocks stacked one atop another, with their narratives unfolding from the top panel down. Different from the dynamic use of panels typifying other forms of manga, artists are confined to working within uniform dimensions and fixed number panels. Although restricted in overall length, the horizontal strips common in other countries allow the cartoonist flexibility in altering individual panel width to produce from one to five panels in the same overall horizontal space. This width variation can serve a range of purposes: as a device for varying the tempo or narrative pace; to emphasize panoramic backgrounds, distance between characters, and even cramped space; or to extend left to right motion. Japanese artists working with vertically formatted strips are not afforded such luxury. With few exceptions, they must create their short humorous narratives using the same four rectangular panels. Only very rarely do creators bring two panels together to make a taller frame or turn one panel into a thought bubble for the one below, extending the tail of the bubble down into the lower panel. In newspapers these strips are usually topped with a small banner carrying the title and the creator's name (in some cases the banner is located vertically to the right or left side of the strip). The characters are inevitably drawn in a simple cartoonish manner with minimal background, and as such, they are not dissimilar to a US strip such as the enormously successful *Peanuts* (1950–2000) by Charles M. Schulz. This choice of simplicity is, at least in part, pragmatic due to the fast pace demanded of artists in producing daily strips. Moreover, their relatively small size on the newspapers page makes highly detailed drawings unsuitable (the average size of each panel is currently around 3 (h) × 5 (w) cm). Each episode, while serialized, is typically a self-contained story; longer, well-defined overarching narratives are rare.

Yonkoma manga appear in the top left-hand corner of the last or penultimate page of a newspaper. Even today most continue to be printed in black and white, although color strips are gradually becoming more common. Those in national papers or syndicated to multiple regional papers target a broad audience, and, as such, they are reserved in the choice of theme and the use of humor so as to avoid offense. Their language usage and content are intentionally made easy to understand in an effort to cater to a wide age demographic, often including text glosses in simple phonetic characters (*hiragana*) to enable even elementary school readers access to the more difficult Sino-Japanese *kanji* text. There is also a tendency to evade references that demand local knowledge, even though strips printed only in regional papers can make their content very localized. One example is Masahiro Mukaoka's *Golden Wedding Anniversary Tosa Diary* (*Kinkon Tosa nikki*, 2004–) in the *Kochi Shimbun*, in which the elderly protagonist couple speak in Tosa dialect. This employment of language is part of the comic strip's local appeal. Its humor arises to a degree from the contrast between the familiar, if somewhat old-fashioned, dialect, and the Standard Japanese language of the strip's other characters and the surrounding news articles.

For some readers of newspaper dailies, the *yonkoma manga* is the first thing they turn to. It is not unusual for readers to collect newspaper comic strips by cutting them out and clipping them together or pasting them into scrapbooks. This is a practice that has continued since at least the 1920s. Popular *yonkoma manga* from newspapers, magazines, and even websites are also published as collections in book form.[4]

Media History

The earliest multipanel strips appeared in Japanese newspapers and magazines around 1890. Over the next decade, they would surface only intermittently. A great number were redrawn from overseas periodicals such as the American *Puck* and *Life*, and the German *Fliegende Blätter*. These tended to be untitled gag strips of varying lengths without recurring characters. Many were pantomime (or silent) strips, and in those with text, the narration or dialog was routinely positioned outside of the panels. At times, the strips were split into individual panels and placed among unrelated text articles, usually one per page, so their narratives unfolded over several pages. This began to change in 1902 when the newspaper *Jiji Shinpō* introduced a weekly comics page called *Jiji Manga* in the hope of lightening its image and harnessing some of the popularity that it knew newspaper comics pages had gained in the United States. The cartoonist Kitazawa Rakuten was charged with creating character-based strips of two to ten panels, which he achieved by populating his strips with a number of named humorous characters, including clumsy country bumpkins, a well-to-do dandy, and mischievous children. The success of the page encouraged other newspapers to employ cartoonists, but it took until 1923 for Japanese newspapers to embrace daily character strips wholeheartedly. Three early hits were the Japanese translation of US cartoonist George McManus' *Bringing Up Father* (1923–40); Asao Yutaka's *Easygoing Papa* (*Nonkina tōsan*, 1923–26), which took its cue from McManus' strip; and Shōsei Oda and Kazuichi Kabashima's *Shō-chan's Adventures* (*Shō-chan no bōken*, 1923–25), which was inspired by a UK strip.[5] Each of these ran initially as four-panel strips in a two-tier, two-column shaped grid (*tanoji*) form. Among these, it was *Shō-chan's Adventures* that eventually settled on the now common vertical format,[6] and although *Shō-chan* was an adventure strip, other humor cartoonists began to follow its lead in terms of format. By the mid-1930s, titled character strips with speech balloons in the vertical *yonkoma* format became the standard in newspapers.[7] It was possibly the popularity of newer strips such as Ryūichi Yokoyama's *Fuku-chan* (1936–71) that concretized this form.

Four-panel strips flourished in the postwar period. Evidence suggests there may have been well over 700 *yonkoma manga* titles run in various newspapers throughout the country.[8] The most notable national long-runners were the abovementioned *Fuku-chan*, a little boy with childish but off-kilter logic; Machiko Hasegawa's feisty but bungling young woman *Sazae-san* (1946–74); Sanpei Satō's hapless lowly office worker *Fuji-san Tarō* (1965–91); Masashi Ueda's mischievous boy *Kobo-chan* (1982–; *Kobo, the Li'l Rascal* in English), and Hisaichi Ishii's third-year elementary school student *Nono-chan* (1997–), who is incapable of applying herself to the things required of her. All of these comic strips revolve around a titular character who is usually a social type taken from everyday life. This thematic trend is thought to have emerged in the 1930s when humor in the manga industry more or less bifurcated with newspaper manga focused mainly on daily-life situations contrasting with magazine manga that leaned toward fantasy and adventure, or nonsense and erotica.[9] Renowned manga artist Osamu Tezuka enumerated a number of sources of humor in manga: the unexpected, the irrational (situation) gag, the everyday (experience) gag, the thought gag, slapstick, and wordplay. He felt, however, that the mundane type of humor generated by familiar environments at home, work, or school, was not only the most widely used form of humor in manga but also the most appropriate for newspaper *yonkoma manga*. This was despite his belief that the same themes could readily be turned into black humor for publications aimed at narrower audiences by adding a bit of venom.[10] This emphasis on the everyday means many strips can delve into social satire to offer quite pointed critiques of social behavior.[11] No different from characters deployed in other genres of comic (or humorous) expression, such as comedy films and theater, animation, jokes, and gag cartoons, protagonists are regularly cast in recognizable stereotypes. Their personality or character flaws, namely their impatience, naivety, overexuberance, erroneous logic, or inability to follow "common sense" social rules are the source of both their troubles and the strips' humor. They exhibit little ability, if any, to reflect on these foibles, and are hence condemned to repeat their mistakes. In reading these strips, adoring fans bring to bear their expectations and knowledge of the personality failings as well as the world or the setting of the characters, and in the process hope for a similar emotional experience each time. This leaves creators with the daunting task of delivering the humorous experience without betraying expectations and without becoming overly repetitive or clichéd, thereby losing the interest of their readers.

While newspapers have long been linked to the four-panel strip, its popularity is by no means restricted to their pages. In the twenty years after the war, humor magazines aimed at adult audiences boomed. These publications were filled with Japanese and overseas gag cartoons and multipanel strips. A four-panel silent strip by US cartoonist Bob Battle, titled in Japanese *Ijiwaru jiisan* (*Old Man Mischief*, 1956–62),[12] was serialized in *Manga Tokuhon* and became, for example, the inspiration for Machiko Hasegawa's hilarious *yonkoma* serial *Granny Mischief* (*Ijiwaru bāchan*, 1966–71).[13] Recent decades have seen the publication of a number of specialist magazines. The oldest and best known – the monthly *Manga Time* – began in 1981 and currently boasts a circulation of approximately 120,000 copies. Another, *Manga Life*, is home to an enduring classic, Mikio Igarashi's *Bonobono* (1986–), which features endearing humorous episodes of sea otters, squirrels, and other forest animals. The online version of this magazine, *Manga Life Win,* has given birth to the zany schoolgirl series *Pop Team Epic* (2006–) by Bkub Okawa.

Monthly and weekly manga magazines and general interest magazines also run *yonkoma*. Popular examples include the "office ladies"-centered strip *OL Revolution* (*OL shinkaron,* in *Comic Morning*, 1989–) by Risu Akizuki; Kenji Sonishi's offbeat strip *Neko Ramen* (in *Comic Blade*, 2006–12) about a cat who runs a ramen noodle restaurant; and Kiyohiko Azuma's work that was driven by eccentric schoolgirl characters *Azuma daioh* (in *Comic Dengeki Daioh*, 1999–2002). These series are aimed at smaller audiences and narrower demographics. As such, they are able to focus on much quirkier humor, breaking away from the familiar everyday themes and conventions of newspaper strips. They are often more in tune with youth cultures, can more easily broach subjects generally considered taboo, and can more readily reject the standard *ki-shō-ten-ketsu* narrative structure discussed below. Yet, despite this greater diversity, it is still the newspaper four-panel comic strip that is most associated with the *yonkoma* form.

The comic strip, just like longer-form comics, enjoys considerable popularity as a participatory culture. *Yonkoma* make up a significant segment of *dōjinshi* (fanzine-like self-published manga). The organizing committee of the largest *dōjinshi* buying-and-selling event, Comic Market (Comiket or Comike), has even asked all creator participants to produce and submit a single-panel cartoon or four-panel comic strip report on the event.[14] Annual *yonkoma* competitions take place regularly and are run by manga facilities with support from local governments (such as Kōchi's Yokoyama Memorial Manga Museum and Toyoshima's Tokiwasō Museum), print and online publishers (such as Take Shobō and Saizensen), as well as newspapers and national government agencies. The *yonkoma* competition of the newspaper *Asahi Shimbun* in 2021 attracted upward of 7,000 entries. In the same year, Japan's Ministry of Justice held a competition on the theme of the "prevention of reoffending" (*saihan bōshi*) for four-panel and single-page strips with the winning works to be employed on posters in a campaign to reduce youth crime. In 2009, the national broadcaster NHK, along with the help of veteran manga artist Kazuo Umezu, produced an eight-part television introduction to drawing *yonkoma* that was accompanied by a textbook. Workshops for school-age children are also quite common, and *yonkoma* competitions and workshops have even been organized outside Japan. In the United Kingdom, for example, the latter were held in 2020 to promote Japan-UK cultural exchange, and from 2021 a *yonkoma* category has been added to the annual Manga Jiman Competition.

Narrative Structure

The most common way to explain the composition of *yonkoma manga* is the use of the concept *ki-shō-ten-ketsu*. Originating in China during the fourteenth century to describe the ideal structure of select forms of classical poetry, *qi cheng huan he* (起承転結) was subsequently introduced to the Korean Peninsula and then spread to Japan in the sixteenth century as *ki-shō-ten-ketsu* (also written with the same characters). When applied to narratives, it calls for a four-stage structure of an introduction, development, denouement (or turn of events), and conclusion. In this sense, it is a conventional story pattern. In Japan, *ki-shō-ten-ketsu* is utilized to explain and to teach a logical organization for all types of text, from essays and business letters to movies.[15] Despite the looseness of its interpretation and application, the concept remains almost unquestioned as the lens through which to understand and create *yonkoma*. Osamu Tezuka felt that this structure is key to any manga, be it a strip or a long-form story.[16] Moreover, in the case of a humorous *yonkoma*, he stressed the importance of not revealing the gag in the first three, or *ki-shō-ten*, panels. For him, the fourth, or *ketsu*, panel should provide an unexpected turn of events or punchline (*ochi*).[17]

The idea of equating *ki-shō-ten-ketsu* with *yonkoma manga* appears to have coincided with the evolution of the four-panel format as the standard convention in Japanese newspaper comic strips. In 1927, Ippei Okamoto released a series of twenty-seven articles on how to draw manga at home, subtitled in English "The Home A.B.C. of Caricature." In the twelfth installment he focused on the *ki-shō-ten-ketsu* concept to elucidate the functioning of four-panel strips. He noted that there is no limit to the number of panels that can be used in a strip, but he found that four panels were both convenient and pleasingly in sync with Chinese poetic structure. For the third step, however, Okamoto replaces the character *ten* (転) with *san* (山 mountain) because he believed that it is the climax of the narrative, rather than simply a change in direction. He went as far as to suggest that when making a *yonkoma manga* the creator should begin by drawing the third panel.

Figure 2.1 Example of a *yonkoma* (four-panel) comic strip, from Ippei Okamoto, "The Home A. B. C. of Caricature," *Asahi Graph* (April 6, 1927), 15. The characters for *ki-shō-ten* [here *san*]-*ketsu* are indicated from top left to bottom right.

Okamoto offers an example with the story of a couple who go on a cherry-blossom viewing picnic (Fig. 2.1). He begins with the third panel (bottom left), in which he has drawn the couple sitting on a picnic blanket; the husband reels back in surprise, spilling his drink. When his wife asks what the matter is, he exclaims that the sake his wife had just poured him was sour. This unexpected turn of events is the source of the strip's humor. Okamoto then advises moving to the proceeding second panel, which should illustrate the situation leading up to the incident and here shows the happy-faced couple settling down under a flowering cherry tree. Next is the first panel that indicates the direct cause of the incident in the third and has the couple preparing to leave home for their picnic. The husband mistakenly pours vinegar into his flask, with an identically shaped sake bottle untouched to the side. In the final panel, the wife looks on in surprise at her husband's actions and asks, "We've just got home, what are you doing?" The husband, wearing a disappointed look, punches over the bottle of sake in the kitchen, saying to it, "This is your fault."

Later artists placed emphasis on different panels and approached the process differently. In his book on how to draw *yonkoma manga*, Kazuo Umezu, like Osamu Tezuka, puts the stress on the fourth panel. Umezu likewise cautions against revealing too much in panels two and three, and plays down their significance.[18] For Umezu, what is of utmost importance are the first and the concluding fourth panels, which he sees as bearing the most affective impact. He argues that in a good *yonkoma* these two panels are inextricably linked – the emotions or feelings expressed in the first panel should be completely reversed by the punchline in the fourth.[19] In his textbook on making strips, Umezu outlines the following four steps in the creation process: (1) before drawing, casually chose anything familiar to you from everyday life as a starting point; (2) think of a fourth panel that turns this beginning completely on its head; (3) once you have decided on the beginning and end, write it down; and (4) finally, draw the comic strip as a rough sketch based on your script, then review it to produce the finishing touches.[20] Every creator of *yonkoma manga* ultimately brings their own individual perspective to the form, and in doing so, develops their own method. Masashi Ueda's newspaper strip *Kobo-chan*, the longest running *yonkoma manga* of this type, is representative.

In the first panel of this cartoon (Fig. 2.2), Kobo-chan's grandmother stands outside the family home, indicated by the fences and power pole,

Figure 2.2 Masashi Ueda, *Kobo-chan*, *Yomiuri Shimbun*, September 12, 1984.

and calls to her grandson: "Kobo-chaan, dinner!" (*Kobo-chaan, gohan yo – !*). In the second panel, Ueda pans back to a long shot, so we can see that Kobo-chan's grandmother has moved to another location in the neighborhood, all the while calling, "Kobo-chaan, dinner!" Visible in the foreground is the back of a recycled paper collection truck, a sort of Chekhov's gun by not giving away, but nonetheless rendering understandable, the final punchline. In the third panel, Ueda moves back even further so we can see entire houses in the neighborhood, with Kobo-chan in the foreground playing with friends. Kobo-chan turns toward the voice in the distance that has suddenly become so loud he can now hear his grandmother's "Kobo-chaan, dinner!" The fourth panel presents the gag punchline, the reason why the grandmother's voice has carried all the way to the park. The recyclable paper collector returns to his truck with bundles of used paper from the house outside of which he is parked, only to find that a stranger – Kobo-chan's grandmother – has appropriated the truck loudspeaker that is normally reserved to announce the paper collection in the neighborhood. He casts a look of disapproval at her as she blushes with embarrassment.

The *ki-shō-ten-ketsu* formula as demonstrated here can be used to explain the structure of the majority of conventional *yonkoma manga*, but it is limited as a critical concept. First, it is not unique to this form of manga; it can be applied to most orthodox narratives in any media. Second, and more importantly, it does not explain how the humor in *yonkoma manga* is produced. To unlock how the various levels of humor might operate in this form beyond Tezuka's aforementioned list of humor types, elements such as caricature, transgressions of social taboos, stereotypes, satire, irony, parody, hyperbole, incongruity, and superiority (victim humor) should be considered. In other words, a deeper engagement with the theories of humor studies is necessary.[21]

One possible approach in the examination of *yonkoma manga* within humor studies is the treatment of the form as a joke through the application of the linguistic script-based semantic theory of humor (SSTH).[22] According to this theory, the strip would be treated as text within which two normally incompatible scripts (or frames of understanding) exist. The punchline suddenly brings these two scripts together, shifting from the primary script to the secondary and underscoring a humorous incongruity. In the Kobo-chan example above, the primary script is one family member calling to another family member to come home for dinner. The secondary script is a recycled paper collection truck with a loudspeaker. And the punchline is the coalescing of these two somewhat incompatible scripts through incongruous logic in the final panel. This linguistic approach requires modification in order to more fully account for medium specificity, particularly in visual aspects such as the drawing style and the four-panel structure that carries an expectation of humor. Nevertheless, it tells us more about how humor functions than the application of the concept *ki-shō-ten-ketsu* which, to reiterate, is not specifically about humor but rather about narrative structure.

Not all *yonkoma manga* strictly conform to the *ki-shō-ten-ketsu* structure, as noted above. It is not uncommon for the development of the narrative to continue into the third panel, with the turn of events and conclusion compressed into the final panel. Moreover, in the late 1980s and early 1990s there were a number of new wave *yonkoma manga* creators working in magazines, including Sensha Yoshida and Kotobuki Shiriagari (now working for the major newspapers, *Tokyo Shimbun* and *Asahi Shimbun,* respectively), who often ignored the rules of *ki-shō-ten-ketsu* by having no clear *ketsu*, or conclusion. It has been argued that this actually underscores the strength of the established *ki-shō-ten-ketsu* formula since part of the humor of these strips is that they are breaking the rules of or parodying this structural convention. It seems that the reliance on this entrenched narrative pattern concept is unlikely to be discarded at any time in the near future.

Conclusion

Over the last century, *yonkoma manga* have developed primarily within newspapers to become a significant component of Japanese comics culture. As printed newspaper circulations continue to decline and news companies head toward a more competitive online presence, the future of four-panel strips in newspapers may well be in the balance. Nonetheless, what is clear is the continuance of the form. Specialist *yonkoma manga* magazine sales still remain strong, with specialist online sites and fan-cultural variants on the rise. At least for the immediate future newspapers will remain the primary platform for these strips.

Despite its potential drawbacks and limits, the concept of *ki-shō-ten-ketsu* offers a helpful framework in structuring *yonkoma manga* and explaining their composition. Yet the examination into how humor in this form actually operates has to date been largely ignored. Notwithstanding the existence of a number of humorous genres, as well as the broad use of humor in all forms of manga, its workings have not yet received the academic attention they deserves. There is a genuine and a much overdue need for manga studies to engage with established theories of humor and to explore the extent to which they accommodate manga.

Notes

1. See Hiroshi Odagiri "Manga truisms: On the Insularity of Japanese Manga Discourse." In *Comics Worlds and the World of Comics: Towards Scholarship on a Global Scale*, edited by Jaqueline Berndt (Kyoto: International Manga Research Center, 2010), 53–66, http://imrc.jp/lecture/2009/12/comics-in-the-world.html.

2. For example, after the 2011 earthquake, tsunami, and Fukushima nuclear-reactor meltdown in northeastern (Tōhoku) Japan, Shūji Akagi reported on daily life in the disaster-affected region in a weekly comic strip of varied format, but mostly the vertical four-panel style in the *Chūgoku Shimbun*. Tenten Hosokawa's monthly essay manga in *Kobe Shimbun* is usually comprised of a banner and three tiers of panels taking up roughly a quarter of the newspaper page.

3. "Chōsa deta: Hakkō busū," *Pressnet: Nihon Shinbun Kyōkai*, November 2021, www.pressnet.or.jp/data/circulation/.

4. Some long-running *yonkoma manga* have been collected into volumes, such as Hasegawa's *Sazae-san* (68 vols.) and Masashi Ueda's *Kobo-chan* (111 vols.). Both have also seen Kodansha bilingual editions (1997–2015). Other translated collections are *Granny Mischief* (Tokyo: Kodansha, 2001–02), *OL Revolution* (Tokyo: Kodansha, 2005), *Neko Ramen* (Los Angeles: Viz, 2006), and *Pop Team Epic* (New York: Vertical Comics, 2015).

5. For impact of foreign, in particular American, comics on the formation of manga as "audiovisual comics" see Eike Exner, *Comics and the Origins of Manga: A Revisionist History* (New Brunswick, NJ: Rutgers University Press, 2022).

6. Isao Shimizu, *Yonkoma manga: Hokusai kara 'moe' e* (Tokyo: Iwanami Shinsho, 2009), 58–62.

7. This can be seen in the exhibition catalog. Newspark, ed., *Shinbun manga no me: hito seiji shakai* (Yokohama: Newspark, 2003).

8. Nihon Shinbun Manga Kenkyūsho, ed., *Shinbun manga sōmokuroku: shohan* (Tokyo: Nihon Shinbun Manga Kenkyūsho, 2019).

9. Yoshihiro Yonezawa, *Sengo gyagu manga-shi* (Tokyo: Chikuma Shobō, 2009), 28–31.

10. Osamu Tezuka, *Manga no kakikata: nigao-e kara chōhen made* (Tokyo: Kobunsha, 1998 [1977]), 130–41.

11. Social satire is common in newspaper *yonkoma manga*, but political satire is limited. Examples include Norio Yamanoi's *Samitto gakuen* (*Summit School*) (*Asahi Shimbun*, 1993–96), Kenī and Ramada's *Nagata-chō gekijō* (*Nagata-chō Theatre*) (*Mainichi Shimbun*, 1993), and some work by the award-winning political cartoonist for the *Tokyo Shimbun*, Masaaki Satō.

12. The original English title of this strip could not be tracked down.

13. Machiko Hasegawa, *Uchiakebanashi* (Tokyo: Asahi Shimbun Shuppan, 2022), 88.

14. A Comic Market Organizing Committee official Twitter (now X) account message of January 16, 2017, described the event report task and provided a template.

15. For example, scriptwriter Hideo Okuni, who worked on a number of Akira Kurosawa films, also used this concept.

16. Tezuka, *Manga no kakikata*, 124–29. Manga artist and educator Kunio Nagatani concurs with Tezuka, suggesting the importance of mastering the *ki-shō-ten-ketsu* structure of *yonkoma* to create any manga work. Kunio Nagatani, *Manga no kōzōgaku!* (Tokyo: Index Shuppansha, 2000), 82.
17. Tezuka, *Manga no kakikata*, 124–25.
18. Kazuo Umezu, *Umezu Kazuo no ima kara kakeru! Yonkoma manga nyūmon* (Tokyo: NHK Shuppan, 2009), 98.
19. Umezu, *Umezu Kazuo*, 84–85.
20. Umezu, *Umezu Kazuo*, 80–87, 98.
21. On the three "classical" theories of humor, see John Morreall, "Philosophy of Humor," *The Stanford Encyclopedia of Philosophy*, Fall 2020, https://plato.stanford.edu/archives/fall2020/entries/humor/.
22. For an overview of SSTH, see Salvatore Attardo, "A Primer for the Linguistics of Humor." In *The Primer of Humor Research*, edited by Victor Raskin (The Hague: Mouton de Gruyter, 2008), 107–15.

3

JOON YANG KIM

Astro Boy and the "Weaponized" Children of Wartime Japan

While Japanese animation dates back to 1917, the year when the three pioneers, Ōten Shimokawa, Sumikazu Kōuchi, and Seitarō Kitayama, are reported to have each created their first animated shorts, the history of anime can be said to have begun with the 1963 animated television series, *Astro Boy (Tetsuwan Atomu)*, in terms of format (one thirty-minute episode per week), style (limited animation), production system, and transmedia relation.[1] Produced eleven years after the inception of the eponymously titled manga series, this animated TV series aired in the United States several months after its first broadcast in Japan. Further, the use of the term "anime" in the Japanese context seems to have been triggered by Osamu Tezuka's defense of the *Astro Boy* anime series against those who rejected it for using the technique of limited animation: In their view, full animation was one of the requirements that indicated quality. But Tezuka stated, "*Astro Boy* is not an animation but a TV anime *(terebi anime)*; it is not supposed to be a show of movements but stories."[2] As regards such narrative motivation, the *Astro Boy* series was also a forerunner of the themes and motifs that are easily found in today's anime, including technology, android robots, mechanical others, posthuman-ness, and child soldiers. This chapter is intended to shed light on the ideological and political origins of those conventions, placing the pivotal *Astro Boy* series within an overlooked type of media ecology developed before and during World War II.

Robots and Imperial Japan's Wartime Ideology of Science

Undoubtedly one of the most popular Japanese anime and manga characters, Astro Boy has been considered by many in Japan and abroad as a pathbreaking icon in the discourse on postwar Japanese popular culture. This posthuman android character and the many other robot figures on and beyond the screen that have followed it have served to narrativize postwar Japan as a leading player in technology. Japanese culture has frequently been approached with a techno-Orientalist gaze – in other words, a revised version of Orientalism in dealing with technologized non-Western countries.[3] In this regard, anime, together with manga, has continuously been subject to two preconceptions, particularly since globalization in the mid-1990s. One is their alleged association with postmodernism, which is closely involved with techno-Orientalism, and the other is their extrapolated link to traditional art forms such as illuminated handscrolls (*emaki*) or woodblock prints (*ukiyo-e*) in an effort to establish an often nativist genealogy of the medium. In effect, both preconceptions have helped to obscure or elude the nation's uncomfortable wartime period, during which time animation and comics witnessed remarkable development.[4]

Eschewing these discursive conventions and focusing instead on the ideological context of media in wartime Japan, this chapter revisits Astro Boy against the backdrop of the state policies of imperial Japan that foregrounded science (*kagaku*). During the Fifteen-Year War (1931–45), science was conceptualized by the Japanese government as a kind of weapon that would lead to victory. Propaganda that emphasized modern, and thus scientific, warfare spread throughout the empire. War-oriented or war-friendly science was not only promoted within the Imperial Japanese Army (IJA) but also within nonmilitary, child-oriented spaces such as elementary education, magazines for children, manga, animation, and the toy industry.[5]

The *Astro Boy* manga began in 1952 as a "science adventure story" (*kagaku bōken monogatari*), and its 1963 anime adaptation introduced Astro Boy as a "child of science" (*kagaku no ko*) in the lyrics of the opening theme song. Significantly, the latter term is found in an earlier android-themed manga, *Puchar in Wonderland* (*Fushigina kuni no Puchā*; hereafter *Puchar*) by Fukujirō Yokoi. Its serialization in the monthly boys' magazine *Shōnen Club* began in 1946, six years before the release of the *Astro Boy* manga.[6]

Yokoi's manga plays a crucial role in two aspects that connect Astro Boy to the wartime policy of science and equally to his still under-researched precursors. First, the term "child of science," present in both Yokoi's 1947 manga and Tezuka's 1963 anime, is itself a discursive agent. It assists in placing Astro Boy within a historical framework spanning a broader period, without simply diverting the discussion of the character to iconographical or textual references, for example, Pinocchio. As already one of the most popular manga artists during the Fifteen-Year War, Yokoi greatly influenced Tezuka who was an enthusiastic reader of Yokoi's works.[7] Yokoi appears to have rarely used the term "child of science" in his wartime manga, but the field of children's literature provides a clear equivalent in Ranpo Edogawa's *Stories of a Science Boy* (*Kagaku shōnen monogatari*, 1942–43). Under this title, Edogawa's later installments of his serial for *Shōnen Club*, initially titled *Clever Ichitarō* (*Chie no Ichitarō*), revolve around the fictional elementary school boy Ichitarō. Notably, Ichitarō, the "science boy," is not an android but a human, and as such different from Astro Boy who is similarly called a "child of science." Representing both machine and human, this semantically mysterious overlap becomes more complicated when Yokoi's *Puchar* is brought into focus.

In the futuristic narrative of Yokoi's *Puchar* manga, a "child of science" refers principally to the human boy named Puchar but also to the android boy Pely, the mechanical substitute of Puchar's cousin who died in a train accident. Furthermore, Puchar is depicted as forming a brotherly relationship with Pely. In this new human-machine relationship mediated by a human child's death, "child of science" does not simply refer to androids as creations of science or the peak of humans' demiurgic, world-making, intelligence. It likewise connotes the next generation of children, who would go beyond the divide between human and nonhuman, organic and mechanical, real and fake, in human-centric and Cartesian terms. Problematizing the military traits of Astro Boy and his intratextual and transtextual siblings – brothers for the most part – the following section explores how the state policy of science was enacted and carried out to forge this new type of child by mobilizing and manipulating the human body.

Human Bodies Incorporated into Weaponry

More detailed than the manga upon which it is based, episode 1 of the 1963 *Astro Boy* anime adaptation presents Astro Boy as an android similar to Pely in *Puchar*. After all, he is conceived by Dr. Tenma as a mechanical copy of his son, Tobio, who died in a car crash. Astro Boy is not merely a perfect copy of Tobio – he is a materialization of the excess desire of his human creator-father. As indicated by the phrase "seven powers" in the theme song of the anime series, Dr. Tenma's new son is endowed with superpowers including jet flight, retractable machine guns (built into his hips), searchlight-like eyes, and super-hearing ears, all of which surpass human abilities and are found in jet fighters or combat drones. Generally, in every episode, Astro Boy's superhero performance paves the way for these kinds of military aircraft operating to detect, locate, target, and destroy enemies.

Astro Boy's military status is not clearly narrated in the first 1963 anime series, but it is highlighted in episode 1 of the 1980 full-color series remake. When Astro Boy is going to be booted up in a laboratory at the Ministry of Science, a research staff member warns that the robot is a new weapon with machine guns built into the body. In a later scene in the episode, such criticism of Astro Boy as a weapon is also made by the prime minister who orders Dr. Tenma to dispose of the robot because it is extremely dangerous (their antimilitary stance corresponds to Article 9 of the Japanese Constitution, which outlaws war). Astro Boy – depicted as a devoted friend of humans in manga and anime – has principally been linked to postwar Japan's pacifism as stated in the Constitution, but it is noteworthy that imperial Japan's policy of military science implemented during the war years was also profoundly influential. Seemingly unaware, Dr. Tenma creates not a copy of his real son but a child simulacrum that is also a weapon.

The portrayal of humanlike robots as weaponry in animation or manga can be traced back to the early 1930s – that is, to the beginning of the Fifteen-Year War.[8] In Gajō Sakamoto's 1934 manga, *Tank Tankurō*, for example, the body of the eponymous main character resembles a hollow cannonball with many holes through which human body parts, aircraft wings, a propeller, and machine guns protrude.[9] Clearly named after a tank, at this time a new weapon, he fights foreign enemy soldiers (presumably Chinese or Russian) on the battlefield. Tankurō also looks more like a human samurai warrior in a suit of armor equipped with modern weapons than a flying military robot in human form. Whatever the case, the figure of Tankurō presents a human body incorporated into a larger structure of weaponry, just as the other military human characters in the manga. Interestingly, this human-mechanical hybridization emerged against the historical backdrop of military accidents involving the IJA, including the Siberian Intervention (1918–22) and particularly the Shanghai Incident (1932). The latter is indicated by three historical suicide bombers (*bakudan san yūshi*), who are depicted as peripheral characters in the manga.

Tankurō's body, grafted into weaponry and mechanical devices, might be considered as purely fictional and imaginary, similar to Marvel's Ironman and other superhero characters. It could be conjectured that these manga figures should not be taken seriously as they were intended for children. Indeed, during the course of the 1930s the imperial Japanese government began to criticize manga and other forms of entertainment for children as fictional and not scientific.[10] This stance was related to the definition of modern scientific warfare upon which the empire's future relied. In 1938, the government even introduced new guidelines for the improvement of children's publications. It condemned manga as vulgar and urged all publishers to treat artwork as scientific material for child readers, precisely by visualizing the function and essential features of weapons, such as bombs, tanks, and aircraft.[11]

To ensure their economic survival under such political pressure, creators in the sectors of children's culture sought to transform the fictional into the scientific by demonstrating that the former can contribute to the development of the latter – ultimately, to be victorious through scientific warfare. Children's magazines seem to have served as one core media in this transformation. For instance, *Mechanization: Magazine of the Science for National Defense* (*Kikaika: Kokubō Kagaku Zasshi*), launched in 1940 with the support of the army, delivered elaborate and exquisite images of real and imagined weapons, along with advertisements of toy weapons and DIY instructions of how to make miniature fake weapons, including models of robots with movable hands and legs.[12] The magazine's depictions of weapons perceptually undermined the divide between the real and the fictional, between life-size originals and miniature fakes. Not every illustration represented a weapon in realistic fashion, however. Many made weapons look spectacular in combat and further provided their readers with an anatomical view of the military objects. Seeing the interior of weapons with the ironclad surface of a tank, for instance, partially peeled off, while human soldiers were shoehorned inside as emotionless, machine-like cogs, satisfied technical curiosity undisturbed by considerations of human mortality. Seemingly anything fictional was accepted as "scientific" as long as it served the state's policy of warfare. In this sense, science or scientific warfare in imperial Japan was deemed the only standpoint from which something would be accepted as real and from which reality should be seen. What happened to children's bodies in a literal sense under the state-led and warfare-driven transformation of the fictional into the real is discussed in the following section.

Children's Bodies between Real and Fake Weapons

Not long after its formation in 1940, the second cabinet of the prime minister, Fumimaro Konoe, issued the national motto of the "science-doing mind" (*kagaku suru kokoro*).[13] This was also the title of a book by physiologist Kunihiko Hashida, who served as Minister of Education in Konoe's cabinet. In addition to the transformation from the fictional to the scientific, and thus "real", the motto of the "science-doing mind" accelerated the dissemination of the state ideology of science, which permeated everyday life. For example, in an essay published in 1942, Hanako Muraoka likened the act of dealing with gas-stove valves to taking part in air-raid drills in that both involved gas (although there were differences between the fuel gas of the former and the chemical weapon of the latter), and she stressed that housewives should make a "science-doing mind" their priority across all scenes of domestic life.[14] This suggests that any act, however small, was coupled with warfare in terms of the discursive device of science.

By the early 1940s, the state ideology of science had impacted housewives and their domestic worlds, but the influence of this ideology also played out in children's miniature model toys. Miniature aircraft were highly valued because they assumed a significant role in the promotion of military science. As early as 1939, the Ministry of Education incorporated the activity of building these and other miniature weapons into the elementary school curriculum. Even after the outbreak of the Asia-Pacific War in 1941, the toy industry apparently did not suffer from the state policy of science to the same degree as manga, animation, and other cultural industries for children. Although it was difficult to manufacture metal toys because metal was an indispensable resource in the making of weapons and other war provisions, the toy industry did not have to redefine its own miniature-type products in line with the government's discourse on science. These toy products were already generally regarded by the government as practical and effective for understanding modern technologies, such as the railways and aircraft that the empire had sought to import during the modernization process from the late nineteenth century onward.[15]

As the war intensified, miniature model toys became modified into objects that not only promoted but also embodied the fascist concept of a "science-doing mind." They were intended to mobilize young children, most notably, fifth and sixth graders in elementary school, to serve the war effort and to shape them into future soldiers. One of the most explicit expressions of this change is the introduction of miniature models in children's magazines as if they were real weaponry, with catchphrases like "Miniature models are weapons." This undermined the difference between the two at a perceptual level. As noted above regarding the magazine *Mechanization*, children were surrounded by sophisticated and refined illustrations of real weapons, which were often difficult to distinguish from fake versions in miniature. Referred to as "little citizens" (*shōkokumin*), children were expected to engage in the war effort on the same terms as the adult nation (*kokumin*). The identification of toys as weaponry in the industry and mass media served to prepare children for the battlefield, tempting them with jet fighters or tanks to volunteer for the war effort. Miniature models of weapons were to an extent indistinguishable from real weapons, and this perception continued even in the aftermath of the war. When the Allied GHQ banned the design and construction of actual aircraft in Japan at this time, the toy industry voluntarily halted the manufacture and sale of model aircraft due to the (mis)understanding that the new military policy imposed by the United States also applied to their products.

Both elementary education and children's publications sought to nurture a romantic, fetishistic sense of weaponry in children through the physical, tactile, and kinesthetic experience of building and playing with model weapons. In his 1942 book, *Models of Weaponry* (*Heiki mokei*), the educationist Sōichi Yokoi emphasized that for children the act of using their hands to build model weapons was a form of experiential (even natural) pleasure that contributed to the development of the empire. Such a performative process can be said to have tuned children's bodies to the mechanical structure and function of weaponry. This was precisely the connotation of the title of the aforementioned magazine *Mechanization* – namely, becoming a machine through a series of acts of "doing science" in everyday life. In 1940, physicist Tokio Takeuchi stated that it was necessary to *rebuild* the way of life of all Japanese by establishing a Ministry of Science (ultimately not realized) in order to make Japan a powerful country.[16] His opinion suggests that the empire's wartime policy of science not only addressed human-made products and objects but also human beings themselves: "People working on the home front were robotified by the state."[17]

The robotification of humans and the fear of physical consequences can be observed in Noboru Ōshiro's 1941 manga *Pleasant Ironworks* (*Yukaina tekkōsho*).[18] In the narrative, the father travels with his little son in a large balloon around China and its vicinity – at this time colonized in part by Japan – to visit ironworks. Both wear the same type of full-body protective suit made of steel that gives them a robotic appearance. Then, the son suddenly disappears, and his father searches for him. He finally locates the protective suit that he believes is his son's (in fact, it is not), but it is empty. This scene makes readers suspect that the little human boy's body was completely replaced by mechanical parts. The father's encounter with more of the same robotlike metal suits creates the horrifying sensation that human beings, including children, have been eviscerated, hollowed out, and mechanized.

Astro Boy as Sound Detector and Military Aircraft

In the first half of the 1940s, elementary school children across Japan were being perceptually and physically tuned to weaponry through an interaction with miniature models, and their bodies were mobilized to partake in the warfare of the real world. An aspiring young cartoonist, Osamu Tezuka, witnessed this firsthand as he completed elementary school in 1941. He drew some scenes of child mobilization in one of his earliest manga, *Until the Day of Victory* (*Shōri no hi made*, ca. June 1945).[19] In one scene with an air raid, an elementary school teacher asks his young students to use their abilities of absolute pitch to detect the sound of military aircraft and to identify their numbers. A little girl then reports the pitches (or musical notes).

This scene is a literal representation of the sound-detecting drill that was a regular part of the Japanese school curriculum at this time.[20]

The Imperial Japanese Navy (IJN) played a leading role in introducing this drill to elementary education in 1941. The music educator Kōkichi Oida worked as a theorist who claimed and advocated the usefulness of absolute-pitch training in the detection and identification of enemies in aerial warfare. This inspired the IJN captain Hideo Hiraide, who noted in a speech at an elementary school: "Today, it seems to be the time when a war of music happens."[21] The absolute-pitch training transformed six- to thirteen-year-old children into pitch- and enemy-detecting machines. Experiments for the training treated these "little citizens" as if they were human radars.

This wartime music education sheds new light on the character of Astro Boy. In the episode "Shootout in the Alps" (*Arupusu no kettō*) from the *Astro Boy* manga, he is seen as equal to humans. Still, he is anxious about not being a real human, only a human simulacrum or a subhuman (rather than posthuman) entity, (self-)ranked lower than humans in the anthropocentric hierarchy. In one scene, he suffers from his inability to enjoy music, saying to a human friend that music sounds merely like a succession of musical notes or pitches. This recalls a postwar report on the student subjects of absolute-pitch training who noted that they were unable to enjoy music because of this childhood experience during the war.[22] The loss of musical sense dovetails with Astro Boy's own suffering. It should be noted, however, that one of his seven superpowers is the ability to hear 1,000 times better than a human, an ability created by Dr. Tenma, who in the storyworld is also the head of the Japanese Ministry of Science. Astro Boy's superhuman hearing power functions as a high-performance radar, and it might have been as great an achievement for Dr. Tenma as the pitch-telling children were for Oida, Hiraide, and other agents of the state policy of science. Their "scientific" feats left both the child robot and the empire's children with an everlasting sense of loss and pain.

Astro Boy is not simply a copy of the original human child Tobio, who is his namesake and who does not possess superpowers. For Dr. Tenma, the robot might have represented the ideal that human children should strive for. Astro Boy is a sound detector and also a kind of jet fighter equipped with machine guns and, as such, distinct from Tobio. These differences between the two equally relate to the concept of life for the human child Tobio. Unable to survive a car crash when driving the futuristic antigravity vehicle, Tobio's organic body is too fragile to endure the physical and kinetic shock caused by the vehicle's high-speed accident, which would not have fatally wounded Astro Boy's mechanical body. Yet Tobio may be reconceived from the perspective of a "child of science" in that the use of this term applies to the human boys Puchar and Ichitarō as well as the robots Pely and Astro Boy. This double signification of a "child of science" calls for the extension of imperial Japan's policy of warfare, science, and children to include the death and unnarrated life of Tobio as the antecedent of Astro Boy who is his posthuman, posthumous successor.

Tobio's premature death is emblematic of the human children who were driven to extremes under the empire's critical military situation. Running short of troops in the first half of the 1940s, the army and navy enforced the recruitment of "boy soldiers" (shōnenhei) by taking advantage of the reformed system of elementary education, the so-called school of the nation (kokumin gakkō) that consisted of six primary grades and two advanced grades. But the military recruitment of children fifteen and older began in the 1920s with preparatory training courses for the army and navy. In 1943, the eligible age was lowered to fourteen, which meant that the military could conduct recruitment-promoting activities among thirteen-year-old children in the eighth grade – last grade to leave the school of the nation.[23] Dissatisfied with the number of children who applied for the boy soldier program because of a fascination with weapons or because of poverty, the military pushed schools and teachers to cooperate in the recruitment, which in effect approximated a form of conscription. Tezuka was himself forced to "volunteer" for the boy soldier program but was rejected due to his myopia.[24]

In addition to this de facto conscription, children thirteen and younger faced another future threat of death. At the end of the war, the military sanctioned suicide attacks (tokkō or kamikaze), developing a new type of weaponry exclusive to these special missions, such as a bomb-laden air-craft manned by a human pilot or a torpedo modified for a human driver: "Bombs were the master while human beings were the servant."[25] In children's magazines, these "disposable" types of weapons were often envisioned as robots radio-controlled by humans who are preferably located in safe places far from the battlefield. In the real world, children undergoing the "child soldier" program were exploited to function as the "driving units" of those suicide-attack and other forms of weapons. The acceptance of fourteen-year-old students in a tank-crew training school for boy soldiers meant that some students weighed as little as 31 kg and were as short as 136 cm – not tall enough for their feet to reach the gas pedal.[26] Their survival on the battlefield was not valued by the army and navy – in effect, humans were forced to work as robot substitutes.[27]

Returning to the human child character Tobio, both intratextual and transtextual research elucidates how the Astro Boy anime and manga are concerned with the lives of the children of imperial Japan's children, who were threatened by the military program and the suicide-attack operations promoted and publicized in newspapers, newsreels, and children's magazines. In episode 105, "General Astro" (*Atomu shōgun*), in the 1963 *Astro Boy* anime, our protagonist lands in a country called Migurushiya, where ten-year-old human children have been drafted as soldiers by a dictator because of the shortage of adult troops during a protracted war, an echo of imperial Japan's historic child soldiers. Astro Boy, together with a group of young rebels who escaped the draft, liberates all the Migurushiya children. This episode demonstrates that the reference to "child soldiers" was still expected to resonate with the television audience in 1960s Japan.

In fact, the depiction of child soldiers in "General Astro" was preceded by Tezuka's 1954 manga, *The Man Who Would Destroy the World* (*Sekai o horobosu otoko*), in which a human boy, Ryōichi Ichinoya, is drafted as a child soldier to pilot a jet fighter soon after his older brother perished in air combat during a future world war between the allied forces of Asia and Europe. This structure of military conflict is clearly a fictional extension of the Asia-Pacific War. Ryōichi closely resembles Tobio, not to mention his mechanical copy, Astro Boy. The resemblance between the two across narratives can be viewed in terms of Tezuka's famous "star system," whereby one and the same character was employed to play different roles in different works, not so dissimilar to a Hollywood movie star. Given Tezuka's star system as a character-casting strategy and the chronology of the two manga narratives, it is plausible to assume that the human character named Tobio was later cast as Ryōichi. Although luckily still alive at the end of the 1954 manga narrative, Ryōichi might have eventually died (like his older brother) in a combat that had yet to unfold in the narrative world. In this sense, it can be argued that in Tezuka's oeuvre Ryōichi delivers the ante-mortem history of the human Tobio, which is only minimally recounted in the 1952 *Astro Boy* manga and the 1963 anime adaptation.

Conclusion

Astro Boy has often been labeled posthuman, but he can also be associated with imperial Japan's wartime state policy-cum-ideology of science. This permits a problematization of militaristic and superhuman traits exhibited on-screen by the robot figure. In light of the historical term "child of science" as a critical link between robot figures and human children in the real and the fictional worlds, Astro Boy emerges as an icon of loss, sadness, pain, and even death. He is more the product of imperial Japan's military-scientific experimentation with human bodies than a representation of a marvelous achievement of human intelligence or an exquisite harbinger of the posthuman. As such, Astro Boy and his siblings might better be conceptualized as *subhuman*, in contrast to *posthuman*, a term that is too future-oriented to evoke the cruelty experienced by wartime children, who were mechanized and weaponized only to die young, both in Japan and in its then colonies. Subhuman figures will continue to fascinate, possess, and speak to anime viewers and manga readers in the form of robots, ghosts, or monsters. This invites us to question what first brought them into existence and what happened to the first generation of a postwar manga and anime population – namely, children who lived through the Fifteen-Year War in Japan and elsewhere in its East Asian neighborhood.

Notes

1. Mitsuteru Takahashi and Nobuyuki Tsugata, *Anime gaku* (Tokyo: NTT Shuppan, 2011), 11; Marc Steinberg, *Anime's Media Mix* (Minneapolis and London: The University of Minnesota Press, 2012), Kindle, 70.
2. Tetsuwan Atomu DVD Box 3 Deita Fairu, (Nihon Korombia, 2002), 45.
3. See Chapter 8, "Techno-orientalism and Japan panic," in David Morley and Kevin Robins, *Spaces of Identity: Global Media, Electronic Landscapes and Cultural Boundaries* (New York: Routledge, 1995).
4. Eiji Ōtsuka, "An Unholy Alliance of Eisenstein and Disney: The Fascist Origins of Otaku Culture," *Mechademia*, 8 (2013): 252.
5. Eiji Ōtsuka, *Taisei yokusankai no media mikkusu: "Yokusan Ikka" to sanka suru fashizumu* (Tokyo: Heibonsha, 2018), Kindle.
6. Below I am referring to the complete reprinted edition of *Puchar* (Tokyo: Tōgensha, 1975).
7. Isao Shimizu, *Yokoi Fukujirō: sengo manga no toppu rannā* (Kyoto: Rinsen Shoten, 2007), 23–25.
8. Haruki Inoue, *Nippon robotto sensōki 1939–1945* (Tokyo: NTT Shuppan, 2007), 44.
9. Translated edition, *Tank Takuro: Prewar Works 1934–1935* (Seattle: Fantagraphics, 2011).
10. Eiji Ōtsuka, *Mikkī no shoshiki: sengo manga no senjika kigen* (Tokyo: Kadokawa, 2013), 162.
11. Ōtsuka, *Mikkī no shoshiki*, 157–60.
12. Inoue, *Nippon robotto*, 260–63.
13. The Japanese term *kokoro* not only refers to the mind but also has other meanings, such as heart, emotion, will, memory, spirit, and soul.
14. Eiji Ōtsuka, *Kurashi no fashizumu* (Tokyo: Chikuma Shoten, 2011), 192–94.
15. Hiroshi Matsui, *Mokei no media ron* (Tokyo: Seikyūsha, 2017), 58–59; below, 82–83.
16. Tokio Takeuchi, "Kagakushō setchi," *Shinseinen* (October 1940), cited in Inoue, *Nippon robotto*, 8.
17. Inoue, *Nippon robotto*, 414.
18. First edition, Tokyo: Nakamura Shoten, 1941, reprinted Tokyo: Shogakukan, 2005.

19. In Osamu Tezuka, *Tezuka Osamu sōsaku nōto to shoki sakuhinshū* (Tokyo: Shogakukan, 2010).

20. Ōtsuka, *Taisei yokusankai*, Kindle, 2490–93.

21. Hazuki Saishō, *Zettai onkan* (Tokyo: Shogakukan, 1998), 65–66. The title of Hiraide's speech was "Daitōa sensō to ongaku" (The Greater East Asian War and Music).

22. Saishō, *Zettai onkan*, 70.

23. Takashi Suzuki, "Rikukaigun shōnenhei (shigan) chōbo taisei no kakuritsu katei," *Nihon no kyōiku shigaku*, 45 (2002): 123–41.

24. Osamu Tezuka, "Shūrenjo to dassō," https://tezukaosamu.net/jp/war/entry/16 .html.

25. Masayasu Hosaka, *Tokkō to Nihonjin* (Tokyo: Kodansha, 2005), 169.

26. Takehiko Matsumoto, "Fujisan to Nihon rikugun no shōnenhei yōsei: rikugun shōnen senshahei gakkō shōkō," *Yamanashi Gakuen Daigaku hōgaku ronshū*, 76 (2015): 250.

27. Inoue, *Nippon robotto*, 376.

PART II

Drawing and Movement

4

OLGA KOPYLOVA

Graphic Style in Anime and Manga

Japanese TV anime, as understood today, dates back to 1963, when Osamu Tezuka recreated his own manga *Astro Boy* (*Tetsuwan Atomu*) for the screen. A tremendous hit, *Astro Boy* set a precedent for the successful cross-promotion between the two media.[1] Since that time, manga and anime have remained interconnected through their characters, narratives, audiences, and visuals. The connection between the visuals of the two mediums is most strikingly revealed through line drawing (*senga*), which continues to constitute the material and semiotic basis of the two media and forms their aesthetic core. In this sense, graphic style provides a useful vantage point from which to explore the relation between them, one that inevitably involves a discussion of movement. The history of on-screen movement of drawn images in traditional 2D anime has been intertwined with movement expressed by and inherent in the still drawings on the printed manga page.

Manga-typical devices for rendering movement largely prefigured and informed the limited animation techniques seen in Japanese TV anime. Traditional hand-drawn animation is achieved through a series of key and in-between frames, which indicate the "first and last positions of a movement"[2] and phases in between those extreme positions, respectively. Limited animation is, first and foremost, associated with a smaller number of frames per second to create movement – twelve, eight, or sometimes even fewer, as opposed to twenty-four in full animation. During the two decades following the launch of *Astro Boy*, however, TV anime acquired an arsenal of other time- and labor-saving devices, which included replacing the actual movement of the figure on-screen with emphatic freeze-frames (*tome-e*) or rapid cuts between still shots. In these instances, animation derives from the "dynamically immobile image,"[3] which does not represent movement but rather implies it through dramatic poses, camerawork, or pictorial runes such as motion lines. While dynamically static images can be traced back to manga and other forms of graphic narrative, they have nonetheless become a staple of TV anime.

Recent decades have witnessed new developments, including the tendency to resort to fully animated sequences at key points of the narrative in order to produce visual spectacle[4] and the increasing reliance on 3D computer-generated (CG) animation. These new trends and technologies are currently reshaping the basic anime look. At the same time, the significance of line drawing in anime has risen in prominence since the early 2000s, with hand-drawn aesthetics and its CG-based imitations recognized as one of the distinguishing features of Japanese anime in the current 3D-oriented global market. A reexamination of the multifaceted dynamism of manga and anime drawings and the interdependence of movement and graphic style enables a reassessment of aesthetic and material connections between these two distinct media forms, as well as similar links between traditional 2D anime and new 3D CG cel-look animation.

Graphic Style and Movement in Anime and Manga

Early TV anime borrowed extensively from manga's narrative techniques, expressive devices, and aesthetic solutions. Moreover, the majority of intermedial adaptations followed in Tezuka's footsteps from manga to anime. The graphic style of manga drawing thus provides a touchstone against which to analyze the anime image.

In graphic narratives, drawing is characterized by parameters such as the use of color and shading; the degree of detail (i.e., the visual density of the image); the level of "iconic abstraction,"[5] which determines how characters, objects, and backgrounds are rendered on a spectrum from naturalistic to cartoonish; the types of graphical projection as pertains to the treatment of space and volume within panels; and the quality of lines and strokes, which partially depend on the instruments and materials employed. Not all of these parameters are equally important for intermedial comparison. For instance, with the development of digital painting and photography, animators have come to utilize much broader color palettes, together with sophisticated color schemes and shading techniques. The majority of manga serials, however, are monochromatic, which makes color coordination secondary in the comparative analysis of anime and manga aesthetics. The following discussion therefore focuses on iconic abstraction, the visual density of the image, and the quality of the line. Each directly impacts the expression of movement – the represented and the implied – in a still drawing. At the same time, these parameters are affected by the movement of the animated image. Moreover, line quality is related to the movement inherent *in* the drawing that precedes the depiction (and recognition) of any specific object. Such prefigurative movement bears special significance for animation.

Iconic Abstraction and Visual Density

Individual artists and drawing traditions are distinguished first and foremost by the level of iconic abstraction, which describes the visual treatment of characters and the implementation of pictorial formulas in visual narration. Such formulas range from basic drawing conventions, which involve abridging some parts of the depicted object and accentuating others, to various shortcuts and sleights of hand that might, among other things, enhance the visual appeal of the character image. An example of the former is drawing a nose in manga, which varies from a single dot in the "cute" style exemplified by Kagami Yoshimizu's *Lucky Star* (2003–), to seminaturalistic representations in titles such as Kentarō Miura's *Berserk* (1989–2021) or Hiroaki Samura's *Blade of the Immortal* (*Mugen no jūnin*, 1993–2012). Common "cosmetic" tricks include the omission of double chins for leading characters, regardless of their pose and camera angle, dramatically twisted poses and bent limbs as exemplified by Kōta Hirano's *Hellsing* (1997–2008) and Hirohiko Araki's illustrations, and warped perspective.[6] The level and manner of iconic abstraction in presented characters, along with the intensity and frequency of expressionistic distortions, are the most obvious and readily reproducible aspects of graphic style. Occasionally, they become idiosyncratic enough to serve as a personal signature, as is the case with the aforementioned Hirano. An artist's approach may of course change with time. In many long-running manga series, the visual treatment of characters evolves over years, sometimes passing through a number of distinct stages. Again, Miura's *Berserk* is an obvious example while a more recent case is Gamon Sakurai's *Ajin: Demi-Human* (2012–21). It is also possible for a graphic narrative to combine several levels of abstraction, with the overall look of the work determined by their interplay. For instance, manga artists commonly resort to an exaggerated cartoonish style, or "super-deformed" expression, in comical scenes (with the cuter variety known as *chibi*). The cartoonish style facilitates visual gags and the representation of emotions and moods, but these are not its only advantages.

Although unrelated to movement per se, the inherent malleability of the character drawing, which permits an oscillation between more naturalistic and super-deformed versions,[7] imbues the drawing with an element of dynamism. Moreover, switches between the default style and its distorted version may be used in lieu of other types of motion, and this is especially the case in anime.[8] The super-deformed drawings share a close affinity with anime's limited animation: Cartoonish style allows for rapid transitions between exaggerated expressions, and "jerky" animation often reinforces the comical effect of distorted figures.[9] Moreover, simplified forms and highly conventionalized expressions are easier to animate. On the one hand, exaggerated, distorted character drawing reduces the work for both manga artist and animator; on the other, it serves as a dynamically immobile image. It is no wonder that this stylistic device has become a mainstay in manga and anime and one of the long-lasting visual links between the two.

Iconic abstraction involves a selective representation of an object, and thus, it overlaps with another aspect of graphic style – namely, the degree of detail. While iconic abstraction concerns character images, the latter is a subset of what I refer to as "visual density." Visual density in manga is determined by the amount and distribution of visual information, including verbal text, balloons, and pictograms in addition to drawn images, in a panel and on a page. The density of the drawing is decided not only by the amount of detail but also by the application of textures and multiplication of lines, which may or may not have a figurative function.

Lines, in particular, often multiply in the form of hatching, which is itself a multipurpose tool. In academic drawing, hatching is the primary means by which to articulate shapes and to create an illusion of volume through shading; it similarly reflects the texture of the depicted objects. A manga artist may acknowledge this tradition, yet many dispense with academism. For the most part, hatching in manga helps to convey a certain mood or to indicate a surface, implying, rather than representing, volume. Screentones have been used for similar purposes since the early 1970s. They are considered a comparatively neutral and inobtrusive device,[10] whereas hatching tends to noticeably saturate or even oversaturate the image. Not surprisingly, it is regularly implemented in *kimegoma* or *misegoma* – that is, highlight panels that mark intense narrative points. Such panels are meant to make the reader pause, frequently through a change in graphic density. *Kimegoma* usually contain the most intricate drawings on a page and are characterized by an abundance of small details and elaborate shading. Such an oscillation of visual or graphic density in response to the demands of the narrative is contingent on a flexible approach to the image already demonstrated with iconic abstraction. But flexibility also exists in a more general sense, as there is no fixed standard in terms of visual density. Some artists exploit the aesthetics of the empty, unmarked page, others pack each panel with visual information.

Hand-drawn animation has inherent limitations that can hinder any attempt to reproduce on-screen the source work's visual complexity line-by-line, with the difficulty of animating an image growing proportionally to the number of lines and the degree of detail. This means that source images are streamlined with smaller details abridged. Hatching in most cases is removed altogether. In recent years, series like *Berserk* (Liden Films,

GEMBA, 2016–17) and *Shadows House* (Clover Works, 2021–) have tried to imitate hatching via digitally applied textures, but the results amount to approximation at best. To some extent, the simplification is set off by the same flexibility that underlies the use of highlight panels in manga. In the medium of anime, this flexibility likewise exists on multiple levels. For instance, anime employs "ratio dynamism,"[11] whereby complicated action sequences utilize a higher number of frames per second to achieve a visual spectacle of smooth, sophisticated animation. It also exhibits variable graphic density such that the number of lines on-screen increases in freeze-frames with an equally dramatic effect. The ultimate form of this expressive device is termed "harmony," developed and popularized by director Osamu Dezaki in hit manga-to-anime adaptations such as *Aim for the Ace!* (*Ēsu o neraé!*, 1973–74), *The Rose of Versailles* (*Berusaiyu no bara*, 1979–80), and *Joe of Tomorrow 2* (*Ashita no Jō 2*, 1980–81). In harmony, visual density is achieved by rendering the image in a painterly manner, with nuanced coloring and hatching applied to both the background and the characters.

Parallels between the two media are obvious, although the devices at play are not necessarily identical. There are multiple ways to signal the importance of a highlight panel, including its size and position on a page. By contrast, in a freeze-frame, it is the combination of stillness and graphic density that is impactful. While the painterly freeze-frame provides visual spectacle in an isolated moment, backgrounds continuously enrich the anime image. The introduction of cel-animation in the United States in the mid-1910s brought about the physical and conceptual separation of the two planes: animated characters and static background. This innovation greatly facilitated the development of commercial animation; it also enabled animators to invest more time and labor in backdrops. The new practice of balancing intricate backgrounds with simplified characters was established in the United States in the first half of the twentieth century,[12] and later perfected in Japan. It culminated in a stylistic convention that remains the mainstay in the anime industry. While the quality of production and materials may vary, the result is usually a relatively detailed background painting that implies depth through the use of linear and aerial perspective. The disparity between characters and background in terms of drawing style, volume, and detail has become so entrenched in anime aesthetics that the harmonization between the two visual planes still reads as a type of special effect.

In manga, meanwhile, the background can assume more diverse roles and appearances. In principle, the background is easy to omit since it is not the primary means of enriching the image: The location or stage of a narrative event (the visual background space) is usually introduced in an establishing shot, whereas backdrops detailing the characters' surroundings are often absent in medium shots and close-ups – that is, when the visual focus is more or less exclusively on the character. Of course, a nonfigurative background can become visually dense when it includes ornamental patterns or pictograms, but the stylistic disparity between the layers of the drawing can be emphasized or eliminated with equal ease. The changeability of manga backgrounds expands the expressive potential of the medium. The majority of these stylistic variations never find their way on-screen, however, as they are obstructed by anime's tendency to standardize the treatment of backgrounds in service of balancing the degree of detail and movement under budget and time constraints.

Moving Lines: Movement in the Line

Comics critics maintain that every visible stroke of a drawn picture is a trace of the artist's drawing hand and thus points to the creative impulse and labor of a particular individual.[13] Such a personal touch is already apparent at the prefigurative level – that is, before the reader recognizes objects and scenes on a page. As such, the quality of linework may induce intense affective reactions on the one hand and serve as a sign of strong subjectivity on the other.[14] But understanding the drawing as a product of an individual's efforts has another implication. A line or a stroke represents not only the mood or the worldview of its implied maker; it also signals the gesture that went into its making.[15] In other words, it evokes the movement of the drawing hand on a literal, somatic level. Any mark on the surface, be it an analog page or a digital screen, is therefore imbued with its own dynamism.

Of course, this dynamism fluctuates depending on the scale of the gesture and the roughness of the resultant mark.[16] Unmodulated, clear lines reveal little about the process of their production when compared to the bold brushstrokes or frenetic crosshatching often encountered in action or horror scenes, which directly convey energetic gestures. For the same reason, vigorous pencil hatching can effectively replace or reinforce motion lines, imparting the same sense of rapid movement. The internal dynamism of the hand-drawn image is not determined by the quality of marks alone, but rather by their relation to the illustrated object. The sketch is considered the most immediate and most dynamic form of drawing not only because it lays bare any hesitation or deliberation on the part of the creator, but also because its strokes do not coalesce into a definitive, final outline, as a sketch is always incomplete. The viewer must close the gaps by adding their own imaginary strokes, and yet this closure is transitory, with the ensuing shapes always open to reinterpretation. It is for that reason that even a drawing comprised of uniform, neat lines may feel unstable, implying movement on a very basic level. This is seen, for example, in Haruko Ichikawa's *Land of the Lustrous* (*Hōseki no kuni*, 2012–).

As mentioned earlier, the "gestural expressiveness of the line"[17] is an essential part of graphic style. It might even serve as a principal parameter for drawing distinctions between individual artists and larger trends, such as the "organic" and "inorganic" periods in the history of postwar manga.[18] The question then arises whether anime is able to replicate this important aspect of the manga image. Insofar as a line or a stroke is taken to refer to the work of a specific artist, it is impossible to reproduce it on-screen, unless the artist animates their own drawings. But the internal dynamism of the line still persists in traditional hand-drawn animation. To what degree this comes through is determined by the nature of animation as a media form that involves several types of movement and by the trends that influence the medium in a given era.

Two contrasting types of movement may emerge in fully animated sequences: the inherent dynamism of the line and the ostensible movement of a figure.[19] The viewer's gaze gravitates to the latter, while the "figural force"[20] (the implied motion) of the lines is subsumed by the moving form they outline, only to resurface in moments of stillness. This tendency is reinforced by the preference of uniform lines and solid, definitive forms that characterize many mainstream animated works, starting with Disney. Anime is no exception: Neat and even contours have remained a default in the industry for almost three decades. This does not mean, however, that anime has no use for the expressive potential of the line.

Movement inherent in the manually produced mark is bound to play a crucial role in anime because it lies at the core of the dynamically immobile image. This kind of motion precedes the dynamic poses of character figures, compositional tricks, camerawork, and so forth. Nowhere is this prefigurative movement more apparent than in harmony shots, which present the viewer with an entire complex of "indexical artefacts of embodied gesture"[21] – in other words, brushstrokes, expressive linework, and hatching coalesced into a single image. Yet the use of expressive lines in anime is not restricted to such special cases. For one thing, Japanese TV anime has not always relied on neutral linework, particularly in its early years when it was still referred to as "TV manga" (*terebi manga*), a term well suited in terms of content and expression. In the late 1960s and the early 1970s, manga-to-anime adaptations became the norm, and animators strove to imitate the graphic style of the source works. This proved challenging as it coincided with the first "organic" phase in the history of postwar manga when artists experimented with tapering, uneven, or

overlapping lines. Their reproduction in hand-drawn animation is difficult insofar as clear-cut forms and smooth transitions between frames are
industrially required. The easiest compensation was to increase still shots
and sectioning, a technique that involves selectively animating parts of the
image such as a character's mouth or limb. Mangaesque linework and limited animation ended up in a mutually reinforcing relationship. Expressive
lines imparted the anime image with dynamism, at the same time steering
it away from actual animation and toward "TV manga" in an almost
literal sense.[22]

Tellingly, the move of the anime industry toward clean lines and even
outlines in the late 1980s coincided with a new interest in fully animated
sequences, spearheaded by the work of Katsuhiro Ōtomo and Mamoru
Oshii. Even that shift did not completely erase expressive linework, however. In addition to harmony shots, character close-ups with little or no
actual animation have continued to employ tapering lines, open contours,
and hatching. Furthermore, the 2010s witnessed the reemergence of varie-
gated linework on-screen. Nonetheless, this does not signal a simple return
to the "organic" phase of the late 1960s. Nowadays, anime adaptations do
not necessarily seek to reproduce the gestural qualities of lines found in their
source works. Experimentation is inspired by the influx of new technologies, rather than the medium of manga itself.

Coda: Graphic Style, Movement, and New Technologies

Manga drawing generates a sense of movement on multiple levels, some
of which are unrelated to the contents of the image. In hand-drawn TV
anime, this inherent dynamism was at times repurposed or substituted with
other types of movement, and diverse manga styles were streamlined to fit
conventions and technical demands. New technologies slowly but steadily
reshape the basic anime image, opening new avenues and closing old ones.

The digitization of anime production caused a first wave of change.
Drawing, coloring, and photography particularly benefited from the introduction of digital tools that greatly expanded the expressive arsenal of traditional 2D anime. Specialized software has simplified the task of creating
clean outlines; at the same time, it has significantly reduced the costs of
labor and the time required to combine idiosyncratic linework with actual
animation. An increasing number of mainstream anime such as *Demon
Slayer: Kimetsu no Yaiba* (2019–) and *Toilet-Bound Hanako-kun* (*Jibaku
shōnen Hanako-kun*, 2020) have been experimenting with colored or irregular contours, as well as lines of wavering thickness. The same applies
to coloring. The application of gradients and textures to the character

plane has become a norm since around 2010. The impact of digitization on photography cannot be underestimated either. Besides the various digital effects, the opportunity to integrate multiple heterogeneous materials (e.g., 2D and 3D CG elements) into the same image and to manipulate an unlimited number of layers has led to a deepening sophistication of limited animation techniques. Generally speaking, the production of visually dense images has become much easier.

The addition of gradients, textures, blur, and other effects at the photography stage of production has also facilitated the reduction of the stylistic disparity between background and character planes without sacrificing graphic density of the former or movement of the latter. Just as with linework, the old conventions persist, and manga-to-anime adaptations do not necessarily strive to replicate the interplay of characters and backdrops that characterizes the source work. Still, the possibility of new approaches is noteworthy.

Digital tools have greatly enriched anime visuals and the medium's expressive range. But what can be said about 3D CG animation, which has finally begun to gain ground in the industry? 3D CG has become the means to realize on-screen the more complicated, nonlateral movement of complex, detailed objects. For a long time, these objects were limited to vehicles, weapons, and battle robots. The principle was then extended to groups of armored humanoids, allowing for more involved crowd scenes and battle panoramas. From 2010 onward, progressively more series have been made with the entire cast modeled and animated in 3D. Even so, there is a reason why 3D CG has only dealt with ostensibly inorganic objects for several decades: 3D character models have been notorious for their inorganic feel that cannot be mitigated solely by cel-shading (a nonrealistic rendering technique designed to make 3D images look flat through the use of hard-edged shadows and outlines in 3D models). Cel-shading is widely embraced in the contemporary anime industry as the primary means to replicate the look and feel of hand-drawn animation. But no matter how closely cel-shaded characters may evoke the flatness of their 2D counterparts, they lack the gestural force found in traditional drawing. After all, linework in cel-shaded animation is an artificial addition that is typically generated with the help of specialized software, even if various manual corrections are usually required when creating character models and executing the second half of the production process. The resulting absence of implied motion makes 3D models appear static and stiff compared to their hand-drawn equivalents. The problem may be solved by introducing textures and other elements to the cel-shaded image that evoke embodied gestures. To date, these attempts have often been hit-and-miss.

The handling of the differing levels of iconic abstraction in cel-shaded anime poses another challenge. Exaggeration per se is not unattainable in 3D CG, as evinced by children's anime such as *Chi's Sweet Home* (seasons 3–4, 2016–18). Yet such works use cartoonish character designs as their baseline. It is impossible to simply transform a more realistic 3D model into a super-deformed version. Another model needs to be made from scratch, and its own changeability will also be limited. Likewise, deliberate distortions frequently employed in traditional anime (and manga) for expressive or aesthetic purposes are unachievable in 3D CG animation.

These setbacks beg the question of whether the attempts to reproduce the aesthetics of 2D anime in 3D CG are viable. Various operational and technological discrepancies prevented the complete replication of manga imagery in 2D anime. On the level of the line drawing, however, the two media have much in common. Both manga and 2D anime allow creators to instantly alter aspects of the graphic style, be they the quality of lines, the degree and manner of iconic abstraction, or the amount of detail. This multifaceted dynamism is absent in the type of 3D CG animation embraced by the anime industry today. As a result, this type of animation has no direct access to expressive devices developed in and shared by 2D anime and manga. In principle, these devices can be imitated, yet the process often becomes too costly to be feasible. It is telling that most of cel-look animation's current challenges regarding style and expression are solved with the assistance of traditional techniques, including intricate hand-painted backgrounds that suffuse cel-shaded images with the warmth of a human touch, sequences animated entirely in 2D for scenes that involve super-deformed characters or require more evocative facial acting, and so forth. This is not to suggest that 3D CG imagery is inferior to the older media forms. It is, however, important to acknowledge that certain kinds of movement cannot be achieved by computing but only through the act of drawing, even if new technologies make it possible to emulate the cel-look.

Notes

1. See Marc Steinberg, *Anime's Media Mix: Franchising Toys and Characters in Japan* (Minneapolis: University of Minnesota Press, 2012).
2. Paul Wells, *Understanding Animation* (New York: Routledge, 1998), 36.
3. Steinberg, *Anime's Media Mix*, xiv.
4. José Andrés Santiago Iglesias, "Not Just Immobile: Moving Drawings and Visual Synecdoches in Neon Genesis Evangelion." In *Anime Studies: Media-Specific Approaches to Neon Genesis Evangelion*, edited by José Andrés Santiago Iglesia and Ana Soler Baena (Stockholm: Stockholm University Press, 2021), 19–48. Open Access.

5. Scott McCloud, *Understanding Comics: The Invisible Art* (New York: Harper Perennial, 1994), 46.
6. Notably, exaggerated body language is not limited to the Japanese comics scene – suffice to recall Burne Hogarth's anatomical studies.
7. Hōsei Iwashita, "Kyarakutā o miru, kyarakutā o yomu." In *Manga kenkyū 13 kō*, edited by Masahiro Koyama et al. (Tokyo: Suiseisha, 2016), 166–67.
8. Jaqueline Berndt, "More Mangaesque than the Manga: 'Cartooning' in the Kimetsu no Yaiba Anime," *Transcommunication* 8, no. 2 (2021): 171–78. Open Access.
9. Stevie Suan, "Anime's Actors: Constituting 'Self-hood' through Embodied and Figurative Performance in Animation," *The Japanese Journal of Animation Studies* 19, no. 1 (2017): 3–15.
10. Fusanosuke Natsume, "Sukurīnton ga manga ni motarashita 'unmei'," in *Manga no yomikata* (Tokyo: Takarajimasha, 1995), 68–74.
11. Santiago Iglesias, "Not Just Immobile," 25–29.
12. Donald Crafton, *Shadow of a Mouse: Performance, Belief, and World-Making in Animation* (Berkeley: University of California Press, 2013), 144–212.
13. Jan Baetens, "Revealing Traces: A New Theory of Graphic Enunciation." In *The Language of Comics: Word and Image*, edited by Robin Varnum and Christina T. Gibbons (Jackson: University Press of Mississippi, 2001), Kindle, 1822–1952. See also Miho Takeuchi, "Sen kara toraenaosu 'gekiga': Saitō Takao o chūshin ni." In *Global Manga Studies* 3, edited by Jaqueline Berndt et al. (Kyoto: Kyoto Seika University International Manga Research Center, 2013), 175–99. http://imrc.jp/lecture/2011/10/3.html.
14. McCloud, *Understanding Comics*, 118–37.
15. Paul Atkinson, "Movements within Movements: Following the Line in Animation and Comic Books," *Animation: An Interdisciplinary Journal* 4, no. 3 (2009): 265–81; Jared Gardner, "Storylines," *SubStance* 40, no. 1 (2011): 124: Graphic Narratives and Narrative Theory: 53–69.
16. Thomas Lamarre, "Manga Bomb: Between the Lines of Barefoot Gen." In *Comics Worlds & the World of Comics*, edited by Jaqueline Berndt (Kyoto: International Manga Research Center, 2010), 245–85, http://imrc.jp/images/upload/lecture/data/262-307chap18LaMarre20101224.pdf, reprinted as "Believe in Comics: Forms of Expression in *Barefoot Gen*." In *Mangatopia: Essays on Manga and Anime in the Modern World*, edited by Timothy Perper and Martha Cornog (Santa Barbara: Englewood Libraries Unlimited, 2011), 191–207.
17. Atkinson, "Movements within Movements," 278.
18. Kentarō Takekuma, "Dōgu to tatchi no hyōgen henkenshi: koseitekina 'sen' o umidasu no wa jidai ka, dōgu ka?," in *Manga no yomikata* (Tokyo: Takarajimasha, 1995), 38–51.
19. Atkinson, "Movements within Movements," 265–81.
20. Lamarre, "Manga Bomb," 277.
21. Pat Power, "Animated Expressions: Expressive Style in 3D Computer Graphic Narrative Animation," *Animation: An Interdisciplinary Journal* 4, no. 2 (2009): 117.
22. Kōji Takase, *Anime seisakusha-tachi no hōhō* (Tokyo: Film Art, 2019), 41–42.

5

SHEUO HUI GAN

Motion and Emotion in Anime

Disney's use of the multiplane camera from 1937 onward was a turning point for the notion of space and depth in cel-animation (i.e., animated film that uses drawings on transparent celluloid sheets). A square steel structure measuring approximately 3 m high, and 2 m wide and deep, this device has a top-mounted camera that shoots vertically down at several flexible planes that hold the painted cels, allowing them to be positioned at different levels. A sense of depth is created by calculating the distance between the camera and the planes. The closer planes are used for moving entities, such as characters, and the farthest for backgrounds.

The operation of a multiplane camera is labor-intensive: It necessitates several technicians to set up the right lighting and the planes for each single shot such that they meet the requirements of the cinematographer. The division between foreground, middle ground, and background, as well as the possibility of realizing tracking shots, facilitated a new model for visual representation in cel-animation.[1] The resultant photorealist depth and a character animation that more closely resembled real-life motion served as the production standard of the animation industry worldwide until the Disney Studios began to use digital techniques in the late 1980s.

Today, the multiplane camera might seem obsolete, but what it embodied, its concept of space, depth, and movement in 3D space, lives on in the multilayering that is a given feature in most software applications and in the basic principles of character animation such as squash and stretch. This chapter focuses on how the multiplane camera was used in Japan and what it signified to Japanese animators. Some creators attempted to bypass the aesthetics commonly connected with it, interrelating mimetic and allusive representation, or motion and emotion, in their storytelling through a synthesis of cinematic techniques derived from live-action film and through drawing conventions derived from comics.

Multiplane Camera in Japan

In prewar Japan, the multiplane camera was viewed as a foreign device that helped to modernize the domestic, then still workshop-based, production system. Film director and animator Hakuzan Kimura apparently used a self-crafted animation stand.[2] Noburo Ōfuji, another Japanese pioneer famous for *chiyogami* cutout animation, had constructed a wooden apparatus with different layers to generate a sense of space in his works, the most notable examples being the wave sequences in his short films *Whale* (*Kujira*, 1952) and *The Phantom Ship* (*Yūreisen*, 1956).[3] While he followed Disney's practice in mounting the camera on top of a vertical apparatus, he placed the light sources at the bottom and utilized glass plates for the planes.

In the late 1950s, the multiplane camera saw an industrial employment designed to emulate the Disney style. This began with the *Legend of the White Serpent* (*Hakujaden*, 1958) by the Tōei Dōga (from 1998 onward, Toei Animation). In the trailer for that film, Tōei president Hiroshi Ōkawa revealed the studio's ambition to become the "Disney of Asia." This statement was enhanced through a series of cuts showing the production system: drawing, tracing, coloring, painting backgrounds, and shooting with a multiplane camera, a high-rise steel structure much larger and certainly more impressive than the previously employed domestic stands. Disney's multiplane camera represented a new level of efficiency: a division of labor that facilitated the increased standardization of the production process.

Disney animations were already popular in 1930s Japan, and the fascination with them in the 1950s coincided with an era of global recognition of Japanese cinema. Film directors, including Akira Kurosawa, Yasujirō Ozu, Kenji Mizoguchi, and Kon Ichikawa, were applauded, but animated film lagged behind. It was mainly restricted to shorts made by independent creators. These were often limited to the educational genre, despite exceptional wartime productions such as the two animated feature films funded by Japan's Navy Ministry, *Momotaro's Sea Eagles* (*Momotarō no umiwashi*, 1942) and *Momotaro: Sacred Sailors* (*Momotarō: umi no shinpei*, 1945), which both employed a multiplane camera.[4] Tōei seized the opportunity and demand for animated feature films at this time to expand commercially and aesthetically with the use of multiplane camera technology. The adoption of Disney's techniques assisted in ensuring Tōei's success in the postwar Japanese market. This involved filming performers for each scene to guide the animators and subsequently synchronizing the live-action footage with meticulously planned imitations of camera movement in animation.

The introduction of the multiplane camera strengthened the admiration for realistic visuals. It also intensified the debate between proponents of "full" and "limited" animation, production modes that are based on different concepts of motion: Full animation leans toward fluid and smooth movement, while limited animation prefers a graphically stylized type.[5] In line with Disney's standards, Tōei promoted a rather narrow type of animation that focused primarily on character movement in terms of design and cinematography. Quantifiable elements, such as the number of drawings inserted between key frames (i.e., the foundational drawings to mark the start and the end of an action), became crucial to determine the "quality" of a production. Using eight frames or less per second (i.e., shot on three, or limited animation) was considered inferior to twelve frames or more (i.e., shot on two, or full animation). Seen from the standpoint of Disney and Tōei, it makes sense to consider full animation, and especially feature-length productions intended for theatrical release, as an estimable approach. In comparison, limited animation has often been viewed within the industry as low standard, associated as it were with restricted budgets and serial narratives meant for TV broadcasting.

Bypassing the Multiplane Camera

The valorization of smooth lifelike motion contributed to the dominance of the multiplane camera. Yet this preference limited the exploration of alternative ways of animated storytelling. After directing *Journey to the West* (*Saiyūki*, 1960) for Tōei, Osamu Tezuka commented that the studio's strictly planned production process was too rigid for him.[6] Inflexibility was in part due to the multiplane camera, which necessitated not only careful planning but also hierarchies, and thus left no room for impromptu ideas. In order to foster experimentation and collaboration among animators, Tezuka founded his own studio, Mushi Production, in 1962. Shortly thereafter, he was contracted to create his first TV anime series of thirty-minute episodes, *Astro Boy* (*Tetsuwan Atomu*, 193 episodes, 1963–66). The extremely low budget that he accepted would become the unfavorable standard for serial anime, and it was met with harsh criticism from colleagues. Ironically, Tezuka's experience at Tōei motivated him to produce animation in a way that resembled what he had initially opposed. But without the standardization and division of labor, Tezuka's studio would probably not have had a head start in making anime series for TV, among them *Kimba the White Lion* (*Janguru taitei*, 52 episodes, 1965–66) and *Princess Knight* (*Ribon no kishi*, 52 episodes, 1967–68).

To meet the requirements set for TV series, Mushi Production animated motion in "limited," but nonetheless innovative ways. Aural elements (monolog, dialog, soundtrack, and sound effects), which conveyed complex narrative information about the characters, complemented highly stylized visual designs with only a few elements selected to depict motion. Tezuka's success in popularizing such a "selective" approach triggered many efforts to reinterpret the norms of realism tied to the multiplane camera – that is, to engage the audience by drawing upon elements other than visual and mimetically represented physical motion. This is precisely what brought emotional movements to the fore, for both animated fiction and the viewer. Emotional movements do not necessarily rely on rationality, standardized color tones or realistic visuals to elicit a response, but more often on abstract, exaggerated, and stylized forms, in which the manner of representation itself becomes the center of the attention and appeals intuitively to the viewer. Yet the economic necessity demanded of a TV series was not the only reason that the multiplane camera was bypassed. Mushi Production also employed its selective animation to enact bold experimentation in shorts, such as *Pictures at an Exhibition* (*Tenrankai no e*, 1966) and *Jumping* (1984), and in three animated feature films, *One Thousand and One Nights* (*Sen'ya ichiya monogatari*, 1969), *Cleopatra* (1971), and *Belladonna of the Sadness* (*Kanashimi no Beradonna*, 1973).[7]

Over time, Tezuka's selective approach changed the notion of "limited" animation. Instead of presuming a general lack of animated movement, awareness increased that the impression of motion is not to be assessed in isolation and that it relates various elements within a shot, a scene, or a collection of shots and sequences. Motion can be suggested by different sets of still images or shots lacking extravagant actions work to complement one another, visually and aurally. Furthermore, animated movement – previously conceptualized mainly as relating to characters' bodies and their visibility – became more closely linked to narrative, and movement that did not add to the storytelling began to appear superfluous. It was this linkage of rhythm and design to meaning that helped to reduce the fixation on quantity (i.e., frames-per-second) and the urge to model motion on real-life physicality.[8]

Gisaburō Sugii's works are representative of these conceptual shifts. Sugii was initially employed at Tōei before he joined Mushi Production where he directed many memorable TV anime series. In his later feature-length animations he experimented with a slow-paced aesthetic. Films, such as *The Night on the Galactic Railroad* (*Ginga tetsudō no yoru*, 1985) and *The Tale of Genji* (*Murasaki Shikibu: Genji monogatari*, 1987), include very long takes, slowly panning the camera to allow room for the drama to evolve within panoramic scenes and to indicate the mood of the characters through the tiniest of motions. This again is augmented by close-ups in silence that conjure up intimacy through a haptic sense of visuality. Sugii equally

explored depth with slow horizontal and vertical pans or zooms, highlighting the grain and textures of things and utilizing clever sound designs. While
not entirely refraining from the conventional shot/reverse shot editing, Sugii
complemented it with cutaway shots, alternating those with longer takes
and slower pacing to create a more stylized spatial relationship between the
characters and their environment that would serve nonverbal storytelling.

Sugii was not alone in this experimentation. His colleague at Mushi
Production, Eiichi Yamamoto, startled viewers with unique effects such as
long tilts in the aforementioned *Belladonna of the Sadness*. An even earlier example was the black-and-white feature film *Band of Ninja* (*Ninja
bugeichō*, 1967) directed by Nagisa Ōshima and distributed by Art Theater
Guild, a collective of Japanese New Wave filmmakers. Ōshima, best known
for his innovative and controversial approach to live-action filmmaking,
adopted a graphic narrative by Sanpei Shirato, employed still images from
the original pages and edited them in a highly dramatic fashion. Motion was
introduced through the multivariant montage of close-ups, zooms, pans,
tilts and stills, as well as a gripping audio track.[9] This "selective" approach
differed fundamentally from the majority of animated films, which were
inclined to tell their story through mimicking live-action cinema – in other
words, through the combination of sequencing as external montage and
mise-en-scène as internal montage.

Conceptions of Anime-Specific Movement

In Japan, the history of the multiplane camera did not eventuate as Tōei
had initially planned. Mushi Production, for example, used layers but
not by means of Disney's expensive device. Its very existence nonetheless inspired animators to find approaches other than the Disney model
to suggest three-dimensionality and spatial depth. What has come to be
known as anime on a global scale distinguishes itself from other forms of
drawing-based animation by selective, or partial, movements of 2D characters set against a static 3D background.

The Japanese animation industry moved toward digitalization in the 1990s.
From the outset, computer technology – commonly regarded as a digital continuation of the multiplane camera – has been widely adopted to streamline
the production process (e.g., scanning, coloring, and cleaning up) and only
sporadically to change visual representation. Traces of the latter are primarily
found in 3D environments for backgrounds and in visual effects for fighting
scenes or weather particles. Even now, with sophisticated technologies, many
productions in Japan hold on to pre-digital traditions of rendering space
and motion, including "frozen" moments and jerky moves. Studio Ghibli,

Studio 4°C, A-1 Picture, Kyoto Animation, TMS Entertainment, Production I.G, Ufotable, and Science Saru have all employed digital animation to fabricate an artificial reality instead of emulating the visual logic derived from live-action cinema. This also applies to the acting style of the characters. With the multiplane camera, the 3D agility of characters and their ability to communicate emotions through body movement (or embodied acting) have often been regarded as the pinnacle of performance in animated film. But anime, most notably in its serial format, has likewise embraced figurative acting.[10]

As noted above, conceptions of anime that rest on binary oppositions – limited versus full animation, embodied versus figurative acting, or cinematic versus drawing-based – miss the actual aesthetic appeal of this form of animation. Anime is characterized by an assemblage of different visual properties, and parts that appear particularly "animeesque" play their role in a specific context. Thus, "anime-ic movement"[11] is certainly a key characteristic of anime, but narrative rhythm is usually sustained by juxtaposing a somewhat immobile shot or sequence with a fast-paced one, regardless of whether the dynamism is achieved visually or aurally. Sequences interrelate with other sequences, especially those before and after.

Many anime productions have been consciously adopting properties of the movie camera, such as focal length and lenses to imitate the effects of depth of field, motion blurs, and zoom. In contrast to film and photography, animation is fabricated frame by frame to create the illusion of movement. It does not need to take on board the effects generated by camera lenses. But the convenience of production software such as Adobe After Effects has enabled animators to employ properties of the camera lens that affect the field of vision and to move the inbuilt virtual camera through the visual space, something that the multiplane camera was unable to do because it was in a fixed position. When required, other cinematic techniques mimicked in anime are the close-up, framing, character blocking, and shot/reverse shot. In short, anime today entwines "animetism" with "cinematism" to a variable extent. Anime's visual language can be seen as a result of a constant negotiation. Its elements are shifting on a spectrum, responding to existing anime norms, film forms, technologies, platforms, funding patterns, and the cross-pollination of practices among creators and audiences that no longer necessarily demand the simulation of photorealism.

Anime's Appeal in Practice

In order to engage the viewer's imagination and prompt participation, anime borrows from live-action film, draws emotions but in a manner distinct from manga, foregrounds metamorphosis but not inevitably that of physical shapes, and it visualizes the invisible. The recent anime series *Demon Slayer: Kimetsu no Yaiba* (two seasons, 44 episodes, 2019–22) is representative of this approach.

Set in prewar Japan, *Demon Slayer* begins with the protagonist Tanjirō Kamado joining a privately formed demon-slayer corps after all his family have been killed by demons, except for his younger sister Nezuko. The story tracks his journey to fight demons and find a cure for his half-demonized sister. The opening sequence of episode 1 is full of suspense (00:01–00:59). It starts with a point-of-view (POV) shot of Tanjirō breathlessly walking in a snowy forest. This is followed by a close-up of him: He enters the shot, together with some quick glimpses of a teenage girl on his back, who has visible blood stains on her forehead. While the audio track conveys Tanjirō's emotions and his vow to save his sister, the pair are portrayed with different framings and angles. These range from close-ups to medium shots, intercut POVs, tracking shots, and ultimately a crane shot moving away from them and upward to reveal an overview of the forest. In sharp contrast to the previous disturbing scenes, this final shot juxtaposes the peacefulness of the snowscape with Tanjirō's uncertainty.

In a flashback sequence shortly thereafter (03:31–03:53), Tanjirō leaves his family to sell charcoal in town. Seen in a wide shot, viewers observe him descending through the wood at a distance. The virtual camera follows him as he moves across the screen from right to left, as if in a live-action tracking shot. In both POV instances, the imagery imitates the deep focus and changing focal length of live-action camerawork: Diverse elements come into view – first the pigeon in the foreground and then the trees in the middle ground – before we see Tanjirō (Fig. 5.1a). Such "cinematism" recurs throughout the series (Fig. 5.1b, 1c).

In episode 24 "Rehabilitation Training" (*Kinō kaifuku kunren*), Tanjirō and his two supporting characters Inosuke and Zen'itsu are receiving medical treatment; then they go through training sessions to rebuild their strength after an intense fight. The episode has significant comical and emotional moments, which are depicted through a change in drawing style. Standing in sharp relief to the earlier film-realistic shots, this alteration invites playful visual engagement with the otherwise often violent narrative (Fig. 5.2a–c).

Figure 5.2a illustrates the feelings of Tanjirō and Inosuke after their physical exercise. The respective sequence starts with a quick tilt-up and then four straight cuts to the static shots where the actions take place. Shifts in the character design range from thinner bodies, unemotional eyes, dropping shoulders, and exhausted gliding gestures to variations in style that include 2D drawings reminiscent of traditional cel-animation and colorless

Figure 5.1a.1-4 Imitation of camera lenses and its effects in tracking shot.

Figure 5.1b The foreground is blurred, imitating a wide-angle shot.

Figure 5.1c The size of Tanjirō's hand is exaggerated, imitating the lens effect.

pencil sketch outlines. The heightened state of the characters' physical and mental exhaustion is communicated through thickened character outlines and slight distortions, and furthermore by turning them into flattened paper figures that move in a slightly wavering manner. As the characters' conditions are communicated visually with a minimum of dialog, this particular sequence is an exemplar of emotional expression conveyed solely through changing visual imagery. Whereas filmic montage creates meaning based on a compilation of multiple cuts, here it is generated in an anime-specific way – namely, from multiple drawings in different styles. Another way in which anime goes beyond visual mimesis in its representation of emotion is the abrupt metamorphosis of an anime character into a dwarf version of themselves, a so-called *chibi*.[12]

Drawing in anime involves multiple levels, as evidenced by the types of lines used. Motion and impact lines are typical expressive devices of comics. They generally visualize speed or blows and also enhance the intensity of

Figure 5.2a.1-3 The change in character design and drawing style of Tanjirō and Inosuke indicates their unspeakable tiredness after the rehabilitation training.

a mood or a situation. They may even guide the gaze of the comics reader from one panel to the next. Similar lines appear in *Demon Slayer*, but not always with the same placement or the same effect as in manga. Figure 5.2b is a compilation of screen shots from various moments illustrating Zen'itsu's distress or emotional outburst. The shots are framed in medium close-ups from above the head to mid torso and focused on Zen'itsu's facial expression. The lines vibrate slightly while the animation is otherwise kept to a minimum, and the movements of mouth and hair are rendered in a simple loop. Together with the intensely colored backgrounds drawn in a radiating pattern, the animated motion lines act like emotion lines, heightening Zen'itsu's outburst and momentarily altering his visual properties.

Figure 5.2b.1-3 These selected screenshots show Zen'itsu bursting into hysterical excitement in different scenarios. The non-diegetic background colors, the painted outgrown pattern in the background, the animated impact lines, and the heightened character outline further fictionalize and iconize the character.

The emotional outburst can be understood as a form of metamorphosis: Characters lose their usual look. But as distinct from the sequences where Zen'itsu fights, this transformation does not increase his power, nor does it drive the plot. It playfully underlines Zen'itsu's temperament that often switches between being easily intimidated or acting courageously, between being cool-headed or edgy. Thus, the visual changes seen in the emotional outbursts function as stand-alone imagery that engages the viewer, effortlessly reaching far beyond the narrative, for example, by triggering the creation of memes or reaction icons.

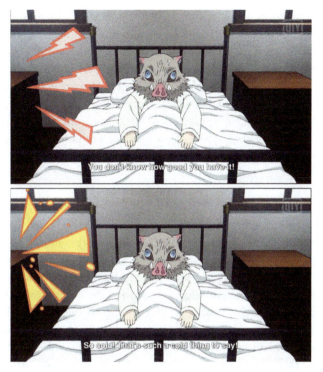

Figure 5.2c.1-2 Inosuke's stillness is contrasted with Zen'itsu's frantic high-pitched voice coming from outside the frame, indicated by the color-shifting shapes.

To indicate sound, manga employs onomatopoeia, mimetic words that are frequently treated as integral elements of design. Early silent animated cartoons borrowed speech bubbles from comics. Today's animation does not rely on such visual techniques anymore, even though anime still uses graphic elements occasionally. In Figure 5.2c, animated flashes and triangles signal offscreen voices. This may seem redundant since we can actually hear them when watching the anime, but their visual inclusion is nonetheless entertaining, among other things as a reference to the manga that many viewers may know. In *Demon Slayer*, they also heighten Zen'itsu's comical appearance, marking him as talkative in contrast to Inosuke, who stays in bed, surprisingly immobile and expressionless. This visual juxtaposition shows onomatopoeia being adopted differently from the manga context. In the anime, they serve the "metamorphizing" of sound and emotion.

Likewise, anime-specific is the visualization of invisible elements, particularly force, energy, or aura. The three main characters in *Demon Slayer* – Tanjirō, Inosuke, and Zen'itsu – all exhibit hyperesthesia: Tanjirō has exceptionally good smell, and Inosuke and Zen'itsu are extremely adept at using sound to navigate. Compared to the manga, the anime series further dramatized these qualities by foregrounding them visually. Often, they are animated more stylishly than the characters in the same shot, especially during fight sequences, when the time of narration is extended. One example is Tanjirō's water-breathing technique. When he uses it, wave-like forces fill the screen space panoramically. These sequences are animated in a dynamic manner that plays with graphic ratios (i.e., enormous effects and smaller characters) and prioritizes visual sensations with bright colors and patterns, as seen, for example, in episode 20 (05:26–06:20).

Concluding Thoughts

The history and aesthetics of the multiplane camera offer insights into crucial characteristics of anime, precisely because this device has not been fully implemented in Japan. In principle, anime builds on assemblages of techniques derived from live-action cinema, drawing-based animation, and graphic fiction of the manga lineage. Typically, the animation of movement is not limited to the characters; it also applies to the background and to various graphic elements, including motion lines and script. Likewise, the visual representation of movement – or the lack thereof – does not exist in isolation, rather as a contextual element that affects the other elements embedded within a shot and sequences.

The aesthetic achievements of Disney's *Snow White and the Seven Dwarfs* (1937) are usually accredited to the use of the multiplane camera.[13] But they also relied on other technical innovations, not least Technicolor, rotoscoping, and the effectiveness of character design such that each character has a unique persona.[14] The multiplane camera was a groundbreaking invention, and Disney employed it as a branding tool to differentiate his studio's work from others. But in our digital age, the multiplane camera with its means for creating a sense of depth is no longer at the center of animated storytelling, although it can appear appropriate for certain narratives. The search for reality simulation has shifted, however, to more sensational forms of virtual depth, such as the immersive quality of an IMAX film or an Oculus VR world. In these cases, the materiality of drawings and other nonphotographic elements has become more important as an alternative way to convey narrative information, including that surrounding the characters and their settings.

The attraction and the success of Japanese TV anime is mainly due to their serial nature in which there is ample screen time to put forward and play with multiple visual elements within a storyline. The interchange of visual styles relating to character or background is often a carefully constructed performance aimed at captivating the audience. This is seen, among other things, in frequently employed medium shots and close-ups. Varied drawing styles and graphic elements enhance the emotions of the characters in an imaginative, fantastical, and even absurd manner. Acted out against realistically rendered background settings – prominently landscapes and buildings – they clearly resonate with audiences.

Notes

1. Marc Steinberg, "Realism in the Animation Media Environment: Animation Theory from Japan." In *Animating Film Theory*, edited by Karen Beckman (Durham: Duke University Press), 287–300.
2. Thomas Lamarre, "The Multiplanar Image," *Mechademia*, 1 (2006): 125.
3. For the image of Noboru Ōfuji's camera stand, see the following printed catalog and online source: *The Catalog for the Exhibition: The Japanese Film Heritage – From the Non-film Collection of the National Film Center*. National Film Center (The National Museum of Modern Art, Tokyo, 2004), Japanese Animated Film Classics – Noboru Ōfuji Memorial Museum, National Film Archive of Japan, https://animation.filmarchives.jp/en/oofuji.html.
4. See Akiko Sano, "Momotarō umi no shinpei no jikken to senden." In *Sensō to Nihon anime: Momotarō umi no shinpei to wa nani datta no ka*, edited by Akiko Sano and Hikari Hori (Tokyo: Seikyūsha, 2022), 135–55.
5. Maureen Furniss, *Art in Motion: Revised Edition: Animation Aesthetics* (New Barnet: John Libbey Publishing, 2017), 133–50.
6. Sheuo Hui Gan, "A Reevaluation of the Importance of Mushi Pro's Three Adult-Oriented Animated Films in the Development of Japanese Animation," *Cinema Studies*, 2 (2007): 66. See also Osamu Tezuka, "Boku no jinsei gekijō," in *Tezuka Osamu zenshi sono sugao to gyōseki* (Tokyo: Akita Shoten, 1998), 84–87; originally serialized in the newspaper *Tokyo Shimbun* in 1967.
7. Sheuo Hui Gan, "Prefiguring the Future: Tezuka Osamu's Adult Animation and Its Influence on Later Animation in Japan." In *Proceedings of Whither the Orient: Asians in Asians and Non-Asians Cinema Conference*, edited by Joel David (Gwangju: Asia Culture Forum, 2006), 207–24, https://amauteurish.com/wp-content/uploads/2020/08/proceedings-final.pdf.
8. In a similar vein, "ratio dynamism," "use of visual and sound synecdoche," and "moving drawings" are discussed by José Andres Santiago Iglesias, "Not Just Immobile: Moving Drawings and Visual Synecdoches in *Neon Genesis Evangelion*." In *Anime Studies: Media-Specific Approaches to Neon Genesis Evangelion*, edited by José Andres Santiago Iglesias and Ana Soler Baena (Stockholm: Stockholm University Press, 2021), 19–48. Open Access.
9. Yuriko Furuhata, "Audiovisual Redundancy and Remediation in Ninja Bugeichō," *Mechademia*, 7 (2012): 249–62.
10. Figurative acting, or performance, often consciously borrows from or responds to a set of established codified expressions and gestures. See Donald Crafton, *Show of a Mouse: Performance, Belief, and World-Making in Animation* (Berkeley: University of California Press, 2013), 15–57. See the discussion of

Crafton's concepts in Stevie Suan, *Anime's Identity: Performativity and Form beyond Japan* (Minneapolis: University of Minnesota Press, 2021), 108.

11. Caroline Ruddell, "From the 'Cinematic' to the 'Anime-ic': Issues of Movement in Animation," *Animation,* 3, no. 2 (2008): 123.

12. Jaqueline Berndt, "More Mangaesque than the Manga: 'Cartooning' in the Kimetsu No Yaiba Anime," *Transcommunication,* 8, no. 2 (2021): 171–78. Open Access.

13. See Christopher Holliday and Chris Pallant, "The Depth Deception: Landscape, Technology and the Manipulation of Disney's Multi-plane Camera in Snow White and the Seven Dwarfs (1937)." In *Snow White and the Seven Dwarfs: New Perspectives on Production, Reception, Legacy,* edited by Chris Pallant and Christopher Holliday (New York: Bloomsbury Publishing, 2021), 61–77.

14. Mark Langer, "The Disney-Fleischer Dilemma: Product Differentiation and Technological Innovation," *Screen,* 33, no. 4 (Winter 1992): 343–60.

PART III

Sound

6

BLANCHE DELABORDE

Hearing Manga

Manga often feels very loud, although it is not an audiovisual medium. A diversity of sounds are represented in its pages, ranging from spoken dialog or internal voices to natural sounds and mechanical noises, and even music.[1] In order to communicate these different auditory sensations, manga has various visual tools at its disposal. Some are fairly simple and transcultural. For example, dissonant or loud sounds can be visually expressed through jagged lines, as seen in comics throughout the world. It is also very common to render music with wavy lines emanating from instruments or electronic devices, and accompanied by graphic symbols, such as musical notes or whole musical scores. Other devices to indicate sound are more complex. This chapter will focus on the intersection of sound and writing in manga to develop two main points: first, the representation of voices in manga, including spoken dialog, thoughts, and voiceovers; and second, mimetic words, or onomatopoeia, which can convey much more than sounds.

Voices

One of the main purposes of writing is to represent spoken language in a visual form – in other words, what is written corresponds to a series of sounds produced by the human voice. This is largely applicable to languages using scripts that are not, or are only partially, phonetic, like Japanese. Nonetheless, a great part of what constitutes spoken language, such as inflection, speed, rhythm, and the quality and texture of the voice or its volume, are usually not evident in writing. One way manga suggests distinct voices is through the use of stereotypical speech markers that give a precise idea of each character's age, gender, and social position. Select first-person pronouns and expressive particles at the end of sentences are employed only by certain categories of people. For instance, a dialog using the first-person pronoun *washi* and ending on *noja* will automatically be attributed to an old man, without having to see the character. The overlap

Figure 6.1 Natsumi Itsuki, *Passion Parade*, Hakusensha Bunko edition, vol. 1, 1987, 210–11.

between conventional character types in manga and anime also means that Japanese readers would have been exposed to corresponding voices played by voice actors and thus have vocal references in mind. Moreover, in any type of text, punctuation has historically helped to make up for those parts of speech that are normally lost when written, but manga has developed an even vaster arsenal of visual and narrative conventions to depict voices.

Writing in manga takes myriad forms. Some manga use few variations in script, but many narratives, especially in girls (or *shōjo*) manga, depend on a complex textual network.[2] Figure 6.1, for example, features an ensemble of main dialog (typed, placed in speech bubbles), secondary lines of dialog (handwritten, placed outside speech bubbles), thoughts (in another typeface with a differently shaped bubble), onomatopoeia (hand-drawn with diverse shapes), and even something akin to a caption (like the words "scary face" handwritten in the middle panel of the right page). The semantic content (what the words mean) and their apparatus (how words are presented) therefore offer the clues necessary to categorize these textual elements. Are they inscribed in a bubble? What shape is the bubble? What about the size of the text and its visual appearance? Is it typed or handwritten, and what font is it? Are there expressive variations in the handwriting?

The visual diversity of script in manga creates a rich soundscape. This is due mainly to the use of multiple typefaces and handwriting styles. Many manga narratives employ one font for spoken words and another one for thoughts and voiceovers, which results in a differing resonance. In Figure 6.1, for example, the font of the first bubble to the right of the figure on the left page (containing thoughts) varies from the font of the next bubble (relating spoken words). Here, as is often the case, the thoughts are written in a Gothic font, characterized by strokes of an even thickness. This gives a drier and airier feel than the font for the dialogs, a mixed style that employs Gothic for Sino-Japanese characters (*kanji*) and Mincho, typified by inflected strokes reminiscent of brush writing, for syllabaries (*kana*). Thanks to the alternation of fonts, dialog, and thought do not "sound" the same. Sometimes, dialog is written in Gothic typeface, which suggests a disembodied or slightly robotic voice, or a voice transformed by mechanical processes such as the telephone or the radio. In these instances, a distinct type of bubble outline is commonly employed. Dialog might also appear in handwriting, in which case it assumes a secondary position. While such lines are not easily categorized – sometimes they operate as asides, sometimes as part of a dialog – they always convey a more personal feel than the primary dialog lines (in type) and serve to foreground the characters' emotions. Generally, they are not nestled in a bubble but rather integrated directly into the drawings and usually placed in a blank space near the face of the character.

In fact, many manga narratives use a combination of several visual signs, such as typefaces and bubble shapes, to ensure reader comprehension. As with bubble shapes or other narrative conventions, there is no one-size-fits-all rule about which font to apply.[3] Although manga narratives belonging to the same genre and drawn in the same period tend to follow common conventions, each author operates their own choices. Digitalization has greatly facilitated the technical challenges of typesetting dialogs, and certain recent manga narratives, such as *Old Fashion Cupcake* (2020) by Sagan Sagan, have more than ten fonts to transcribe intonations or voices. In other cases, a specific font is tied to a specific character. In *Tokyo Tarareba Girls* (*Tōkyō tarareba musume*, 2014–17) by Akiko Higashimura, for example, each of the two imaginary characters seen by the protagonist in her alcohol-induced delirium has their own typeface. Thus, the variation of typefaces can mean different things, including, but not limited to, the sonority of voices.

Explorations of the "sound" of manga are not possible without a closer look into how writing works in Japanese. The Japanese writing system has several unique characteristics that influence how it is linked to sound and how it is used in manga. First of all, Japanese can be written vertically, from right to left, or horizontally, from left to right. In manga, writing is normally vertical. Another important peculiarity of written Japanese is that it is composed of three scripts: two syllabaries (*hiragana* and *katakana*, collectively referred to as *kana*) that each contains forty-six basic characters corresponding to the same forty-six syllables, and a set of tens of thousands Sino-Japanese characters called *kanji*. Different from *hiragana* and *katakana*, which are phonemic (each character accords with one fixed pronunciation), *kanji* characters are logographic (each having its own meaning and generally several pronunciations). A Japanese sentence is typically written with *kanji* characters for content words and *hiragana* characters for grammatical elements. *Katakana* characters are reserved for loanwords and occasionally to place emphasis on words, in a similar way to italics in English. Japanese students are supposed to know the 2,136 basic official *kanji* characters by the end of high school. Especially in manga aimed at younger readers, such a complex system sometimes necessitates the inclusion of a reading aid that glosses *kanji* characters. This is done by inserting smaller *hiragana* characters on the right when written vertically or above when written horizontally. They are often very small, sometimes barely visible in pocket editions.

This complicated system is also surprisingly lax in some aspects, enabling the glossing system to be used creatively. The reading aid may indicate what someone said in a dialog, whereas the *kanji* will spell out what they actually meant. For example, in a scene where an employee is speaking, the main text may have *kanji* reading "the company," glossed as "we," and the reader will understand that the employee really said "we," referring specifically to their company. Another frequently occurring example is that of a special move in a fight, which is written in *kanji* in the main text but glossed with a cool, English-sounding name. For instance, in *Undead Unluck* (2020–) by Yoshifumi Totsuka, one special move is named "dead road," but written with the *kanji* for "death" and "path," which would usually be pronounced *shidō*. This saves space and clarifies the content of the move. In both cases, the glossing system is not a simple pronunciation guide; instead, it provides other types of information. Another instance of this flexibility of writing in Japanese is how some words, which are usually written in *kanji*, can be written in *hiragana* or *katakana* to suggest that the person saying them does not really comprehend what they signify but only knows how they sound. This particular occurrence has an English equivalent of difficult words written phonetically, except that in the Japanese case, it is not necessarily considered a spelling error.

A last example, which is specific to manga and different from the previous two cases that also apply to literature or other media, is to be found in the orientation of the text. This may signal that someone is not speaking in

Japanese but in English (or any other language with a script running from left to right), even though the text is written in Japanese. In *Akira* (1982–90) by Katsuhiro Ōtomo, horizontally written dialog lines indicate speech in a foreign language while vertical lines relate Japanese in scenes where different languages are spoken concurrently. Clearly, Japanese writing, especially in manga, is not a straightforward representation of the sounds of language, and therefore the visual appearance of the words is vital. This is none more so than in the use of onomatopoeia.

Mimetic Words

Most manga narratives are full of mimetic words, and this varies according to the narrative's genre and the time of creation. The average number of mimetics per page has increased significantly between the 1950s and the 1970s,[4] when onomatopoeia in manga developed most of the characteristics still seen today. Generally, it can be said that the more a manga narrative is aimed at a young audience, the more it employs mimetic words. But, in fact, this is quite difficult to measure because one would have to determine exactly what counts as a mimetic word. In fact, many mimetics in manga are neologisms, which sometimes blurs the boundaries with other types of handwritten texts. Indeed, most mimetics are drawn by hand and placed outside the speech bubbles, directly in the drawings. Moreover, the majority of mimetic words are drawn with expressive effects. This visual aspect is fundamental, but to grasp the importance of the role of mimetics in manga, one must again understand the linguistic characteristics of Japanese.

The Japanese language contains thousands of mimetic words, of which several hundred are commonly found both in speech and in literature. Lexically, onomatopoeias are often divided into two main categories: *giongo*, which mimic sounds, and *gitaigo*, which mimic nonsound phenomena, such as physical appearances, types of movement, tactile sensations, or emotions. Examples of *giongo* could be *dokan* (kaboom), *ban* (bang), or *būn* (buzz or whir), while the range of *gitaigo* could be illustrated by examples including *jī*, which signals a fixed and insistent gaze, *kyun*, which relates the feeling of a heart suddenly squeezing in the presence of one's crush, and *subesube*, which conveys the sensation of a smooth surface. Some words are clearly either sound or nonsound mimetics, but many can assume both functions depending on the context or they can simultaneously mimic a sound and something else. For example, *patapata* is used to express the motion of a flag fluttering in the wind or that of a waving fan, a phenomenon that can, but not exclusively, produce a sound. In other words, the boundary between sound and nonsound mimetics is somewhat porous.

In manga, this distinction is often even hazier, and several elements contribute to this situation. First, paranormal phenomena are a frequent occurrence, and mimetics linked with them can be hard to categorize since there are no real-life referents of these phenomena. Hirohiko Araki's *JoJo's Bizarre Adventure* (*Jojo no kimyōna bōken*, 1986–), for example, famously makes recurrent use of *dodododo* and *gogogogo* (and *dododo*, *dododododo*, and so on) to express a paranormal tension that only characters with magical superpowers can sense. Initially employed for sounds of telluric rumbling and earthquakes, these mimetics gradually came to be associated first with highly dramatic scenes – as seen in Buronson and Tetsuo Hara's *Fist of the North Star* (*Hokuto no ken*, 1983–88) – and then with paranormal activity. Such shifts in meaning contribute to a blurring of the line between mimetics that convey sound and those that do not. Furthermore, the processing of onomatopoeia is the same for both categories of mimetics. One can generally assume that mimetics are read and then resonate in the mind of the reader. Even if the reader "hears" each mimetic word more or less loudly depending on the size of the word, this process does not distinguish between sound and nonsound mimetics. It could be argued that all onomatopoeia in manga is sound, creating a universe with a texture divergent from real life.

Many mimetics that originally imitated sounds are now utilized metaphorically to express feelings. The earliest example is attributed to Ikki Kajiwara and Noboru Kawasaki's baseball manga for boys, *Star of the Giants* (*Kyojin no hoshi*, 1966–71). In one of the last scenes of the manga (vol. 19),[5] the mimetic word *gān*, up to this time employed exclusively to evoke sound phenomena such as ringing bells, indicates a moment of shock for the young hero. The success of this scene gave *gān* a psychological signification and opened avenues to other innovative applications of mimetics in manga. *Gān* also illustrates the influence of manga onomatopoeia on the evolution of the Japanese language, as nowadays, people often use it in everyday life as a way to narrate their own shock. In other cases, mimetic words form part of a larger metaphor and are intertwined with drawing, such as when a character suddenly feels lonely and is shown blown by the wind, accompanied by the mimetic word *hyū* that communicates the sense of gusting wind.

Mimetics are almost without exception written in one of the two Japanese syllabaries, *katakana* or *hiragana*. This means that each mimetic word in manga can be pronounced, with very few exceptions, contrary to onomatopoeia in English or French comics, where an unpronounceable string of letters may surface instead. The fact that mimetic words generally appear written phonetically is of particular interest given that Japanese is one of the

Meaning	Alphabetical transliteration	*Hiragana*	*Katakana*
kaboom	*Dokan*	どかん	ドカン
fixed gaze	*Jī*	じいorじー	ジー
rotating motion	*Kurukuru*	くるくる	クルクル
heart beat	*Doki*	どきっ	ドキッ
sparkle	*Kirakira*	きらきら	キラキラ
aggressive glow	*Giragira*	ぎらぎら	ギラギラ

Figure 6.2 Examples of the transliteration of mimetics words.

few languages – if not the only one – that offers a choice between a phonetic and a nonphonetic manner of noting most words. Using the syllabaries instead of Sino-Japanese characters is one way to foreground immediacy. To Japanese speakers, mimetics may easily feel like a direct representation of reality, transcribing sounds and other phenomena without any linguistic filter. This sense of immediacy is one reason why onomatopoeia is such a crucial narrative and expressive tool in manga, as it allows for vivid scenes with a powerful immersive feeling.

Although today both *hiragana* and *katakana* syllabaries are employed to write mimetics, that has not always been the case. In early manga published before 1945, mimetics (and also a good part of the dialogs) were written in *katakana*. In the 1950s, *hiragana* began to be employed for mimetic words corresponding to organic sounds such as laughter, sighs, or crying – all other mimetics remained in *katakana*.[6] In the 1960s, *hiragana* were occasionally employed for other mimetics as well, for example, in *Hakaba Kitarō* (1960, later *Gegege no Kitarō*) by Shigeru Mizuki. Their number gradually increased but not uniformly. Nowadays, everything is possible: Some manga narratives use only *katakana*, others only *hiragana*, and yet others both syllabaries in various proportions.

In the latter instance, the alternation is anything but arbitrary. Even though every speech sound in Japanese can be written in either syllabary, their visual characteristics differ significantly. *Hiragana* characters are curved and soft, whereas *katakana* characters are made of straighter lines with sharp edges and angular shapes (see Fig. 6.2). Since at least the 1970s, *hiragana* tends to be used for mimetics associated with light or comical connotations; *katakana* is more often reserved for mimetics having serious or dramatic connotations. One can assume that this is motivated by the psychological meanings generally linked with each type of line. In Figure 6.1, the first three mimetics are written in *katakana*, but the drama of the situation is immediately diffused, and thus, all subsequent mimetics appear in *hiragana*.

The variations of shape in manga's written mimetic words are not limited to the choice of syllabary. There are also diverse graphic effects that are visually and referentially broad-ranging. But some conventions are common to all mimetics: The bigger a mimetic word, the louder the phenomenon it expresses. This results in a great scope of sizes, with some onomatopoeia being barely visible, while others, in extreme instances, take up almost the height of the page. Another convention that appears common to all mimetics deals with the quality of the lines. Soft and rounded shapes are associated with less dramatic phenomena than angular or jagged shapes, regardless of the original form of the written character. These conventions are widely shared across all genres of manga, and even in comics from other parts of the world,[7] although exceptions are inevitable.

Other graphic effects are more specific, however. For example, some mimetic words are drawn as if they were material objects made of stone or ribbons and placed on the ground or floated in the air. Such effects were fairly common during the 1960s, as seen in Osamu Tezuka's work, and today they are mainly seen in humorous narratives that tend to play with the conventions of manga. In fact, convention dictates that written words are not meant to be visible to the characters: In the storyworld, the sounds or the sensations themselves exist but not their written signifier. The materialization of mimetics goes against this rule and is often used as a source of gag, for example, in scenes where characters interact with speech bubbles or panel frames.[8] In one gag from *Dr. Slump* (1980–84) by Akira Toriyama, for instance, a handwritten scream is grabbed and employed as a blunt weapon by the Akane character. While such materializations are obvious, recent manga narratives feature others and more ambivalent ones.

These exemplars could be described as a sort of semimaterialization. The mimetic word is not present in the storyworld, and as such the characters are unable to perceive it. Nonetheless, it still undergoes the physical effects of the phenomenon it represents. A mimetic word that conveys shock, for example, may be written with split, broken, or trembling characters, as if they had suffered the blow themselves. A mimetic word expressing movement can be drawn as if it were itself moving. In Figure 6.3, manga artist Hirohiko Araki uses his trademark doughy or flabby effect at the bottom of the right-hand page to show the tension that distorts *dogyūn*, an original mimetic word that relates the way in which the Star Platinum character grabs the rope.

Likewise, when mimetic words are partially hidden by characters or objects, they seem quite literally to enter the spatial depth of the storyworld. This has not always been the case, as onomatopoeia was first placed in the foreground. In early manga, such as *Norakuro* (1931–41) by Tagawa Suihō,

Figure 6.3 Hirohiko Araki, *JoJo's Bizarre Adventure*, Shueisha, vol. 16, 1990, 194–95.

the application of mimetic words was sporadic, and they appeared in neutral parts of the drawings. Progressively, as onomatopoeia use increased so did occurrences of mimetic words hiding larger portions of the drawings, including parts of the characters, as in Figure 6.1. From the 1970s onward and especially in the 1980s, they came to also be situated in the middle ground. This evolution may be traced to the multilayered conception of manga space put forward by experimental creators of *shōjo* manga in the 1970s. In Figure 6.3, the abovementioned *dogyūn* is partly concealed by the rope and seems to pass behind it. In other examples, the illusion of onomatopoeia entering the background is suggested by foreshortening. Such placement and depth effects are very common in manga today.

Several other phenomena equally merit mention. One is the use of the vowel-lengthening symbol (*chōonpu*), which was originally a simple straight line. It surfaces frequently in onomatopoeia because of its malleability. Figure 6.1 features two instances of the same symbol. In the second panel, the mimetic word *uwā* above the little girl, which expresses her cry, contains a vertical line, and in the panel at the bottom right, the mimetic word *shīn* that relates silence has a horizontal line. In many mimetic words, however, the shape of the line is modified, and on occasion even includes loops. In Figure 6.3, the very wavy line immediately to the right of the rope is actually a vowel-lengthening symbol, although barely recognizable as such.

Another noteworthy phenomenon is the case of the voicing symbol, or sonant mark (*dakuon*), which consists of two small lines or dots affixed to the top right corner of certain *kana* to note voiced consonants. In linguistics, voicing refers to a vibration of the vocal cords during the emission of a sound. In Japanese, this applies to obstructing the consonants p, t, k, and s, which respectively become b, d, g, and z (or j). In contrast to the Western alphabet, where different letters denote voiced and unvoiced consonants, Japanese only uses this diacritic symbol, affixing it to the various *kana* characters that indicate syllables with these consonants.

What could be seen as a detail is in fact significant because in Japanese mimetics, voicing is associated with a coherent set of intensive and pejorative connotations, regardless of the target consonant. Indeed, mimetics with voiced consonants usually connote a massive, heavy, unpleasant, or dirty phenomenon. This can easily be seen in mimetic words that exist in both unvoiced and voiced versions. For example, *kirakira* describes a pretty sparkle, whereas *giragira* indicates an aggressive glow (see Fig. 6.2). It is no wonder therefore that many variants of classic mimetics in manga exhibit the voicing symbol, particularly in fight scenes or in dramatic moments. Each of the mimetics in Figure 6.3 begins with a voiced consonant and employs the voicing symbol. Through the decades, the size of the voicing symbol has gradually increased in relation to the size of the characters to which it is affixed, and it has gained visual prominence in a number of manga narratives. The inclusion of the voicing symbol is even sometimes extended to *kana* that should be invoiceable, especially those that correspond to vowels alone. In many cases, what appears to the reader's eye is less the exact representation of sound than the connotation of performed voicing that assists in dramatizing a scene.[9]

Conclusion

Sound is undoubtedly an essential aspect of manga. A number of tools allow a visual expression of sounds in the storyworld, even though these tools often fulfill other narrative functions. Mimetic words play, for example, a material role in the overall page structure and in the way it guides the reader's gaze. Furthermore, variations in the appearance of writing, such as the use of several fonts, may not only correspond to a variation in sound but also to a divergence in enunciation or in the narrative status of the text. Manga communicates diverse qualities of sound through visual effects applied to writing. Taking this visual element into account frequently adds a layer of difficulty when translating manga into other languages with completely different writing systems.

Although similar to onomatopoeia in comics from other parts of the world, mimetics in manga present several particularities, the first being the range of phenomena they are able to convey. Compared to mimetics in spoken language or literature, the use of onomatopoeia in manga also tends to present many neologisms and variants of common mimetics, and applies many more voiced and long vowels. It seems that these linguistic characteristics are in part due to choices made by authors based on visual parameters. Mimetics are not the equivalent of sound effects. Indicative in this regard is the integration of written mimetic words, often for comical effect, into anime since the 1970s. Mimetics are not merely a stopgap in the absence of sound but rather an essential expressive and narrative tool that imbues manga pages and dynamically immobile anime imagery with a diversified sensory texture.

Notes

1. Kunio Nagatani, *Manga no kōzōgaku* (Tokyo: Index Shuppan, 2000), 210–21.
2. Giancarla Unser-Schutz, "Language as the Visual: Exploring the Intersection of Linguistic and Visual Language in Manga," *Image[&]Narrative*, 12, no. 1 (2011): 1–22, www.imageandnarrative.be/index.php/imagenarrative/article/view/131/102.
3. Naoki Shirahata, "Fukidashi wa nani o tsutaeteiru ka?," in *Manga no yomikata* (Tokyo: Takarajimasha, 1995), 138–45.
4. Fusanosuke Natsume, "Gion kara 'on'yu' e," in *Manga no yomikata* (Tokyo: Takarajimasha, 1995), 126–37, esp. the figure on page 132.
5. *Kyojin no hoshi* (Star of the Giants), Kindle, 160–200.
6. Robert S. Peterson, "The Acoustics of Manga." In *A Comics Studies Reader*, edited by Jeet Heer and Kent Worcester (Jackson: University Press of Mississippi, 2009), 163–71.
7. Scott McCloud, *Making Comics: Storytelling Secrets of Comics, Manga and Graphic Novels* (New York: Harper, 2006), 147.
8. Fusanosuke Natsume, *Manga wa naze omoshiroi no ka* (Tokyo: NHK Shuppan, 1997), 80–84, 180–82.
9. Blanche Delaborde, "L'iconicité de l'écriture dans les mangas: le cas des onomatopées et des impressifs," *Japon Pluriel* 12, ed. Julien Bouvard and Cléa Patin (Arles: Philippe Picquier, 2019), 389–400.

7

MINORI ISHIDA

Voice Acting for Anime

The basic expressive means and narrative techniques of anime have developed within the environment of television broadcasting. On-screen movement in TV anime is often limited and is only one part of an otherwise still character drawing. Such limited, or "selective,"[1] animation, seen in Japan in *Astro Boy* (*Tetsuwan Atomu*, dir. Osamu Tezuka, 1963–66), radically reduced production time and costs. It also enabled the broadcasting of weekly thirty-minute episodes. The success of *Astro Boy* led to its emulation in other series, thus making limited animation the cornerstone of anime production. The extremely selective approach to visual movement on-screen has significantly impacted the recognizable shape of anime. For animators, the key issues are what parts of a drawing, or a character image, should move and how. "Selective animation," together with camerawork, created a unique rhythm of pronounced modulations between stillness and movement that is the foundation of anime's visual expression.

In terms of character construction, feature-length animated films by Disney, for example, tend to express personality by means of "embodied performance," in which each character possesses a unique set of gestures and mannerisms that directly indicate their personality. In contrast, Japanese anime has developed a shared repertory of poses and movements that go beyond single characters or individual works, foregrounding "figurative performance."[2] But like "selective animation," "figurative performance" alone cannot create outstanding characters: In fact, their construction relies heavily on voice, making voice performance vital in bringing a character to life.

Similar to visual animation techniques, voice performance in TV anime has been shaped by the specifics of the production process. In Disney feature films and Hanna-Barbera TV animations, voice recording precedes animation production. Working within the model known as "prescoring," animators follow voice actors. In Japan, prescoring was implemented in the 1940s in animated films, including *The Spider and the Tulip* (*Kumo*

98

to chūrippu, dir. Kenzō Masaoka, 1943) and *Momotaro: Sacred Sailors* (*Momotarō: umi no shinpei*, dir. Mitsuyo Seo, 1945). Prescoring was also adopted in the early feature-length films of the studio Tōei Dōga (from 1998 onward, Toei Animation), such as *Magic Boy* (*Shōnen Sarutobi Sasuke*, dir. Taiji Yabushita, 1959) and *The Orphan Brothers* (*Anju to Zushiōmaru*, dir. Taiji Yabushita, 1961). Sometimes additional voices were recorded after the completion of the animation production in order to achieve a more precise synchronization with the images.

In *Astro Boy*, however, the voice was exclusively recorded after the completion of the animation (or at least the storyboard), which required voice actors to synchronize their performance with the drawings. Subsequent weekly TV series adopted this cost-saving method known as *afureko* ("after recording"),[3] and it has since become the most common model of voice recording in the anime industry. Both the production flow and the limited animation techniques employed in TV anime are structured around the *afureko*. As a consequence, it exercises considerable influence on the form of anime. The following discussion examines the relationship between visuals and voice as well as the voice actor's contribution to character construction. It also touches upon the ways voice actors perceive themselves and their work.

Reliance on Voice: *Astro Boy*

In limited animation, voice contributes substantially to the narrative. For example, many scenes in *Astro Boy* rely more on the expressive and explanatory power of the voice than on the animated image. In episode 1, Dr. Tenma weeps over his dead son's body. The image on-screen remains still throughout the shot, making it impossible to interpret without sound. Here, the coherence of the narrative is maintained through the vocal track.

The creators of *Astro Boy* understood the crucial role of voice acting. Eiichi Yamamoto, formerly a chief animator at the studio Mushi Production, where the series was made, explained the relationship between voice and limited animation as follows: "When a real person speaks, their mouth takes various shapes. But we limit those to three: closed, open, and half-open. We then repeat those in random order, at eight drawings per second. Just four in-betweens [three in-betweens for the mouth + one for the face] are enough to animate dialogs of any length."[4]

Yamamoto's explanation implies that the importance of voice in animation is proportional to the reduction of the characters' body movements. Furthermore, simplified, rather than naturalistically smooth, movement makes it possible to animate characters talking at length. American animators, not only Disney but also the Fleischer brothers, who practiced an alternative style to Disney, attempted to emulate realistic mouth movements in order to synchronize character images with voices ("lip-syncing"). Even in the work of United Productions of America, a pioneer of limited animation that profoundly influenced the *Astro Boy* creator Osamu Tezuka, mouth articulations are much more intricate than in TV anime. The absence of lip-syncing in Japanese anime appears exceptional in the history of animation globally.[5] Such shortcuts have been implemented to reduce production costs, but they additionally provide an opportunity to express the characters' emotions through voice acting. Skillful voice actors are in fact indispensable in breathing life into characters.

Since *Astro Boy*, there have been many examples of visual direction that rely on voice acting. One of the most outstanding is in the final two episodes of *Neon Genesis Evangelion* (*Shinseiki Evangelion*, 1995–96, dir. Hideaki Anno). These surprised viewers with their unconventional collage of different visual materials, ranging from rough sketches to photo footage. But even if the visuals seemed at times chaotic, the characters conveyed their thoughts and feelings clearly – by voice.[6] It was thanks to voice acting that the unusual visuals made sense.

The Dubbing Controversy of 1962

The voice actor occupies one of the central creative positions in anime production, and yet, voice actors for anime and other types of TV programs were not initially acknowledged as true performers. Although the history of voice actors in Japan coincided with the launch of radio broadcasting in 1925, voice acting was treated as a sideline for stage or cinema actors until the mid-1960s. The reasons for the ongoing prejudice against voice acting were alleged during the Dubbing Controversy (*Atereko Ronsō*) of 1962, one year before the airing of *Astro Boy*. It reminds us of the low status of the voice acting profession before its eventual integration into the anime industry.

The Dubbing Controversy erupted on February 19, 1962, with an article by the famous stage and cinema actor Eijirō Tōno in the widely circulated newspaper *Tokyo Shimbun*. In it, he attacked the new practice of dubbing for telefilm and TV series, which with hindsight can be considered a predecessor to voice recording in anime because dubbing actors are also expected to synchronize with the visual performance on-screen (in fact, many voice actors continue to perform both types of jobs even today). For Tōno, dubbing actors were little more than "marionettes," who adjusted their voices to original performances by foreign actors. He believed true acting meant creating a character through one's own means, while dubbing was a smothering practice potentially damaging a voice actor's reputation. Actors engaging in this practice, Tōno maintained, could become mentally ill if they were only allowed to perform like puppets, and therefore they should be remunerated fairly.[7] A week later on February 26, Tōru Abe, a dubbing actor for the TV series *The Third Man* (NTA Film Network, BBC, 1959–65), countered Tōno's assertions in the same newspaper. Abe argued that dubbing was a valid form of employment for an actor, emphasizing that "the most important task [for the actor] is to adequately reproduce the character's feelings and personality in Japanese."[8] The actor Daijirō Natsukawa supported Tōno's view regarding the notion of mental suffering, claiming that dubbing required a set of technical skills rather than artistic performance. In this regard, they had more in common with a TV announcer or a tour guide.[9]

Audience Attention to Voice Actors

The concept of acting promoted by Tōno and Natsukawa was too narrow, however, to accommodate the new types of voice acting emerging in the early 1960s. Despite the misconceptions and biases, audiences began to show interest in voice actors because of dubbed TV dramas. In 1965, just three years after the Dubbing Controversy, the stage actor Nachi Nozawa participated in the dubbing of the American TV drama *The Man from U.N.C.L.E.* (Metro-Goldwyn-Mayer Television, 1964–68), a role he continued until the end of this extremely popular Japanese broadcast in 1970. In response to public demand, articles about dubbing actors appeared in the magazine *Television Age*, which ran from 1960 to 1981 and specialized in foreign series airing in Japan. The enthusiastic reactions to dubbing actors by fan critics in the magazine have been described on reexamination as representing "the first voice actor boom."[10] The number of positions available to stage, cinema, or radio drama actors increased with the arrival of weekly TV anime as a new standard format for Japanese animation.

Since the early 1970s, anime viewers have paid greater attention to voice acting. Yoku Shioya, who performed the protagonist in *Triton of the Sea* (*Umi no Toriton*, dir. Yoshiyuki Tomino, 1972), generated an organized fan following among junior and senior high school girls. Likewise, the popularity of the TV series, *Space Battleship Yamato* (*Uchū senkan Yamato*, dir. Leiji Matsumoto, 1974–75) and its eponymously named film (dir. Toshio Masuda, 1977) sparked what fan critics regard as "the second voice actor boom" and the launch of specialized anime magazines that allocated considerable coverage to voice actors.[11] *Animage*, for instance, published numerous interviews and gravure photographs, together with feature articles dedicated to voice actors. It also established a performer popularity poll, creating a space in which readers could share their fascination with anime voices. *Animage* and other such periodicals encouraged a new appreciation of the profession of the voice actor and were instrumental in the formation of a corresponding fandom in Japan.[12]

Voice Acting for *Afureko*: The Role of Punctuation Marks in the Recording Script

Voice acting for anime is characterized by a number of technical particularities. The practice of *afureko* requires the voice actor to follow a special recording script that adheres closely to the storyboard. This explains why voice acting has been rendered as "an assemblage of acting and characterization within a framework predetermined by others."[13] What this framework is and how it affects voice acting will be examined here using the recording script (*afureko daihon*) and the regular script (*kyakuhon*) for episode 33, "Mother Has Disappeared" (*Kāsan ga inai*), from the anime series *3000 Leagues in Search for Mother* (*Haha o tazunete sanzenri*, 1976, general dir. Isao Takahata).[14]

The recording script for "Mother Has Disappeared" lists the contents of the storyboard per shot. The page is divided into three horizontal rows: The upper indicates the number of the shot, the middle contains visual directions including character action, camera movement, and location, and the bottom has all the character lines. Visual and vocal data comprising the shot are thus treated as two distinct tracks, and yet, they are meant to be entwined in the final animation. Their amalgamation is facilitated by punctuation marks – namely, the comma and the ellipsis. These reflect the distinctive features of voice acting in TV anime.

The protagonist Marco, an Italian boy who has left his hometown Genoa in search of his mother, arrives in a town in Argentina with a family of touring actors. There Marco visits Moretti, a town councilor who may know his mother's whereabouts. Shots 163 to 208 contain the dialog between the two characters. In shot 169, they are sitting opposite one another. In shot 172, Marco is told that his mother is unlikely to be in the town, followed by his astonished reaction in shot 173 (Fig. 7.1).

The exchange between the characters starts with the two lines:

MARCO: But, uncle Merelli ... ...? (*Demo, Mererri ojisan ga ... ...?*)
MORETTI: Listen.[15] (*Sono koto da ga ne*)

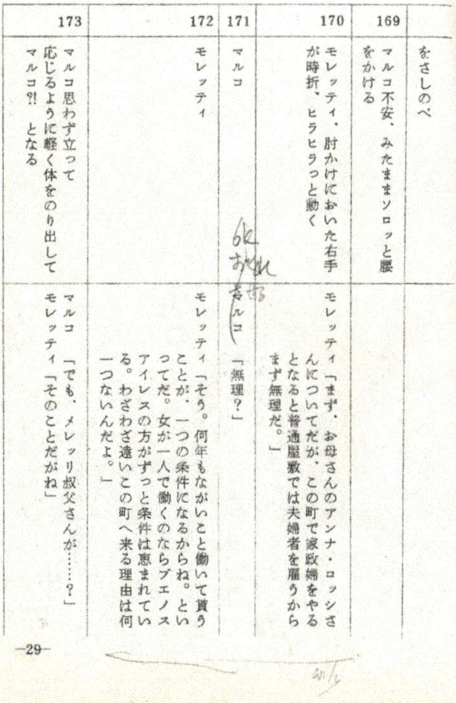

173	172	171	170	169
マルコ思わず立って応じるように軽く体をのり出して マルコ?!となる	モレッティ	マルコ	モレッティ、肘かけにおいた右手が時折、ヒラヒラっと動く	をさしのべ マルコ不安。みたままソロッと腰 をかける
マルコ「でも。メレッリ叔父さんが……?」 モレッティ「そのことだがね」	モレッティ「そう。何年もながいこと働いて貰うことが。一つの条件になるからね。といって女が一人で働くのならブエノスアイレスの方がずっと条件は恵まれている。わざわざこの町へ来る理由は何一つないんだよ。」	マルコ「無理?」	モレッティ「まず、お母さんのアンナ・ロッシさんについてだが、この町で郵政娘をやるとなると普通屋敷では夫婦者を雇うから まず無理だ。」	

—29—

Figure 7.1 Page 29 of the recording script of *3000 Leagues in Search for Mother*, including shot 173 on the far left. Courtesy of Hideo Watanabe, Watanabe Collection.

The corresponding visual direction in the middle row reads:

Marco stands up.
He slightly leans forward to listen to Moretti.
Marco is all "!?"[16]

In the final anime version, Marco jumps from the chair as described in the recording script. Interestingly, the timing of the movement coincides with the comma in Marco's line. Clearly, the comma acts as a cue for the voice actor to synchronize with the visual direction.

In the anime production process, the script outlining the story as a succession of scenes precedes storyboard and recording script. When the script is turned into a storyboard, it is broken down into shots. The director working on the storyboard determines the movements and facial expressions of the characters, measuring the duration and timing of their lines with a stopwatch. In scene 13 of the script, Marco's exclamation appears as follows:

MARCO: But uncle Merelli … …? (*Demo Mererri ojisan ga … …?*)[17]

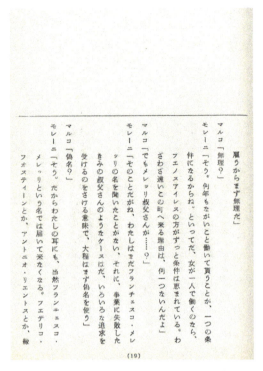

モレーニ「願うからまず無理だ」

モレーニ「無理？」

マルコ「そう。何年もながいこと働いて貰うことが、一つの条件になるからね。といってだ、女が一人で働くのなら、フエノスアイレスの方がずっと条件は恵まれている。わざわざ遠いこの町へ来る理由は、何一つないんだよ」

モレーニ「そう。」

マルコ「でもメレッリ叔父さんが……？」

モレーニ「そのことだがね、わたしはまだフランチェスコ・メレッリの名を聞いたことがない。それに、事業に失敗したきみの叔父さんのようなケースはだ、いろいろな追求を受けるのをさける意味で、大概はまず偽名を使う」

マルコ「偽名？」

モレーニ「そう。だからわたしの耳にも、当然フランチェスコ・メレッリという名では届いて来たくなる。フエデリコ・フオスティーンとか、アントニオ・リエントスとか、樅

(19)

Figure 7.2 Page 19 of the script of *3000 Leagues in Search for Mother*, including Marco's line in the middle. Courtesy of Hideo Watanabe, Watanabe Collection.

The line is the same as in the recording script, except for the comma, which was apparently added later by the episode director, Yoshiyuki Tomino, when he specified Marco's jumping up from the chair. In fact, the script does not describe Marco sitting in the chair; all his positions must have been governed by the director (Fig. 7.2).

The addition of the comma to the recording script, together with the corresponding animation, confirms that the comma marks a breathing interval for the voice actor and the timing of character movements that must match up with spoken lines. The voice actor cannot simply add, delete, or move the corresponding pause. As such, the comma becomes a crucial link between character movements and voice, even if it epitomizes a "framework predetermined by others" to which the actor must adapt.

In recent years, animation is rarely completed before the production moves to voice recording, and it has become common practice to create a "rehearsal video" consisting of still storyboard panels. Voice actors employ it in combination with the recording script to prepare for the recording session. Each shot is accompanied by a rectangle board (*bōrudo*) that designates the name of the speaking character. The board appears when characters begin to talk and disappears when they finish. Even though the rehearsal video is a new tool, the director controls the time frames for character speech. The video and the boards continue to privilege the visual direction over the actor's voice, reinforcing the organizing power of the comma in the age of digital production.

The above similarly applies to the ellipsis, which indicates the absence of spoken words. Even though the ellipsis is widely used in all kinds of scripts, it functions differently depending on the media. In radio drama, for example, the ellipsis may specify any sound apart from human speech. In live-action cinema and theater, it may not be needed as facial expressions and body motions accompany sound.

The visual description for shot 72 in the recording script of "Mother Has Disappeared" is just "Fiorina," and her line in the bottom row reads, "Dad ... ...?" (*Tōsan ... ...?*).[18] In the final anime version, Fiorina's mouth movement stops at the last sound of "Dad ..." and is followed by blinking that continues until the next shot. This movement overlaps with the ellipsis in the recording script, which can be interpreted as signaling changes in facial expression that do not involve talking. A comparable function of the ellipsis is evident in shot 57. The simple explanation in the middle row ("a blink," *mepachi*),[19] combined with an ellipsis in the bottom row of the recording script, results in Marco blinking silently in the final animation.

Both comma and ellipsis serve as director cues. The comma determines the actor's breathing rhythm and permits synchronization of spoken lines with character movements. The ellipsis prompts the voice actor to predict and embody a character's facial movements unrelated to the act of speaking.

Nuance Embedded in Sound

Voice actors do not need to keep mindlessly to the recording script and the visuals since the *afureko* system allows for nuanced performances. This is again evident in the episode "Mother Has Disappeared." Peppino, performed by Ichirō Nagai, is the leader of a traveling puppet troupe. Together with his daughters Concetta and Giulietta, he has just arrived at an inn, where they meet innkeeper Lucia. The middle row of the recording script for shot 62 describes the actions of the characters as follows:

> Peppino receives the key and hands it to Concetta. Lucia pushes the visitor register toward Peppino, who has turned back to her, and Peppino writes down their names. Concetta turns her head to the left and goes out of frame (*FR-O*). Giulietta goes out of frame. Lucia moves only her neck (her elbows remain fixed in place).

The bottom row contains the lines:

CONCETTA: Let's go, Giulietta. (*Sa, Giulietta ikimashō*)
PEPPINO: Goodness, now I can relax. (*Yare yare, kore de teashi ga nobaseru*)
LUCIA: Hew, wait a bit! (*A, chotto!*)[20]

In the final anime version, Peppino's exclamation "Goodness" (*yare yare*) overlaps with a sigh not indicated in the recording script. The sigh is an important means of characterization because it expresses both Peppino's momentary relief after a long journey and the general exhaustion of a traveling artist. This example proves that voice actors can make spoken lines more elaborate, can reveal a character's interiority, and can breathe life into the drawn figures on-screen by adding sounds and sighs. But such additions do not constitute a radical departure from the script. In his voice acting, Nagai stays within the frame shaped by the director, aligning his breathing to the intervals designated by punctuation. This is further evidence that voice acting under the *afureko* system involves extremely nuanced performances synchronized to the predetermined timing down to one 24th of a second.

Ichirō Nagai's Method and Voice Actor's Identity

How do voice actors view performing under the *afureko* system? In 1981, almost twenty years after the Dubbing Controversy, Ichirō Nagai explained his approach to voice acting in the article "Acting Caught by Cells." For Nagai, stage and voice acting are part of the same vocation in terms of character embodiment: Actors need to "match the vector of their cells to the image of the character."[21] "Cell" in this context refers to the actor's bodily sensations, whereas "vector" is used to describe the psycho-physiological alignment with the character. It is necessary to recognize the "vectors" that define a character's mindset – their cognitive, moral, and emotional orientation – as well as the set of external and internal factors that determine their actions. The voice actor must identify these vectors and internalize them to the level of bodily reactions, thus necessitating a thorough analysis of the script, otherwise "they will end up with an inaccurate understanding of the character's behavior. In such cases, there will always be something off with their performance, no matter how hard they try to tune in on the bodily level. The actor's ability to grasp all necessary vectors that shape the character depends strictly on their talent."[22]

By successfully internalizing a character, the actor is able to process its movements as their own, even when standing in front of the microphone. Nagai describes his own voice acting: "Of course, I observed the character moving or opening and closing their mouth on-screen. But, first and foremost, I tried to imagine myself going through the same motions. Again and again. I was able to reproduce this feeling on the cellular level. The work goes smoothly when that happens. My lines are filled with life."[23]

The method proposed by Nagai counters the biased opinion that dubbing does not count as acting because actors cannot utilize their own vocalization, and as he maintains, performers who speak in their "own voice" do not deliver a proper performance in any case. Nagai also believes that the oft-lamented restrictions imposed on the actor by the visuals do have a certain potential: A character's mouth movement, for example, can provide an actor with more valuable clues than an (incompetent) director. In other words, the experienced actor would follow the character's movements rather than listen to the director.

Nagai's approach served him well throughout his twenty years as a voice actor. His description of method in "Acting Caught by Cells" celebrates voice actors as irreplaceable creative professionals directly responsible for bringing fictional characters to life. For him, the performances of voice actors are on a par with film and stage acting. Indeed, since the publication of Nagai's article over forty years ago, voice actors have profoundly enriched the medium of TV anime.

Conclusion

The voice-acting method developed under the *afureko* system is now an integral part of anime. Voice acting for *afureko* facilitates character individuality, even if the visual performance is severely restricted. At the same time, some anime audiences appreciate voice performers and their voices more than performances associated with particular characters. This fascination with voice actors has spawned a vast range of media that depend on the voice even more than anime, including drama CDs, situation CDs, and visual novels.[24] Today, voice actors perform with both voice and physical appearance in the form of concerts and other live events, the popularity of which offers powerful support for the growth of the anime industry. Although restrictions imposed by *afureko* still remain in place, the performer's voice has nonetheless been liberated from them to communicate freely with anime audiences.

Notes

1. Sheou Hui Gan, "Selective animation to iu gainen gihō: "Limited Animation" no genkai o koete." In *Animēshon no eigagaku*, edited by Mikirō Katō (Kyoto: Rinsen Shoten, 2009), 284–89.
2. Stevie Suan, *Anime's Identity: Performativity and Form beyond Japan* (Minneapolis: University of Minnesota Press, 2021), 212–28.

3. Takashi Kayama, "Masaoka Kenzō ni yoru rippu shinku to sono hyōshō," *Animēshon kenkyū/ The Japanese Journal of Animation Studies*, 19, no. 2 (2018): 43.

4. Eiichi Yamamoto, *Mushi puro kōbōki: animēta no seishun* (Tokyo: Shinchōsha, 1989), 106. All translations from the Japanese are by the author.

5. Hiromichi Hosoma, *Mickī wa naze kuchibue o fuku no ka: animēshon no hyōgenshi* (Tokyo: Shinchōsha, 2013), 221.

6. José Andrés Santiago Iglesias, "Not Just Immobile: Moving Drawings and Visual Synecdoches in Neon Genesis Evangelion." In *Anime Studies: Media-Specific Approaches to Neon Genesis Evangelion*, edited by José Andrés Santiago Iglesias and Ana Soler Baena (Stockholm: Stockholm University Press, 2021), 39–43. Open Access.

7. Eijirō Tōno, "'Sei'yū ni kiken teate o: tanin no engi ni awasu kurushimi." *Tokyo Shimbun*, February 19, 1962, 9.

8. Tōru Abe, "Atereko to haiyū: katawa ni naru to wa omowanai." *Tokyo Shimbun*, February 26, 1962, 9.

9. Daijirō Natsukawa, "Bijinesu to warikire: atereko wa tokushuna gijutsu," *Tokyo Shimbun*, March 5, 1962, 9.

10. Shō Kobayashi, "Seiyū shiron: anime būmu ni miru shokugyō seiyū no tenkanten," *The Japanese Journal of Animation Studies* 16, no. 2 (2015): 8.

11. Minori Ishida, *Anime to seiyū no media shi: naze josei ga shōnen o enjiru no ka* (Tokyo: Seikyūsha, 2020), 116.

12. Ishida, *Anime to seiyū no media shi*, 119–28.

13. Ryōta Fujitsu, "Seiyūron: tsūshiteki, jisshōteki ichi kōsatsu." In *Anime kenkyū nyūmon ōyōhen: anime o kiwameru 11 no kotsu*, edited by Masahiro Koyama and Akiko Sugawa (Tokyo: Gendai Shokan, 2018), 103.

14. Both scripts are part of the Watanabe Collection, which is housed in the Archive Center for Anime Studies at Niigata University and contains so-called intermediate materials of anime production (i.e., various materials produced in the different stages of anime production), www.arc.niigata-u.ac.jp/en/research/anime-archive/.

15. Recording script (*afureko daihon*) for episode 33, "Mother Has Disappeared" (1976), 29.

16. Recording script [for "Mother Has Disappeared" (1976)?]. The punctuation "!?" signals Marco's confusion.

17. Script (*kyakuhon*) for episode 33, "Mother Has Disappeared" (1976), 19.

18. Recording script for "Mother Has Disappeared" (1976), 16.

19. Recording script for "Mother Has Disappeared" (1976), 13.

20. Recording script for "Mother Has Disappeared" (1976), 14.

21. Ichirō Nagai, "Saibō de toraeta engi." In *GUNDAM CENTURY RENEWAL VERSION: sora kakeru senshi tachi* (Tokyo: Kisōsha, 2000), 94. The first edition appeared in a special issue of anime magazine *OUT* in 1981.

22. Nagai, "Saibō de toraeta engi," 92.

23. Nagai, "Saibō de toraeta engi," 93.

24. Minori Ishida, "Sounds and Sighs: 'Voice Porn' for Women." In *Shōjo across Media: Exploring "Girl" Practices in Contemporary Japan*, edited by Jaqueline Berndt, Kazumi Nagaike, and Fusami Ogi (London: Palgrave Macmillan, 2019), 286–89.

PART IV

Narrative

8

KŌICHI MORIMOTO

Reading *Story-Manga*

Narrative and Story

Japanese manga is a form of comics that took shape in the twentieth century, and it is distinguished by its genres, narrative tropes, and character types, as well as its expressive techniques. Yet the basic form of manga is not so different from Western comics. The majority of contemporary mainstream manga titles belong to the category of graphic narratives, the primary purpose of which is storytelling. A major attraction of narrative media is naturally the range of stories, but it should be remembered that a "story" is not the same as a "narrative." What stays with us as a story after reading a work of fiction might be fragmentary recollections and impressions left by the characters and any striking scenes, in addition to a fundamental grasp of the plot. As such, the story is a secondary experience grounded in recollection and conceptual synthesis. Our primary encounter with a narrative – that is, our experience of narrative as narrative and not as story – precedes any understanding of the story.

The narrative experience is dependent on the narrator, which is variously defined. It is generally accepted, however, that a creator operates behind the narrator and aims to convey the narrative by means of a specific representational system or set of signs. As in any type of communication, the choice of signs is predicated on how the recipient receives them: Expressions are assembled for their possible effects on reading and viewing. But creators cannot completely control reception since narrative experience is concretely established only through the imaginative commitment of the recipient.

The principal type of event depicted in a narrative is an action performed by a concrete entity that belongs to the fictional world – the "character." Different from natural phenomena, human actions originate in individual intention, which is the product of personal beliefs, desires, and emotions, be it a fictional character or an actual person. The main task of the creator is therefore to make the mindset, thoughts, and emotions of their characters understandable. Recipients are inclined to focus on the interiority of the characters, whether consciously or not, in an attempt to approach their inner state. The intensity of this approximation can vary, from the recipient's simple efforts to find the reasons behind an act to deep empathy. In any case, imaginative synchronization with a character is essential for the narrative experience, and it is crucial in generating "reality as mimesis." The purpose of this fictional reality is not to *refer to* the real world but rather to make the recipient *perceive* the created world. Certainly, a fictional world has the quality of mimesis insofar as the real world is reproduced or imitated. But while historical narrative prioritizes factual truth, fiction is committed to "what sort of man turns out to say or do what sort of thing according to probability or necessity."[1] This probability can only be achieved by mimetic reproduction and is not to be confused with what fiction implies about reality – in other words, fictional narratives aim to communicate a storyworld and characters as self-standing entities.

The three basic components of graphic narrative are image, word, and panel.[2] Narration is carried out through combinations of images, which are usually hand-drawn but can also consist of photographs, or digitally generated materials, and words jointly organized into framed units or panels. As a visible unit, the panel functions to advance the narrative, and it influences how the recipient perceives narrative time. A sequence of panels conveys the temporal progress of events, with various nuances expressed by panel shape and arrangement. The reader must deduce the contents of each panel and track the relationship between panels in order to comprehend what is happening – who thinks, who acts, who does what and how. Readers accumulate visual and verbal information from panels and integrate it into a story that is a mentally reconstructed summary of the narrated events.

The Three Phases of Reading Manga: The Microscopic, Mesoscopic, and Macroscopic

The process of experiencing a graphic narrative involves three phases. The first is the *microscopic* phase, which applies to the impressions and interpretations evoked at the very moment of encounter with visual and verbal components. While experiencing the narrative panel by panel, the recipient also has a slightly broader field in view as they observe the adjacent panels. This might be seen as the *mesoscopic* phase. As the reader continues beyond the single page, the contents are retrospectively integrated, gradually clarifying the nature of the characters and the story as a whole. In this *macroscopic* phase the reader supplements the narrative contents with their own accumulated memory.

Figure 8.1 Moto Hagio, *The Poe Clan*, vol. 1 (translated by Rachel Thorn, Seattle: Fantagraphics Books, 2019), 167–68. Panel numbers were added by the author for ease of explanation. Reading direction from right to left. © 2007 Moto HAGIO/SHOGAKUKAN.

From the reader's perspective, the direct engagement with the narrative occurs during the process of reception. Interpretations and impressions obtained at this stage rest on concrete textual elements or narrative discourse.[3] This discourse is determined by the particularities of the sign systems through which the narrative is conveyed, including words, images, videos, and body movements. Manga as a specific form of comics has acquired various distinguishing characteristics with respect to contents, but these have been premised on the development of specific forms of its narrative discourse. A representative example is a double-page spread from the 120-page narrative *The Poe Clan* (*Pō no ichizoku*, 1972) by Moto Hagio, published in Shogakukan's girls-manga magazine *Bessatsu Shōjo Comic* (Fig. 8.1).

The Poe Clan was one of the shorter stories that led to the long-running serial of the same title (1972–76), and it marked an important step in the evolution of manga's narrative techniques. Authors such as Hagio enhanced readers' synchronization with characters by refining the means of rendering character interiority. A vampire story that belongs to neither the horror nor the gothic genre, *The Poe Clan* is a realistic drama about vampire characters living through different periods and about the people with whom they have relationships. Figure 8.1 features the Englishman Dr. Clifford and one of the vampires, Lady Portsnell. When Dr. Clifford embraces Lady Portsnell, he finds that she has no pulse. Already suspicious about her identity, he is now convinced that she is not human and decides to kill her with a pitchfork. Thus, the identity of the Portsnell family is revealed, signaling the narrative's turning point that eventually leads to a catastrophic ending.

In any narrative experience, the denotative textual content – what is read or viewed – is merely a set of clues for the presentation of the respective event. Each recipient interprets these clues from the text as they reconstruct what is happening and how. Panel 10 in Figure 8.1 contains a relatively realistic depiction interspersed with many suggestive omissions. On its own, the panel offers no hints about what is transpiring. Notwithstanding, the reader understands from the upper panel that Dr. Clifford is trying to stab the woman with the pitchfork (invisible in panel 10), which he must be gripping in his right hand.

A still panel image never represents an isolated moment.[4] Even if the panel appears as if it is capturing a particular point in time, in actuality, it contains more than one. Furthermore, the passage of time within the panel is subsumed by the temporal continuum of the narrative. In the same way, we also know that any given scene is part of a fictional world, its space extending beyond the frame of the drawing. A reader's association with a temporal and spatial continuum is conceptualized by some as "closure,"[5] but this is better understood as supplementation. Whereas "closure" implies a filling in of missing pieces to complete an allegedly incomplete image, a fictional world is always complete as depicted and does not designate beforehand what should or can be supplemented. At the same time, the signs given do not restrict what the reader may imaginatively supplement. Certain supplementations by the reader are more likely than others depending on the organization of a specific text; these range from the most obvious to those that derive from freer and more individual associations. In a broad sense, supplementation is a form of reasoning and as such is an essential part of communication. Narrative discourse in manga can set events in motion insofar as it appeals to the essential human disposition of continuously inferring and supplementing information.

The Microscopic Phase

As a recipient reads, they acquire not only the literal meaning, or propositional content, of what is unfolding. The assault scene in panel 10, for example, emphasizes the contrast between lightness and darkness in a small barn through shadows rendered by lines and solid black inking that spreads to the faces and clothes of the two characters. This extreme contrast impresses the reader, and no doubt deliberately so. The hands are also noteworthy. The man's left hand, which sticks out of the panel, and the woman's two hands are clearly seen, as is the man's right hand in panel 9. His coat and her dress with its complex rippling folds are equally evocative. Together with the dramatic urgency of the depicted moment, these drawings directly relate the psychology of resolve and fear. Some readers may equally interpret lightness and darkness as symbolizing the confrontation between good and evil.

The details of the imagery convey an impression of the scene (i.e., atmosphere, ambience, mood) rather than facts. As a result, the reader is pulled into the event and emotionally attuned to it as if being an actual witness. Instead of recognizing rationally and cognitively what is happening, the reader tangibly experiences the fictional world on an aesthetic and emotional level. Only then can characters emerge as living beings with whom the reader develops a close bond. Taken together, these experiences warrant the pleasure of engaging with a narrative and fulfill the purpose of narrating, thereby allowing the recipient to directly perceive the created world.

Manga has evolved diverse expressive devices to facilitate the recipient's engagement with the fictional world, including unique linework and elaborate shading, pictograms, the shapes of text balloons that adverbially distinguish the modes of dialog and thought, the iconographic application of onomatopoeia, and complicated page layouts necessitated by space limitations. The choice to privilege the use of certain signs over others is likewise important. In many panels of the spread in Figure 8.1, the backgrounds are barely or only vaguely delineated. In addition, the outer borders of panels 2, 9, and 10 are omitted. Such ellipses and blanks encourage the reader to supplement imaginatively the mood of the situation and the interiority of the characters. The ability to utilize the semantic effects of the *zero sign* – the power of absence – is one of manga's most remarkable features.

In general, a realistically rendered drawing occasions objective and literal recognition. But the greater the level of pictorial abstraction, the greater the room for the reader to fill. And this cognitive effort can be rewardingly accompanied by affective impressions. Moto Hagio tends to draw human bodies and faces in a realistic fashion, but as Figure 8.1 demonstrates, visual realism is not the ultimate goal. If we were to borrow cinematic terms, the "camera" remains close to the characters, which evokes an overall impression of spatial and psychological tightness in many of the panels. The lack of explanation about the characters' surroundings and the frequent employment of close-up shots encourage the reader to focus on the interiority of the characters. This effect is most obvious in panel 2, which exhibits an extremely rare technique in the daring omission of the outlines essential for manga characters and the use of only cross-hatched shadows for the forms of a man (Dr. Clifford) and a woman (Lady Portsnell) in an embrace. It could be conjectured that this sketchlike technique immediately conveys the sentiments of Dr. Clifford, whose astonishment and fear threaten to blur the borders of reality itself.

The Mesoscopic Phase

The narrative experience of a single panel and the retrospective macroscopic synthesis are interconnected by a mesoscopic phase. The reader's eye constantly moves from panel to panel, forward as well as backward, and is mostly constrained by the format of the double-page spread – in other words, the two pages within visible range. During this reading process, the progression of time within each panel and the time passing between panels are integrated. While the creator organizes time within and between panels through montage, the recipient reconstructs the narrative time by means of their imagination.

In manga, as in other narrative media, order and duration come to the fore within the temporal organization of the narrative.[6] The small vertically aligned panels 3, 4, and 5 in Figure 8.1 relate the memories of Dr. Clifford, who is portrayed in panel 2. These panels thus constitute flashbacks, or analepses, to the corresponding scenes that appeared on the previous pages. The recollection highlights a character's interiority and at the same time links events separated in time. Even more significant than such order is the duration (or the tempo) of events. Just as a film creates a single scene by stringing several shots together, multiple panels in manga are regularly connected in keeping with the temporal sequence of actions. In Figure 8.1, events are generally depicted as they progress. Panel 1 is different, however, because it is a cutout of a simple outdoor landscape whose temporal and spatial relationship with the events in the middle tier remain ambiguous. It is probably intended to emphasize the gloomy atmosphere of the scene.

Based on the most popular categorization of the relationships between two adjacent panels, Japanese manga have frequently employed aspect-to-aspect transitions, with adjacent panels containing fragmentary images unrelated to temporal continuity: "Most often used to establish a mood or a scene of place, time seems to stand still in these quiet, contemplative combinations."[7] This differs from mainstream comics in North America, which have been dominated by action-to-action transitions. In fact, narrative accentuation, or tempo control, is an important technique in manga, exemplified brilliantly in Kiyohiko Azuma's *Yotsuba&!* (2003–). In this serial, anything resembling a dramatic story is essentially absent; instead, the fragments of the main characters' daily activities are narrated in a minute fashion. But the delicate linework and singular slowness create an atmosphere and humor that captivate the reader.

The Poe Clan depicts events as they unfold, even though the panels are not always interconnected by action-to-action transitions. There is also a subject-to-subject transition. For example, the pitchfork shows in three panels (6, 9, and 11), which can be interpreted as relating Dr. Clifford's focalization. To this end, panel 6 is followed by his profile close-up. Such focalization – the presentation of an event from the perspective of a character – is another crucial means of expression at the mesoscopic level, and it is frequently employed in manga. The thoughts of characters are often integrated directly into the image, as in panels 2 to 5, which are easily identifiable as Dr. Clifford's own recollections and inner monolog. But words outside of the text balloons are not always monolog. Non-framed text can also serve as the narrator's voice, sometimes summarizing events as in novels. Conversely, inner monologs can likewise appear within balloons, with modes of thought and emotion finely articulated through modified balloon shapes. Focalization encourages imaginative synchronization by communicating interiority, and graphic narratives such as manga have developed a range of methods to do so.

When dealing with focalization in manga, it should be noted that images tend to assume a third-person perspective, as they present objects to be viewed. It is impossible, for example, to interpret a panel that contains an entirely abstract drawing as a symbolic expression of a character's state of mind or interiority. This must be inferred from the previous or following panels as in the case of Figure 8.1, or specified in words. The role of verbal elements is vital to comprehending the visuals, as the problems surrounding the expression of a purely subjective perspective in manga indicate.

The Macroscopic Phase

As readers read, they continuously recall to some degree what they have digested up to that point, anticipating what might happen and associating these recollections and anticipations mentally with the events before them, even if done unconsciously. This is another aspect of the recipient's imaginative supplementation. Prospective expectations are constantly corrected and accumulated as a retrospective understanding of the narrative content. This process gradually shapes the comprehension of the macroscopic story. Conversely, such prospective and retrospective interpretations of the chronology of events influence the interpretation at the moment of reading. Dr. Clifford's actions, for instance, are linked with his previous actions and thoughts, allowing the reader to delve further into this character. As a womanizer, he has been trying to win over Lady Portsnell. But on these pages he realizes her true identity, leading to his affection morphing into fear and hatred. In light of this scene, the recipient may reappraise Dr. Clifford's personality, taking into account his shallowness and weakness.

The reader arrives at retrospective and prospective interpretations by recollecting and anticipating events that are not directly visible. This is noteworthy because such interpretations go hand in hand with the supplementation that occurs during the process of reading in order to further facilitate synchronization with the narrative. For the creator, that is, the *mangaka*, this macroscopic phase involves the core task of structuring the work in its entirety by breaking down the narrative into increasingly large units, from scene to sequence (collecting several scenes), to chapter to the piece as a whole, and organizing these units in a nested fashion.

Such structuring is not specific to graphic narratives, but it varies according to media development, and with manga it is necessary to note that since the 1960s even long stories were first magazine serializations before they appeared in book form. Single installments in a magazine may have constituted a sequence, a chapter, or something in between. And, due to its commercial nature, magazine serialization could be paused against the wishes of the creator, based on reader responses or editorial decisions. Thus, the discontinuation of a serial could occur before the entire story was long enough to be published in book format. *The Poe Clan*, for example, was initially planned to finish after a few episodes, even though Moto Hagio envisioned something larger in scale. Ultimately, favorable reader reception led to the work becoming a long serial, eventually comprising fifteen chapters, which were published in five *tankōbon* volumes between 1972 and 1976. Although many manga works have been completed as integrated wholes after lengthy serialization (not unlike novels by writers such as Charles Dickens and Sōseki Natsume), their publication in magazines involved the need to satisfy the reader continuously. Consequently, each installment must contain narrative hooks and radical turns of events, even if it is only intended to be a fragment of the whole. This media-specific institutional constraint has led manga creators to give technical preference to the microscopic and mesoscopic phases. By comparison, the macroscopic conception of the narrative in its entirety could remain vague and tentative.

That the macroscopic level is allocated secondary relevance resonates well with the fact that narrative experience derives from microscopic impressions and interpretations. During the reading process, the recollection of preceding events and the apprehension of those forthcoming are required to reinforce the ongoing changes (the eventfulness of the narrative) and to create the impression of temporal development. As such, the narrative whole can be anticipated but does not necessarily have to be preexisting. Clearly, the attractiveness and consistency of the entire story can affect the appreciation of the work in question. But there are many unfinished literary masterpieces, and these can be understood as complete insofar as they have the power to motivate readers to supplement any missing parts.

The narrative is sometimes extended if a work proves highly popular as a magazine serialization. Such cases abound in boys manga, with representative examples being Akira Toriyama's *Dragon Ball* (1984–95) and Eiichirō Oda's *One Piece* (1997–). The potential variability and multiplication of such narratives also enable media-mix development. Present-day narrative media appear to cling to the maximal potential of marketable content and not to the traditional idea of the individually complete story. Moreover, the technological progression of the medium and its social and cultural influence transform narrative discourse and story contents. This, however, does not change the universal truth that a narrative exists only if a recipient experiences it, nor does it alter the fact that a graphic narrative emerges from a synthesis of microscopic, mesoscopic, and macroscopic phases.

Characters Acting on Their Own

To reiterate, the purpose of the narrative is to create a fictional world with its own reality. Success relies on how well the recipient reconstructs the character actions depicted through the combination of signs available to the medium. The storyworld can only be experienced through active supplementation by the recipient, and this is shaped by medium-specific narrative discourse. Manga strives to generate maximum narrative effect by combining the three elements of image, word, and panel. Maximum narrative effect means that the acting characters present themselves as thinking and feeling beings, with whom the recipient can imaginatively synchronize and share experiences. Manga has developed various narrative techniques to achieve this effect, of which only a handful are touched upon here. The joy of reading manga is derived to a great extent also from the linework of the drawings, which expresses the individuality of the artist, as well as diversity in imagery. But this alone does not constitute a graphic narrative, since the *mangaka* seeks to control what is semantically evoked by these visible signs.

As established above, in manga the convention of magazine serialization has generally defined the manner of production and consumption. Thus, from the creator's standpoint, the process of sustaining the flow of narrative fragments appears to play a greater role than the organization of those fragments as parts of a larger bounded whole, with the story seemingly emerging

on its own from an open-ended, serialized narrative. This is also related to
the fact that in manga, the writer and the artist are usually the same person.
Osamu Tezuka, widely acknowledged as the founder of manga as a graphic
narrative, advised future *mangaka* in a how-to book that for a good story
reliable characters are key: "If you succeed in making a unique character,
you conceive a story for them. Think about what they would do in a certain
situation. As long as their nature is clear, the character will act on their own
without causing any problems for the writer."[8] Tezuka's statement points to
a bottom-up self-organizing process of creation rather than a top-down control of individual movements based on an overall blueprint. Human actions
are irregular, inherently contingent, and swayed by emotions as well as the
unconscious. The notion of characters acting on their own thus suggests
that the depicted actions are reproduced realistically in the strictest sense of
the word. Outstanding skill and talent on part of the creator is undoubtedly
a prerequisite in convincing readers that characters are indeed acting of their
own volition. Recipients expect to see living, breathing persons acting in a
world that stretches beyond manga's still images. After all, it is precisely
in these experiences that we discover the profound joy of reading fictional
narratives.

Notes

1. Aristotle, "Chapter IX, 1451b," *Aristotle's Poetics*, trans. Leon Golden (Tallahassee: Florida State University Press, 1981), originally published 1968), 17.
2. Nobuhiko Saitō, "Manga no kōzō moderu," in *Manga no yomikata* (Tokyo: Takarajimasha, 1995), 220–23.
3. See Gérard Genette, *Narrative Discourse: An Essay in Method*, trans. Jane E. Lewin (Ithaca: Cornell University Press, 1980).
4. See Masao Suzuki, "Shunkan wa sonzai shinai: mangateki jikan e no toi," in *Manga o "miru" to iu taiken: furēmu, kyarakutā, modan āto* (Tokyo: Suiseisha, 2014), 57–86.
5. Scott McCloud, *Understanding Comics: The Invisible Art* (New York: Harper Collins Publishers, 1993), 63.
6. Gérard Genette, *Narrative Discourse*, 35.
7. McCloud, *Understanding Comics*, 79.
8. Osamu Tezuka, *Manga no kakikata* (Tokyo: Kōbunsha, 1996, first ed. 1977), 164.

9

SELEN ÇALIK BEDIR

Anime Narratives and 3D CG Aesthetics

TV anime (*terebi anime*) is easily identified by its reliance on 2D-limited animation techniques, to the extent that it often seems to favor stillness over movement. Despite the assistance that various computer programs offer in maintaining the fluidity and consistency of movement, anime primarily opts for the partial representation of movement, if not its total abstraction. This choice, however, does not necessarily rob anime of its dynamism, as movement is more frequently implied than visualized. Judging by the visible, that is, mostly suspended character images accompanied by sound, the audience can infer the intensity of the action, even though they never get to know the true nature of it. As a result, character emotion overwrites character action and triggers an affective reaction with the conceived intensity resonating physically across the viewers' bodies.[1] Moreover, the persistent abstraction of actual movement brings about a narrative ambiguity, or unpredictability, that typifies anime as much as its dynamic immobility.

In anime, the form that a moving object should take over time, as well as the positions that it should occupy, can be masked in such a manner that it has an affective stimulus on the audience. The suspension of movement over arbitrarily extended periods of time, however, may remove vital clues for establishing the relations of the object-in-action within time and space. The discarding of spatiotemporal consistency makes it impossible for the audience to deduce the laws of motion that apply to the specific storyworld. In fact, apart from the will and emotions of the characters, there may not appear to be any force consistently binding actions to their outcomes. On the one hand, the impossibility of resolving the principles that organize causality in the given storyworld makes it difficult for the audience to rationalize the particularities of action in a specific scene. The audience becomes unable to rely on their understanding of causality for anticipating the future outcomes of present actions. On the other hand, the emerging ambiguity is useful if the aim is to create unpredictable worlds in which everything is possible.

The animation of a storyworld aligns with the type of action to be expected, but in anime the future remains unpredictable. By integrating extreme stillness in the representation of action and without justifying the ambiguities it produces, anime refrains from revealing what may be possible in a given world. Anime narratives let viewers expect the protagonist's victory but do not necessarily detail the steps that lead there. As a result, anime provides excitement since it undermines predictions about how events, episodes, story arcs, or entire seasons will end. Furthermore, if desired, nothing stands in the way of *extended* serialization.

This lucrative deal of extended serialization occasioned by narrative unpredictability, however, seems to contrast with 3D animation. In embracing physics-based simulation, 3D animation creates mathematical worlds in which the forms of 3D objects, as well as such objects' relationship with 3D space, remain consistent during action. Is the anime-specific ambiguity noted above under threat or could it even be entirely lost as 3D animation is progressively and more openly embraced in anime production? If ambiguity or unpredictability is a must-have feature of anime, where does it sit in 3D anime? Moreover, how can this type of animation generate impossible outcomes while following physically traceable actions? Analyses of innovative productions are therefore necessary to consider anime as a media form and to approach its transformation.

Rather than explore deviations from the predominant aesthetics of 3D animation within 2D animation, this chapter focuses on the obvious use of 3D computer-generated (CG) animation in anime production, taking as an example *Gantz: O* by Digital Frontier (2016). Based on the manga of the same name by Hiroya Oku, which was originally serialized in *Weekly Young Jump* (2000–13), *Gantz: O* is an animated sci-fi film that puts a dark spin on the *shōnen* (boys) genre. It maintains the genre's promise of action but targets an older audience by rewriting the famous effort-plus-friendship-equals-victory storyline with a higher mortality rate. For the purposes of this study, the *shōnen* genre is optimal as a case study since it promises considerable action, the particularities of which will be analyzed. The extent to which anime is compatible with 3D modeling and 3D animation in terms of producing unpredictability will also be examined to determine whether the concept of "3D anime" is plausible. The methodology adopted in this study falls under postclassical narratology, due to its emphasis on unpredictability in narration and its attempt to consider the issue in relation to a wider socioeconomic framework. The aim of this chapter is therefore to trace a potential route for the future of anime, as the specific material-technological resources once typifying the medium have irreversibly merged with digitalization.

Defining 2D Anime

It is generally accepted that anime employed 2D-limited animation techniques as these were practically a requirement for serialization on TV in the 1960s. They included the retention of the number of frames-per-second to a minimum, using only one still frame when possible, and recycling cels.[2] Over time, these techniques evolved into a hallmark of anime and contributed to an anime-specific narrative style, rather than existing simply as tools in need of periodic tech updates. A case in point is the fact that the "anime look," down to its 2D flatness and exaggerated stillness, continues to hold ground alongside the use of 3D models and animation techniques.

How exactly does 2D animation affect narration in anime? What in fact is anime? Anime can be seen as a specific medium,[3] closely related to other popular media in Japan and across the globe. Contemporary popular media aim to produce narratives that are composites of the same building blocks, which should be pleasantly familiar to extremely narrative-savvy contemporary audiences. But these narratives must also be unforeseeable enough to keep viewers engaged in a media environment that circulates excessive information. Although these media share the tendency to surprise, they diverge in the ways they attempt to form unpredictable narratives. Contemporary Japanese popular media, including but not limited to manga and anime, rely considerably on emotions for surprise effect. In order to understand why, the notion of unpredictability needs to be clarified.

Whether popular fiction or not, contemporary narratives' relationship with unpredictability extends beyond a simple sales strategy. Knowledge has continued to grow, thanks to scientific developments, since the early nineteenth century, and this has resulted in an awareness of the possibility of finding not one but multiple causes for the origin of everything.[4] To put it differently, the assumption of causal connections between phenomena and their origins has moved toward an understanding of causality as a web of connections, the true extent of which may never be within our reach. The awareness of this change in mindset spread with the advent of new technologies of information storage and sharing, following printing and perhaps reaching their culmination with the internet.

In a sense, the confusion of causality was already reflected in literary realism, as the details of daily life flooded fictional accounts, making it difficult to trace the links between actions and their outcomes.[5] Today, the production and consumption of popular narratives start with the assumption that all seemingly unrelated dots can be interconnected with a little effort. Any fictional encounter is possible, and actions can have any desired outcome that renders the fate of popular characters surprising and open to rewriting.

There are several ways to explain and give plausibility to the unlimited feats of characters, one common scenario being the recourse to alternative realities or multiple universes with internal working principles that are foreign to the audience. Japanese popular narratives, by contrast, specifically rely on the incalculable potential of emotions to justify the unpredictable. For example, heroes of the *shōnen* genre quite often come into great power on the brink of defeat and even after death, simply because they desperately wish to protect their loved ones. Representative works are the extended meta-series of *Dragon Ball* (starting with the first animated series 1986–89, and continuing with *Super Dragon Ball Heroes* from 2018, both serialized by Toei Animation), or the ongoing *One Piece* (serialized by Toei Animation from 1999).

Apart from the plot, the link between unpredictability and emotions in anime is established by the conventionalized use of limited animation techniques, which leave movement and its physical context un(der)drawn and invisible. Many recent titles, such as the latest episodes of *Seven Deadly Sins* (*Nanatsu no taizai*, serialized by A-1 Pictures, 2014–18, and by Studio Deen, 2019–21), still resort to the partial animation of bodies in movement loops, maintaining the gliding effect of the pull-cel technique, and the affective employment of total stillness. Due to anime's heavy reliance on visual abstraction, any sign of physical inconsistency may be seen as a result of stylistic omission. The viewers are unable to verify whether the rules of physics are breached, but even verifiable breaches do not appear to be vital problems, as emotions are most binding on causality. Despite the relative ease in presenting a smoother movement for detailed figures in complex environments with the help of digital tools, recent anime continues to imply action while visualizing emotion. Consequently, it seems as if emotions *somehow* fuel any type of action and produce wild outcomes, which is quite convenient for introducing plot twists. It is also important to note that the centrality of emotions, as the main source of energy for actions and as the decisive factor on their outcomes, seldom gets acknowledged within the storyworld; anime series, as well as original video animations (OVA), do not necessarily present worlds in which unlimited emotional energy is scientifically extracted or collected for some reason. Instead, thanks to its specific use of limited 2D animation techniques, anime tends to fashion physically inconsistent and emotionally organized worlds,[6] where anyone who feels can be a hero.

As anime creators seem increasingly and more openly willing to embrace 3D computer-generated imagery, it is not surprising that such anime-specific conventions are challenged. What happens when anime characters are transferred to intrinsically consistent and calculable, computer-generated

3D worlds? How do they prevail against the odds in a manner that remains animeesque – that is, through the power of emotions – in worlds organized and shaped by mathematics?

Transferring Unpredictability from 2D to 3D Anime

3D CG animation inhabits a place that is not necessarily positive, but is clearly exclusive, as it is strictly organized by linear perspective and Cartesian principles. It is commonly opposed to "expressive animations," even when the goal is to consider "the future for an expressive aesthetics in 3D CG animation."[7] Simply, expressive animation should facilitate creative and emotional viewer engagement: "Traditionally, animation has been one of the most expressive of the visual arts, but in 3D animation, quantitative has trumped qualitative, due in part to … 'the calculative and quantitative tendencies of the computer.'"[8] In complete contrast to 3D CG animation, which remains on the quantitative end of the spectrum, expressiveness in animation appears to surface when verisimilitude vanishes, or when there are deliberate divergences from lifelikeness (photorealism) in favor of exaggeration and metaphorical expressions. Then, computer-generated 3D imagery is arguably at an advantage in building lifelike environments and consistent worlds, while it is not necessarily the most favorable choice for centralizing emotions. The combination of these attributes has led to labeling 3D worlds as "architectures of control," in which digital bodies move under the direction of animators to dazzle the audience with their impressive mimicry of actual human bodies and extended physical abilities.[9]

There are of course multiple strategies to tweak 3D animation, to introduce inconsistencies, and to infuse it with emotions.[10] One example is Chris Landreth's *Ryan* (2004), in which the character design exposes the digital infrastructure of the photorealistic look achieved through 3D imagery. Instead of presenting exact 3D copies of real people as might be expected from an animated documentary, Landreth introduces faces and bodies that colorfully disintegrate with each move as a type of emotional representation.[11] In contrast, *Gantz: O* is a stand-alone animated movie that fully embraces 3D aesthetics, opting for a high level of verisimilitude via 3D modeling and physics-based simulation of motion. Interestingly, while *Gantz: O* employs a heavily computerized animation, it imagines a possible victory for humans in the face of a perfect nonhuman other and does so without taking emotions out of the picture.

In *Gantz: O*, a group of humans are caught in a losing battle against alien invaders, a battle that takes place in a perfectly mathematical game world, where an exact copy of the real-life city of Osaka becomes the fighting arena. These "ordinary" humans attempt to improve their skills as they go along, but training delivers no advantages against the final boss, who has skills of perfect mimicry. Engaged against a rival of at least their own level, it seems that our heroes are all doomed to defeat.

The ideal *shōnen* anime scenario, taking the form of either 2D or 3D animation, seeks the aforementioned promised victory in the incalculable potential of creatures who have feelings. This inexhaustible energy reserve is quite often imagined as the soul, spirit, or emotional capacity of humans against nonhuman others. As established by the *Shōnen Jump* magazine in the 1970s, the boy hero finds an endless store of energy in himself. His energy is infinitely upgraded with the catalyst of friendship and unleashed in critical situations. Yet in the emotionally organized worlds that 2D anime tends to create, this potential becomes a sheer force that eliminates the target or an unimaginable solution conveniently left unvisualized. Although the heroes might remain immobile, they are meant to be in act, caught in a deadlock that feels challenging and dramatic for everyone involved. And while the animated movement is minimized, the final outcome attests that the necessary actions were actually performed. 3D animation, however, has to come up with its own formula to mix photorealistic spectacle with emotions and miracles.

Gantz: O does not imbue action with emotions in the same way as 2D anime; nonetheless it can position emotions as the starting point and trigger for all sorts of action. At the end of this 3D anime, the successful attack of the human team assumes the form of a group ambush, which begins with the protagonist's heartbreaking self-sacrifice. Then, in the transition from 2D to 3D, actions and emotions that were once intertwined, initially have to part ways, only to be reconnected.

Keeping in line with the discussion regarding medium specificity, we should ask where this transition leaves us in terms of unpredictability. If the intertwinement of actions and emotions is also the main source of the unpredictability in anime to keep the viewer engaged, where should we seek unpredictability in *Gantz: O*? A big challenge for this 3D anime is to display the upper limits of humans, although the plot necessitates that the limits of the human body are somehow surpassed. On the one hand, *Gantz: O* embraces 3D animation in order to display movement in the utmost detail, with the aim of presenting tech-boosted human agility and sturdiness as spectacle. On the other hand, the plot in *Gantz: O* challenges the physical potential of the heroes by depicting an enemy that can do everything its opponent does.

How, then, is *Gantz: O* able to visualize the impossible human potential, which should remain identifiable as human at the same time? How does this animation produce impossible outcomes for a physically possible set of actions? The answer lies in the randomization of actions, exaggerated and therefore spectacular, yet still compatible with consistent physical laws. In the final showdown, the characters keep shooting at the same rival from scattered hideouts, such that the enemy will fail to recognize the patterns of attack and to come up with a timely defense/attack strategy. The cornerstones of this process can be listed as below:

- The repetition of imperfect, asymmetrical human actions yields an unpredictable result in time.
- The increase in the number of actors also increases the variety of actions (differing in speed and execution), which helps to exceed the previously set limitations and expectations. The patterns of how a person acts can be detected over time, but the totality of shots fired by a group of individuals is exponentially harder to trace.

Gantz: O yields unpredictable outcomes because its plot reimagines anime's impossible actions as a series of quite possible asymmetrical actions that are visually compatible with 3D animation. In each of these scenarios, the desired outcome is triggered by emotions but produced through continuity of action. The more often an action is repeated and by a greater number of people, the chances of aligning perfect external conditions with the particularly satisfactory action appear to rise. Persevered action, then, is presented as the only hope for miracles in a mathematical world, as it aids in the exploration of a set of infinite possibilities.

Emotions turn into energy through an invisible, unknowable process in the way 2D anime employs limited animation. 3D animation, if it strives for full visibility of movement for the sake of spectacle, can only rely on emotions to kick start another process. In *Gantz: O*, the production of energy out of emotions becomes possible through the characters' endless, mundane striving. *Gantz: O* fills, in other words, the mysterious gap between emotions and desirable outcomes with labor. In a computer-generated world, the struggle for dominance seems to be settled (or calculated) in terms of productivity.

Ceaseless Labor and Post-Fordist Affect in Anime Production

Although setting anime in computerized worlds may generate an expectancy for a sharp break from the past, the use of technological novelties can nonetheless disguise conservative imagination. Closer observations of the form expose historical continuities in creative activities and assist in situating anime in relation to broader social issues.

While limited 2D animation might link action and emotion to open the way for surprising narrative turns that delight viewers, these two are inevitably separated in 3D animation. But *Gantz: O* still adheres to the tradition of Japanese popular narratives by tracing the birth of unexpected outcomes back to emotional outbreaks on the level of its plot. Filtered through 3D technology, however, another aspect of the same story comes to the fore: labor.

Gantz: O amplifies the linearity of causal and chronological alignments between emotions as the start and victory as the final destination; consequently, its 3D animation makes explicit what 2D anime only implies: the direct relationship between characters' emotional state and productivity, or people's ceaseless labor as the miraculous means to victory. Being a 3D anime, *Gantz: O* reinterprets the incalculable human potential as an infinite streak of collective and calculable action fueled by emotions. The collectivity falls in line with the theme of friendship, a vital element in both *shōjo* (girls) and *shōnen* genres, as well as with the function of friends as catalysts of energy upgrades. Moreover, the anime adds direction to this human potential in that persevered action will be rewarded eventually, someday.

As such, the narrative of *Gantz: O* seems to echo the affect-driven labor of an increasingly active audience, who are busy fashioning alternative routes for the development of stories that they cannot predict. In its 3D mode, anime also reminds us of never-ending casual social network games, in which the players' constant actions, at times just the clicking of a button, configure play as the means toward a goal, any goal that will be forever followed by another. An illustrative analogy would be Zynga's famous *FarmVille* (2009). In this game, clicking becomes the sole necessity and the main guarantee for reaching every goal. Moreover, during the endless pursuit of accomplishment – that is, ever-expanding one's virtual farm – it becomes possible to aid other players or to receive their help. Caught in a narrative play, anime viewers resemble these players as they endlessly engage with anime, collectively producing a chain of rewrites until every desirable scenario is created.

The following excerpt from an interview by Hikaru Kurozumi with the *Gantz: O* animation team, director Yasushi Kawamura, and set artist Ryōta Minamoto also suggests such continuity or correspondence between the storyworld and the production studio:

> INTERVIEWER: After I listened to your stories, I find that the office world is the same as the GANTZ [title styled in Japanese] world. You can't go home until the mission is completed.

[Director Kawamura responds by quoting a line from the movie.]

> KAWAMURA: "Do it. We have no other way," we would say at the work site (laugh).
> MINAMOTO: We couldn't see the end.
> KAWAMURA: Who the heck is the enemy, maybe I AM [Nurarihyon] (laugh).[12]

Gantz: O illustrates that the move from 2D to 3D animation techniques does not mean a direct subversion of anime's identity, but rather a change of the lens through which it is seen. Along with the incorporation of realistic settings, the movie seems to handle the relationship between emotion and action (or labor) more directly or more literally than its 2D-animated version. This transition, hinted at in the above interview, calls to mind the familiar image of a factory that is also strangely outmoded. Here, people's lives are consumed by labor on an assembly line, continuously engaging with a menial task that is taxing not in its complexity but continuity, with the hope to collect some rewards eventually.

These references via the image of a factory to Fordist and Taylorist production systems that envisioned human beings as a part of mechanical production, might sound anachronistic when analyzing a recent work. It could be argued, however, that this regression takes place precisely because the world is now engaged in a post-Fordist system of production.[13] Although the unfeasibility of Fordism is generally acknowledged in the twenty-first century, the needs that this project professed to fulfill are not entirely extinguished, as together with collective labor comes the guarantee of accumulating enough wealth to ensure economic stability. Despite the disappointment with Fordism, the fantasy of an almost certain expectation of financial reward is sustained and perhaps grows more affective now that it seems out of reach. The transition period of anime from 2D to 3D appears to reflect the persistence of Fordist imaginary even today, of the goal it sets and the path it paves, minus the immediacy and certainty it once held.

With a better semblance of physics-bound spaces and consistent motion, some new aspects of real life find their way into animeesque narration. In the aftermath of Fordism, the soothing promises of this unfinished project and its familiar rhythm of production nevertheless make an organic appearance in popular culture. The expectation of novelty from cutting-edge animation technologies are, perhaps not surprisingly, thwarted as the past keeps shaping the imaginary that gives rise to these technologies. Or perhaps *Gantz: O* runs on post-Fordist affect – that is, the allure of rewarded labor, especially in an age of unpredictability.

Conclusion

Full 3D animation as seen in *Gantz: O* might seem risky due to the familiarity of anime producers and consumers with 2D aesthetics, and to its paramount function in anime. 2D-limited animation techniques are a part of anime's identity, and this is for no small reason: They imply the activation of an emotional potential without revealing its particularities or how exactly it is put to use. The abstraction of movement proves convenient for the visual representation of an unknown power that is at the disposal of everyone who feels, thus a sign of being human or being humanized. By contrast, 3D animation has had to devise its own strategies about how to visualize this mysterious force in action because it risks dehumanizing the characters by concealing too much or by revealing an extended series of highly improbable feats.

Surprisingly, *Gantz: O* is able to preserve the advantages of both 2D and 3D animation by displaying an exaggerated, albeit limited, "human" physical prowess. It does not stray far from 2D anime in that it recounts a tale of marvelous human potential. *Gantz: O* attempts to locate 2D anime's legacy in a consistent, mathematically organized space, and chooses to show the body in action. It envisions, therefore, the mysterious human potential as a set of ordinary moves that can yield unpredictable results, especially if several actors are involved in action. In other words, 3D anime does not sacrifice the mystery or the force produced by 2D anime, rather replaces the incalculable power of the individual with the banal, asymmetrical, and, in the long term, incalculable potential of a group of people.

In the search for human identity and an unknown means to victory, *Gantz: O* seems to fall back on an old Fordist model of production that promises rewards for continuous collective labor. Although no challenge is insurmountable with ceaseless collective effort, the actual rewards are spectral and forever delayed. Promises of the accumulation of wealth and progress are kept alive on the off chance that the slightest probability will be realized in an unknown future.

In light of the mathematical worlds of 3D modeling and animation, anime narratives seem to resemble never-ending casual social games. The characters of 3D anime, as well as its consumers and producers who at times overlap, face a relentless linearity that allows for tackling any challenges. The only condition is whether there is enough time, despite the mundaneness of the effort exerted.

For the time being, there is no conventionalized way of incorporating 3D elements in anime, nor is there a preferred ratio of meshing 2D and 3D techniques. Although a larger set of productions must be examined in order to have a better understanding of twenty-first-century anime, the unapologetic and unrestrained application of 3D aesthetics in *Gantz: O* points to one possible direction: 3D anime can tell us stories of post-Fordist affect while remaining conveniently and conventionally unpredictable.

Notes

1. Eric Shouse, "Feeling, Emotion, Affect," *M/C Journal*, 8, no. 6, 2005, https://doi.org/10.5204/mcj.2443.
2. Marc Steinberg, *Anime's Media Mix: Franchising Toys and Characters in Japan* (Minneapolis: University of Minnesota Press, 2012), 15–16; see also Thomas Lamarre, *The Anime Machine: A Media Theory of Animation* (Minneapolis: University of Minnesota Press, 2009).
3. Selen Çalık Bedir, "(Re)Playing Anime: Building a Medium-specific Approach to Gamelike Narratives," *Mechademia*, 12, no. 2 (2020): 52–57.
4. See Stephen Kern, *A Cultural History of Causality: Science, Murder Novels, and Systems of Thought* (Princeton: Princeton University Press, 2004).
5. Jacques Rancière, *The Future of the Image*, translated by Gregory Elliott (London: Verso, 2007).
6. Çalık Bedir, "(Re)Playing Anime," 52–57.
7. Pat Power, "Animated Expressions: Expressive Style in 3D Computer Graphic Narrative Animation," *Animation: An Interdisciplinary Journal*, 4, no. 2 (2009): 107–29, https://doi.org/10.1177/1746847709104643.
8. Power, "Animated Expressions," 109.
9. Mihaela Mihailova, "The Mastery Machine: Digital Animation and Fantasies of Control," *Animation: An Interdisciplinary Journal*, 8, no. 2 (2013): 131–48.
10. Alex Jukes, "Emptiness Is Not 'Nothing': Space and Experimental 3D CGI Animation." In *Experimental & Expanded Animation*, edited by Vicky Smith and Nick Hamlyn (London: Palgrave Macmillan, 2018), 119–44.
11. Barbara Robertson, "Psychorealism," *Computer Graphics World*, 27, no. 7 (2004): 14–18.
12. Hikaru Kurozumi, "Interview with Yasushi Kawamura," *Digital Frontier*, (2016): 2, www.dfx.co.jp/en/cgmaking/gantz_O/page02.html.
13. Andrea Muehlebach and Nitzan Shoshan, "Introduction to Special Collection on Post-Fordist Affect," *Anthropological Quarterly*, 85, no. 2 (2012): 317–43.

PART V
Characters

10

LUKAS R.A. WILDE

Characters in the Media Mix
Beyond Narratives

Japanese manga, anime, light novels, and video games are recognized across the globe by specific aesthetics, modes of address, styles of narration, and generic conventions as well as by easily identifiable character types. It has become commonplace for producers and audiences alike that "manga-esque" or "animeesque" characters exist in part independent of, in part overlapping with, the determining systems of media from which they originate.[1] A manga's or anime's success has long been thought to depend on characters rather than story or plot. But fan reception likewise demonstrates that the engagement with characters in secondary productions, or derivative works (*niji sōsaku*), relies to a degree on the creation of actual narratives, such as fan fiction or *dōjinshi* manga. Characters also circulate in nonnarrative media forms, including decontextualized artworks or cosplay performances. It is noteworthy that many characters typifying Japanese strategies of media mix are not grounded in narrative texts, as seen, for example, in Miku Hatsune, a virtual celebrity that appears only as a vocaloid (an artificial singing voice) and within artworks. In other words, "manga-like" or "anime-like" characters are not necessarily connected to media specificity or to media narrativity. This may seem odd since characters are usually defined as elements of a constructed fictional world – a diegesis or storyworld – in narratology, literary studies, or film studies.[2]

Japanese popular and academic discourses offer a systematic alternative, proposing that popular media forms such as manga, anime, video games, and light novels feature protagonists that vary entirely from traditional characters based on narrative representations in novels or live-action films. During the last two decades, the technical term "chara" (*kyara*) – purposefully distinguished from that of *character* (*kyarakutā*) – has been employed to denote fictional beings that seem typical of Japanese popular media. Nonetheless, what separates chara from regular characters, as seen in American comics or Hollywood movies, remains notoriously hard to pin down. The term chara, itself initially an abbreviation of *kyarakutā*, has been part of the Japanese lexicon since the 1950s when it was introduced to differentiate between the fantastic, hand-drawn "fanciful characters" of Disney animated movies from realistic depictions of dramatis personae in literature and film.[3] It was later adopted to denote manga and anime protagonists, such as Osamu Tezuka's Astro Boy (*Tetsuwan Atomu*), created in 1952 for the manga magazine *Shōnen*. By their very pictoriality as iconic, planar line drawings (*senga*) connecting manga, anime, and particularly merchandised toys to a network of media products (i.e., a media ecology), charas were and are still perceived as quintessentially fictional, fantastic, or imaginary. They are somehow independent of narrative because they seem more fundamental (pre-narrative or proto-narrative) if circulating only in material objects, in single, often digital artworks, and in cosplay performances without any preexisting story. Or, they are transcending individual narratives – that is, they become metanarrative or transfictional entities that appear across mutually exclusive fictional worlds and are continuously recontextualized by, but not identified with, the specific, noncontradictory stories in which they might star. Today, the term chara has emerged in a range of different discourses, serving a variety of functions. This chapter presents a map of four representative, albeit contrasting, dimensions of chara in the franchise *Demon Slayer: Kimetsu no Yaiba* (2016–), and traces the extent to which its protagonists Tanjirō and Nezuko Kamado, as well as other characters, can be considered charas exemplifying the "other sides of narrative."

Introducing the *Demon Slayer* Franchise

In 2020, *Demon Slayer* was the highest-grossing movie of all time in Japan and Taiwan. In many ways, the movie's surprising success during the global COVID pandemic is not due to its exceptionality but rather its conventionality. The popularity of *Demon Slayer*, however, could hardly be predicted from its original manga release: Both Koyoharu Gotouge's manga serialized in the magazine *Weekly Shōnen Jump* and the later rerelease (2016–20) in twenty-three *tankōbon* (collected paperback) volumes were only marginally successful. The twenty-six episodes of the first TV anime season produced by Ufotable as the central studio proved extremely popular, so much so that the subsequent story arc was turned into the theatrical release *Infinity Train* (*Mugen ressha*, 2020). In terms of story, the TV anime was mostly a straightforward adaptation of the manga, although the visuals did not remain as close to the manga as expected with such adaptations. Even before an official English version of the anime series appeared, *Demon Slayer* inspired an international fan base through online communication. In Japan, Tanjirō and Nezuko also circulated within an ecology of licensed goods and items, including toy figurines, replicas of Tanjirō's iconic earrings, and McDonald's Happy Meal Stickers.

Like many battle manga for boys, the plot of *Demon Slayer* follows the adventures of a young hero on his quest for self-improvement: The storyworld is set in the Taishō period (1912–26) of prewar Japan where powerful demons (*oni*) with magical powers roam the lands. They are in combat against a corps of demon slayers, a secret circle of mostly unnamed soldiers, and nine highly skilled elite warriors called Hashira. The demons are all offspring of a potent being called Kibutsuji Muzan, who has elevated twelve monsters to the ranks of the most trusted warriors known as the Twelve Kizuki or Twelve Demon Moons. Tanjirō learns of them only after his peaceful life in the mountains is abruptly and brutally ended when Muzan murders his entire family, except for his sister Nezuko who is instead transformed into a demon. Tanjirō's quest to become a demon slayer and to face Muzan and his armies is mainly motivated by his will to save his sister and to find a way to return her to a human form. Fortunately, she has not become a murderous monster but retains her own will and personality. Tanjirō undergoes arduous training under multiple masters, acquires new fighting moves and techniques, and encounters many friends and allies who agree to assist him and Nezuko as their enemies become stronger. These narrative developments clearly correspond with other battle manga for boys. Yet to what extent do Tanjirō and Nezuko exemplify "nonnarrative" charas?

Consequentiality versus Cartoonishness

One of the most important dimensions of narrativity is the presentation of recounted stories as facts arranged around a number of potentially irreversible narrative events that facilitate consequential character development.[4] As is evident from the plot of *Demon Slayer* outlined above, manga and anime *do* offer a storyworld with dramatic events and lasting repercussions. The initial point of departure for a nonnarrative understanding of manga and anime characters (charas) does not contradict this stance, instead, it points to a special type of narrativity that is differentiated from the linearity associated with the literary novel or the live-action film. The evaluation of manga and anime has long focused on book-length works that modeled their storyworlds on contemporary or historical settings, and their protagonists as psychologically profound and complex. Tezuka and the proponents of the later *gekiga* movement – artists such as Yoshihiro Tatsumi, Masahiko Matsumoto, and Takao Saitō – aimed at graphic narratives that were capable of rivaling films and novels in their ability to communicate intricate, developmental storylines; psychologically deep, aging protagonists; a linear progression of narrative events; and the definite ending of the closed work of art. In the 2000s, however, the embracing, as opposed to the downplaying, of manga's artificial tendencies came to the fore due to the new predominance of anime and video games in media usage.[5] Protagonists are thus not confined to any specific story with a beginning and an end. Alternatively, they serve as engines that propel the motors of seriality and transmediality from one iteration to the next.[6] They are connected to the *senga* aesthetics of particular media forms: Their drawn-line pictures accommodate certain types of protagonists whose bodies neither age nor die.

Crucially, such a mode of seriality and narrative inconsequentiality, which traps protagonists in an "eternal present," are typically associated with completely different medial lineages than those encountered in the Tezuka tradition. The former might include prewar manga and animated short films such as *Norakuro* (manga, 1931–41), four-panel gag comics (*yonkoma*) such as *Sazae-san* (1946–74), and especially American newspaper strips or animated shorts like *Looney Tunes* (1930–69) or *Tom and Jerry* (1940–67) in which injury or damage through anvils, explosions, or bullets is never lethal or permanent. In comics and animation studies, this is often described as a "cartoonishess" that mediates between a specific visual style of abstracted, exaggerated body representations on the one hand and a specific "worldness" of narrative inconsequentiality on the other. The "acting style" of such drawn protagonists is likewise not intended to resemble naturalistic method actors but adopts a highly codified figurative manner. Characters' bodies equally remain somewhat imaginary since we usually do not know or are not troubled by the question of what they "actually" look like – that is, whether there is a photorealistic world "behind" the simple line drawings that could be delineated by actors or verbal description.[7] Liberated from the dictates of consequentiality, manga and anime thus generate their own kinds of realities that exist only within the imagination or, more precisely, within media ecologies. In this sense, their protagonists – as charas instead of characters – are entities freed from the shackles of physics, inhabiting their own imaginary realm of ritual and repetition. Both ends of the spectrum are always intertwined, although with different emphases at different times. Tezuka's 1948 manga *The Mysterious Underground Man* (*Chiteikoku no kaijin*) was groundbreaking expressly because its protagonist, an anthropomorphic bunny called Mimio, *did* die at the end of the story, much to the shock of many readers.

In that respect, *Demon Slayer*'s Tanjirō and Nezuko are removed from the chara end of the spectrum as both manga and anime open with the irreversible, even traumatic, narrative event of the death of Tanjirō's family. But while *Demon Slayer*'s excessive battle sequences are about lasting outcomes, the cartoonish media roots remain visible, especially in the anime, and most conspicuously when the narration is interrupted for comic relief and the characters turn into super-deformed dwarf (*chibi*) versions of themselves.[8] These transformations are accompanied by mangaesque pictograms and visual morphemes that highlight their overall artificiality. In these situations, physical violence is of no consequence, played entirely for laughs or the social embarrassment of the heroes. Often, this serves to parody the overall masculinity of warrior characters such as Zen'itsu and Inosuke, resulting in an ironic performance of gender. Such abrupt switches between tonalities or registers – dead serious versus slapstick – lay bare the cartoonish, charaesque roots of both manga and anime. Interestingly, these switches in tonality are emphasized in the anime, which exaggerates the "*chibi*-fication" of the protagonists and the use of pictograms both in terms of quantity and quality. These scenes interrupt the continuous animation of the images, highlighting gaps and interstices through individual stills of exaggerated affects. The "other sides of narrative" – what distinguishes Tanjirō as chara from character – are ultimately the frequent moments when the narrative progress is halted and paused through disparate and discontinuous elements in codified spectacles of cartoonish affects.

Representational Realism versus Ludic Realism

Another, perhaps more obvious, break of the linear narrative in *Demon Slayer* is connected to a different aspect of charas: the "Taishō Secret" post-credit ending sequences that complement every episode. In a kind of paratextual framing, the protagonists, usually Tanjirō and Nezuko, but occasionally others, reappear as commentators who discuss events and revelations in a humorous manner. They also address the viewer directly as a kind of metaleptic mediator between the fictional and the real. On closer inspection, the post-credit sequences resemble video games in which characters likewise feature in a dual role as entities within the represented world and as avatars of the players outside of the narrative.[9]

In recent years, media ranging from manga and anime to light novels and beyond have tried increasingly to emulate the experience of playing games. Such a "ludic realism" places characters in a duplicate, mediating position between the fictional world and the player/viewer. In a way, the avatar in video games has assumed the role of the I-narrator in literature who speaks from a position outside the storyworld but is interpreted as an insider with a coherent personality.[10] Super Mario exists partly outside of his individual walkthroughs precisely because he can die, respawn, and replay his adventures without ramifications. At the same time, he can be imagined to learn from his mistakes, while in reality it is the player who does so. In short, the inconsequentiality of the cartoonish mode has assumed a different medial actualization in video games when and if the player does not identify with a character who is supposed to lead only one life, but with the avatar who has as many lives as the game permits and who lives outside of the narrative world in title screens or game menus.[11]

In fact, countless noninteractive media texts remediate or reflect this constellation, generally with recourse to a plot in which protagonists are stuck in a time loop and able to learn from their deaths by returning with augmented knowledge. Examples might include the light novel and later manga adaptation *All You Need Is Kill* (2004), the media-mix franchises *Re:Zero – Starting Life in Another World* (*Re:Zero kara hajimeru isekai seikatsu*, 2012–), and the manga series *Summer Time Rendering* (*Samā taimu renda*, 2017–). This structure has been taken up so frequently that it is today considered a stable subgenre of *isekai*, or stories that send protagonists to another world where they acquire new powers and abilities. Quite often, gamic elements are explicitly integrated and addressed within the stories themselves. This form of ludic realism based on game experiences has thus replaced the representational realisms based on modern novels. But again, both ends of the spectrum appear in countless variations.

Demon Slayer is interesting in this regard because it does not refer explicitly to video games, even though the aesthetics and virtual camera movements in battle scenes are strongly reminiscent of special attacks in fighting games. In the post-credit sequences, however, Tanjirō and other characters feature as straightforward extradiegetic narrators or commentators separated from the narrative and mediating between the storyworld of Tanjirō and the viewers. Intriguingly, just like the "*chibi*-fication" within the stories themselves, this element was not part of the original manga. It was only added for the anime, highlighting again the successive "chara-fication" of the characters in their transmedia circulation.

Narrative Consumption versus Database Consumption

In another sense, the extended battle sequences and Tanjirō's continuing ordeals with the Hashira and the Twelve Kizuki constitute a different renunciation of "narrative" qualities. As mentioned earlier, *Demon Slayer* is quite conventional in many ways. On a material and aesthetic level, this is true of the character designs, the background imagery, the coloring, the animated movements, and the voice acting. On the plot level, the series employs many familiar tropes, starting from the premise of the whole show to travel throughout the land in a quest to vanquish demons.[12] The relationship between Tanjirō and his sister also follows an established older-brother-to-younger-sister pattern. At the same time, conventions are "resampled" in surprising ways: Tanjirō's personality, the care for his sister, and his humble spirit conform more to character tropes known from female, rather than male, manga genres. Such play with conventionality facilitates a kind of engagement with the characters that has been called database consumption, in contradistinction to narrative consumption.[13] The basic notion is that modern literature attempts a construction of a coherent whole out of the narrative information the text provides, imagining characters as psychological and internally complex, sometimes self-contradictory, but necessarily unique. These, in turn, mirror a worldview in which society is structured by grand narratives, for instance, by a socially shared view on technological progress or liberal democracy.

By contrast, fans approach franchises such as *Demon Slayer* for entirely different reasons: Enjoyment is directed toward surfaces, in aesthetic and narrative terms. The "deep inner layer" of a coherent storyworld and the psychological depth is replaced with an imagined "database" of generic elements that fans acknowledge and reiterate. These elements serve affective pleasures when we see Tanjirō repeat his fixed number of attacks again and again, each time somewhat adjusted but nonetheless recognizable. Familiarity with genre conventions and tropes across texts only heightens the pleasure. Character designs, for instance, feature many identifiable affective elements, such as the colorful hairpieces based on flora or fauna worn by Nezuko (and also Kanao Tsuyuri and Shinobu Kochō) or animal masks such as Inosuke's, that can be traced to countless earlier anime. The show can then be seen as a performance of media literacy celebrating slightly modified conventions. The notion of database consumption helps to identify what makes manga "manga" and anime "anime": not "being from and for Japan" (Chinese and Korean companies distributed the show's production, with global export from early 2021 onward) but rather a series of tropes and discernible elements that are part of the lexicon and repertoire of fans and viewers within the global community.

Importantly, these recognizable database elements are embraced and celebrated instead of downplayed, which distinguishes late-night TV anime such as *Demon Slayer* fundamentally from Japanese animated movies such as those created by Studio Ghibli. For characters such as Tanjirō and Nezuko, this means that their attraction does not necessarily rest on "narrative" qualities such as social representation or psychological complexity. Instead, their appeal is on the surfaces of affective elements constructed around perceivable tropes and designs.[14] This is especially prominent for the nine Hashira whose names, powers, and colorful outfits, which mix Japanese and Western clothing styles similar to the characters in the manga and anime franchise *One Piece* (1997–), are all constructed around a specific element, such as wind, stone, or love, and whose personalities mainly mirror these. Clusters of tropes and conventions thus inspire affective engagement within fan networks. In short, whereas narrative consumption is all about representation – a unique, coherent story within a storyworld or a possible world (diegesis) that to some degree reflects social reality – database consumption facilitates mediation between media forms, texts, and fans with charas as a nodal point. This is especially relevant for aspects of fan participation.

Authorized Works versus Secondary Productions

Characters can turn into charas by stepping out of the narrative world and into the paratexts. Their actual "existence" is less grounded in any individual story or storyworld but instead in their propensity to achieve their own life within participatory cultures. The US-based cosplayer Aki. nei, for instance, posted widely circulating pictures on Instagram impersonating the character Kyōjurō Rengoku as early as November 2019. In the spring of 2021, *Infinity Train* had garnered a considerable degree of international fandom, even though it had not even been released officially on international channels. *Demon Slayer* fan fiction can be found on all major online platforms: around 22,000 alone on Archive of Our Own, and close to 281,000 artworks that were tagged with "#Kimetsu no Yaiba" on Pixiv.net as of May 2024. Fan fiction is thus anything but external to transmedia franchises, and Japanese media culture in particular has proven that secondary or derivative productions are vital.[15] The majority of Japanese *dōjinshi* employ characters that already exist in order to continue their stories, imagining alternative ones by positioning them within different settings and worlds, or by reimagining them with another gender or sexual orientation. The same character (or rather chara) may circulate both inside and outside individual narrative worlds. As a metanarrative (transfictional) chara, Tanjirō can lead countless alternative lives across contexts and works. The legal situation remains highly complicated as the willingness of rights holders to ignore or even encourage appropriation of characters in fanworks depends on various "tacit agreements." In any case, charas are "open source cultural goods" that can and should be remixed and resampled.[16]

Instead of looking at manga and anime as a collection of texts, we might interpret them as an invitation to innovative production and collaboration. What connects these networks is usually the characters of any given franchise, or more precisely the charas, as they are circulating across heterogeneous, mutually exclusive fictions. Often, the original narrative has little to do with these recontextualizations, the charas instead addressing specific desires of smaller collectives and groups. Perhaps more importantly, they mostly appear in artworks and cosplay, media forms that cannot be conceived of as narrative. Crucial for this is once again a visual design that remains recognizable even as it is modified and appropriated. On the one hand, charas in fanworks or cosplay must be identifiable as variations of the same beloved character from the "original" manga or anime. On the other, they bear personal traces of new creators with individual line-drawing styles, handmade costumes, unique narrative recontextualizations, or interpretations in another species, gender, or genre setting. Charas thus constantly mediate between the personal and the social. Such a "life of their own" arises not from traditional authorship but rather from networks of countless individuals. As such, metanarrative (transfictional) charas seem to possess a special "life force," or presence, which transcends the narrative of the source text authored by one person, one group of people, or one given rights holder.[17]

Additional Dimensions of Chara and Nonnarrativity

The four dimensions of chara and the respective "other sides of narrative" introduced above with respect to *Demon Slayer* are certainly not the only ones. Related to the transfictional or metanarrative participatory potential, 2.5D culture (*ni-ten-go jigen*), or interactions with fictional characters in actual real-life settings, also comes into view.[18] Typical examples are sing-along musical screenings and "anime pilgrimages" to locations that are linked to the fictional locations of a franchise or its production.[19] Myriads of charas do not even originate from narrative text, existing only on material "chara goods" or in mediated performances. Aside from the aforementioned Miku Hatsune, examples include "chara-ized" interfaces such as Hiraki Azuma by Gatebox, pure product placement figures like Sanrio's Hello Kitty, or the countless mascots of companies, institutions, and prefectures like Kumamoto's Kumamon. "Working charas" on street signs and instruction manuals serve as imaginary interfaces in real-life places and settings. In such contexts, recipients are encouraged to imagine affective entities to communicate norms and regulations in a less authoritative, "softer" way by exemplifying affects and emotions associated with "right" or "wrong" behavior.[20] All these cases employ the same kind of 2D line-drawing pictoriality, clearly distinguished from the "real world" with which photographic imagery is affiliated. Neither realist nor exactly fictional – in other words, confined to an enclosed narrative world – such working charas are perhaps

better described as virtual actors, actualized within the individual imagination like the parasocial relationships that we might entertain with television
actors and their celebrity personas.[21] What connects all these vastly different phenomena is a shared distinction between characters as parts of closed,
fictional stories or worlds, in contrast to charas as nodal points between
historically changing media practices and conventionalized modes of imagination and participation.

Notes

1. See Luca Bruno, "The Element Factor: The Concept of 'Character' as a Unifying
   Perspective for the Akihabara Cultural Domain," *IMAGE:* Special issue
   Recontextualizing Characters, 29 (2019): 38–59. Open Access.
2. See Jens Eder, Fotis Jannidis, and Ralf Schneider, "Fictional Characters in
   Literary and Media Studies: An Introduction." In *Characters in Fictional
   Worlds: Understanding Imaginary Beings in Literature, Film, and Other Media,*
   edited by Jens Eder, Fotis Jannidis, and Ralf Schneider (Berlin: de Gruyter,
   2010), 3–66.
3. See Marc Steinberg, *Anime's Media Mix: Franchising Toys and Characters in
   Japan* (Minneapolis: University of Minnesota Press, 2012), 40.
4. See Gerald Prince, "Narrativity." In *AXIA: Davis Symposium on Literary
   Evaluation,* edited by Karl Menges and Daniel Rancour-Laferriere (Stuttgart:
   Heinz, 1981), 74–75.
5. See Gō Itō, *Tezuka izu deddo: hirakareta manga hyōgenron e* (Tokyo: NTT
   Shuppan, 2005).
6. For a related account of "serial figures" in American contexts, see Shane
   Denson and Ruth Mayer, "Border Crossings: Serial Figures and the Evolution
   of Media," *NECSUS* (Autumn 2018). Open Access.
7. See Lukas R.A. Wilde, "Material Conditions and Semiotic Affordances: Natsume
   Fusanosuke's Many Fascinations with the Lines of Manga," *Mechademia:
   Second Arc. Asian Materialities,* 12, no. 2 (2020): 62–82.
8. Jaqueline Berndt, "More Mangaesque than the Manga: 'Cartooning' in the
   Kimetsu No Yaiba Anime," *Transcommunication,* 8, no. 2 (2021): 171–78.
   Open Access.
9. See Hiroki Azuma, *Gēmu-teki riarizumu no tanjō: dōbutsuka suru posuto-
   modan 2* (Tokyo: Kodansha, 2007).
10. See also Eiji Ōtsuka, *Kyarakutā shōsetsu no tsukurikata* (Tokyo: Kodansha,
    2003).
11. See Zoltan Kacsuk, "From 'Game-Like Realism' to the 'Imagination-Oriented
    Aesthetic': Reconsidering Bourdieu's Contribution to Fan Studies in the Light
    of Japanese Manga and Otaku Theory," *Kritika Kultura,* 26 (2016): 274–92.
    Open Access.
12. Stevie Suan, "Colorful Execution: Conventionality and Transnationality in
    Kimetsu No Yaiba," *Transcommunication,* 8, no. 2 (2021): 179–91. Open
    Access.

13. See Hiroki Azuma, *Otaku: Japan's Database Animals* (Minneapolis: University of Minnesota Press, 2009).
14. See Jaqueline Berndt, "Introduction: Manga beyond Critique?," *Kritika Kultura,* 26 (2016): 166–78. Open Access.
15. See Sandra Annett, "What Can a Vocaloid Do? The Kyara as Body without Organs," *Mechademia: World Renewal,* 10 (2014): 163–78.
16. See Nele Noppe, *The Cultural Economy of Fanwork in Japan: Dōjinshi Exchange as a Hybrid Economy of Open Source and Cultural Goods* (Leuven: University of Leuven, Faculty of Arts, 2014), 335.
17. See Lukas R.A. Wilde, "Kyara Revisited: The Pre-narrative Character-State of Japanese Character Theory," *Characters across Media. Special-Themed Issue of Frontiers of Narrative Studies,* 5, no. 2 (2019): 220–47.
18. See Akiko Sugawa-Shimada, "Emerging '2.5-dimensional' Culture: Character-oriented Cultural Practices and 'Community of Preferences' as a New Fandom in Japan and Beyond," *Mechademia: Second Arc: Asian Materialities,* 12, no. 2 (2020): 124–39.
19. See Siyuan Li, "Where Is the Sacred Site? Research Notes on Contents Tourism Induced by Kimetsu no Yaiba," *Transcommunication,* 8, no. 2 (2021): 203–11. Open Access.
20. See Shunsuke Nozawa, "Characterization," *Semiotic Review,* open issue (3 November 2013). Open Access.
21. See Thomas Lamarre, *The Anime Ecology: A Genealogy of Television, Animation, and Game Media* (Minneapolis: University of Minnesota Press, 2018).

11

STEVIE SUAN

Character Acting in Anime

Characters are one of the central elements in the production, consumption, and media mixes prevalent throughout the anime industry and fandom. When attention is paid to the ways characters perform and are performed in anime narratives, it becomes apparent that there are certain regularly utilized approaches to the character acting widespread in anime. Two of the most prominent modes of performance have been called embodied acting and figurative acting.[1] Each uses distinct techniques to act out a specific character's personality and, in the process, implies different notions of selfhood.

These performance modes can be seen in the TV anime *Yūri!!! on Ice* (hereafter *YOI*). Released in 2016, this twelve-episode series was directed by Sayo Yamamoto with chief animation director and character designer Tadashi Hiramatsu, and with scripts by Mitsurō Kubo, all working with MAPPA as the central studio of production. *YOI*'s narrative follows figure skater Yūri Katsuki who, after a slump in his career, is coached by his skating idol, Victor Nikiforov. Yūri aims to win the Figure Skating Grand Prix, competing with his rival, the younger skater Yuri Plisetsky (or Yurio).[2] Over the course of the series, Yūri overcomes his anxiety and trains diligently to improve his skating technique, and eventually he develops a romantic relationship with Victor.

Important for the depiction of gay relationships in anime, *YOI* is noteworthy for its character animation as well. Like most other TV anime, *YOI* embraces figurative acting operations to constitute characters but also employs a significant amount of embodied acting. With the aim of exploring the operations of character acting in anime, this chapter will examine the specific utilization of embodied and figurative acting in *YOI* and how these interrelated modes of performance dovetail with the narrative. Through its balancing of embodied and figurative modes of performance, the anime moves between an individualized self whose interior is expressed externally and an open acknowledgment of the interrelation of external others in the performance of self.

Embodied Acting

Let's begin with the very opening moments of the *YOI* series. The first movements we see are of the character Victor ice skating. He glides swiftly and smoothly across the ice, each movement precise, projecting an elegance that seems to stem from inside of him. We do not see the character's facial expressions, however, only his shrouded outline, such that it is just his motions and gestures that convey who he is. Here, Victor exemplifies embodied performance: the acting character moves with distinction, with gestures and at speeds that appear unique to that individual, as if an external manifestation of their interior self. Those expressions are not seen as coming from outside but rather as internally motivated, seemingly exclusive to them. This produces a sense of boundary between the inside and the outside of that character.

Embodied performance is developed from method acting in the theater, a common mode of performing on TV and in movies today, where subtle motions and gestures bring a character to life. Such "realistic" acting was adapted for animation in the 1930s by Disney, and it is often seen as the standard for quality animation.[3] When enacting embodied performance in Disney's works, and to an extent in anime as well, there tends to be a reliance on full animation, with a large number of frames (usually between eighteen and twenty-four) to present a linear, continuous movement that allows the envisioning of the animated character as having an interior presented externally. Smooth, lush movements when transitioning between expressions are prioritized, but sometimes variable frame rates are employed to make movements feel faster or slower. In fact, some characters move faster or slower in general depending on their personality, giving them a sense of uniqueness to even the pace of their movements.

In sum, through embodied acting, characters use their individualized speeds, gestures, and finer details of movement to display their interior emotions and personality externally.[4] In its extreme form, embodied acting can be considered to lean implicitly toward the constitution of individual characters. Put differently, embodied acting tends toward a notion of selfhood that aligns with the modern, autonomous individual – that is, the conception of the human subject that is still dominant in the world today.

Figurative Acting

Returning to the opening scenes of *YOI*, the other character present is a young Yūri, the protagonist of the series. Impressed by Victor's skating, Yūri's hair blows back as if hit by a sudden gust of wind. Yūri then transitions into an older version of himself and his eyes glimmer, before shifting to a look of determination with eyebrows pointed downward. Each of these expressions are not exclusive to Yūri, but are codified elements seen throughout anime. The wind blowing through the hair is commonly used to convey how something had an impactful, almost spiritual effect on a character; the glimmering eyes for overflowing emotion are one of anime's most ubiquitous conventions; and the sudden shift to a look of determination is one commonly performed by many characters that commit themselves to a task. These codified expressions are employed across characters, genres, and studios in anime. They are not unique to one character, and in fact, are overtly performed by multiple characters at once (sometimes in the same scene), exposing how they are sourced from outside of the character. This utilization of such shared codes enacted in combination is an example of figurative acting.

While not isolated to so-called limited animation, figurative acting is prevalent in anime and leans on this technique of animating. Limited animation tends to require fewer frames (usually between eight and twelve per second), sometimes barely including movement at all, such as with the glimmering eyes. To transition between expressions, sudden switches between distinct codes (from glimmering eyes to round eyes for shock) are common. This gives the impression of "jerkiness": instead of continuous movement, there is a sudden shifting between differing image compositions.[5] In some instances, no real movement is present at all, with characters simply striking a motionless pose, which may itself be a conventionalized code. These take advantage of the "dynamic immobility" of the anime image, whereby the poses appear to have characters caught in motion, even in still images.[6] This is part of what enables these characters to jump across media and remain expressive, despite the other media they are present in not overtly moving. Indeed, many of anime's codified poses and facial expressions are taken from the still pages of printed manga.

The optimization of limited animation techniques in conjunction with figurative acting codes is also the basis of much of anime's humor. For instance, in YOI there are numerous sequences where female characters will witness a character's (often Victor's) skating performance and suddenly burst into a nosebleed – a figurative acting code for excitement and arousal. This humor is further underpinned as a tongue-in-cheek, self-reflexive joke for fujoshi (literally "rotten girls") viewers, female fans who consume and regularly produce media with romantic relationships between men, with YOI's romance between Victor and Yūri a particular fan favorite. In any case, the nosebleeds occur to different characters through the series. This also happens with arched eyes for smiling, another figurative acting code repeated by many characters, revealing how such codes are not isolated to any one character (Fig. 11.1). This happens even if that code references a certain character. One widespread example beyond *YOI* are the opaque glasses with hands folded in front of the face and a (usually hidden) conniving smile. Such poses are generally direct references to Gendō Ikari from *Neon Genesis Evangelion* (1995) but are repeated in various other anime (e.g., Hange Zoë in *Attack on Titan*), frequently comedically (e.g., Chiaki Ogaki in *Yuru Camp*).

To give an example from *YOI* that is broadly emblematic of figurative acting, throughout the series both Yūri and his rival Yurio make a number of glimmering eyes and looks of determination. In general, instead of presenting the illusion that it is interior emotions motivating the exterior movements, such enactments of externally sourced expressive codes can be seen as performed externally "on," rather than from within, the characters. Additionally, each instance of figurative acting is dependent on its relation

Figure 11.1a-b Yūri (11.1a) and Yurio (11.1b) smiling with the same arched eyes, evincing how figurative acting codes are not isolated to one character. Here Yurio reveals a rare moment of affection, a stark departure from his usual expressions of irritation that help constitute his *tsundere* character.

to prior iterations of the code to be legible – it cannot stray too far from the recognizable format of the code or it will be indecipherable. Every repetition of the code is thus linked to both earlier and later instantiations of that code, forming a network of connections. Compared to the *individual* characters of embodied acting, the selfhood that figurative acting tends to imply is better described as *particular* characters: They enact a code specifically and as that character, but they are also linked to earlier iterations of those codes and sometimes other character types.

Balancing Acting Modes

The balancing of these two performance modes – embodied and figurative – is actually a theme within the narrative of *YOI*. For instance, the abovementioned opening scene makes the embodied performance of Victor appear so unique as to be a goal to strive for, which is what causes the determined figurative acting expression of Yūri. In fact, the story takes its departure from a skating performance where Yūri is secretly filmed while performing the supposedly individual skating routine of Victor, which incites Victor to visit Yūri in Japan. Such a reenactment displays the operations of figurative acting: Yūri is citing (repeating with minor differences in a distinct context) the movements and routine of Victor.

Indeed, referential reenactment is precisely how figurative acting functions. Each codified movement is reiterated, a citation of a prior enactment of that code. Eventually, the new enactment itself may become the source for a further citation of that code. As the process continues, the codes most often cited, such as the arched eyes for smiles, are connected to a vast network of other citations of that code. The citation of Victor's performance, moreover, shows the expansive capacities of figurative acting. Any movement or expression that is repeated with a degree of frequency and rigidity – that is, without much deviation between each iteration – can become a figurative acting code. At the same time, it brings to the surface how figurative and embodied acting are not isolated but rather mutually implicated in one another, even to minor degrees. No performance of any code could be an *exact* duplication because it has to at least differ in terms of where and when it is reenacted, and the codes do change over time. Moreover, any embodied performance that is completely unique would not be understandable – there is some repeated element in the shape and curvature of every smile, for instance, although the subtleties are individual.

But there is also a certain tension between figurative and embodied acting, as each mode is somewhat inflected in the other in each performance, even if it is only slightly. To some extent, this is directly visualized in the opening credits of the show itself, repeated at the beginning of every episode. Performed through the key animation by the opening's chief animator Sung Hoo Park, the sequence starts with a focus on Yūri. With expressive linework and elegant motions, it seems that these are the sole movements of Yūri, a display of his interiority through his externally presented figure skating routine – that is, as embodied acting. Here, the precise manipulation of frame rates presents the graceful transition between slow and fast moves. Initially, this may give the impression of being individualized to Yūri, but a spinning jump suddenly turns the figure into Victor, who himself performs a routine that seems to be a continuation of Yūri's. Once again, the movements appear like embodied acting, an individualized expression. But Yurio enters next, along with Yūri himself skating around Victor. Afterward, Yūri and Yurio are seen performing together, both of them executing the same motions. The focus transitions to Yurio skating in unison with Victor, then Yūri with Victor, each pair moving in sync with the other (Fig. 11.2a–b). Finally, all three spin together, with Yūri and Victor leaving to one side,

Figure 11.2a-b Yūri and Yurio skating in unison (11.2a), followed by Yūri with Victor (11.2b), each individualized movement repeated by the other characters, evincing the tensions between embodied and figurative acting.

and Yurio spinning out to leave on the other side. There is then another transition back to Victor's initial entrance. Afterward the pattern repeats a number of times before the title sequence ends with them all spinning away.

Here a question arises with all these movements repeated and performed in unison: how can these individual movements be reiterated? By definition, something individual cannot be repeated or it would no longer be individual. Thus, the short opening sequence highlights the tension between these two modes of acting – the individualized external expression of interiority (embodied acting) and the refined reenactments of codified movements (figurative acting) – which is subsequently explored throughout the series narrative.

Acting across Modes

It is important to note that figure skating is itself dealing with these tensions. As a competitive sport, there are decided upon, or rather, codified moves (e.g., triple axel) that each skater must perform. Skaters do not make up these movements but spend years honing them, refining their implementation of those moves. At the same time, individualism comes to the foreground, as the skaters aim to perfect their performance and express their individuality through the subtleties of their specific execution. And this is precisely what the quest of Yūri is about: How can he balance the two dynamics of enacting a highly refined figurative acting performance of codes while presenting a sense of embodied performance's individualism?

Notably, the whole plot of episode 3 works with these tensions. Victor choreographs two routines for Yūri and Yurio, each to dissimilar compositions of the song "In Regards to Love" – Yūri performs the version titled "Eros" (implying a theme of the affection of sexual desire) and Yurio the version titled "Agape" (implying a theme of the affection of family). The point is to challenge the two athletes to go beyond their comfort zones, gain confidence in their abilities, and engage a personal meaning for the theme of the music that they can manifest in their embodied performances of the routine. This exploration of individual expression is mirrored in the production as well, with different animators performing the animations for the characters, involving animation directors Yumiko Nakamura, Noriko Itō, and Min Bae Lee, and figure skating animation directors Junpei Tachinaka and Eiji Abiko.

The other aspect of this episode's narrative is learning how to actually execute the complex skating moves that Victor combined to compose the routines for each of them. Yet Yūri feels that he should not copy Victor exactly. Instead, he wants to master the movements, finding his own conception of

Eros and expressing it in a personalized way. Meanwhile, Victor continues to push Yurio toward attaining a personal understanding of Agape despite his technical proficiency. Yurio achieves this when he has an introspective moment meditating under a waterfall, remembering the devotion of his grandfather. It is his internal examination that lets him externally enact his interpretation of Agape. Similarly, Yūri gains his understanding of Eros through an epiphany that the Eros he feels most comfortable with is not masculine but rather feminine. His subsequent enactment, though, is not portrayed as something that is entirely predicated on some internal core. After his realization, Yūri wakes up his former ballet instructor to have her teach him how to perform a feminine Eros – in other words, the successful articulation of his interiority is presented as dependent on learning modes of expression from an external source.

Significantly, it is Yūri's technically flawed performance – where he trips during one of the complex maneuvers – that wins the competition, even though Yurio's performance was more technically precise. In the next episode, Yūri explains the figure skating scoring system and how his wins are usually due to him making up for his technical misses through his presentation score. The opposite seems to have been the case for Yurio (at least to him personally), as Yurio's internal monologue reveals that he is spending more time concentrating on the movements than on the interior emotion of Agape, apologizing in his mind to his grandfather for this indiscretion.

The personalized expression of the figure skating performances as leaning toward the interior expressed externally like embodied acting is also displayed in episodes 6–8. Each of the figure skaters provide an internal monologue, explaining their inner thoughts that are then, in terms of the narrative, articulated externally through their specific movements as they perform their routines. The skaters' subtleties of movement are diverse, all presenting a distinct take on the thematic of love that was assigned for that competition (episodes 6–7). At the same time, the very fact that these are "routines" points to their iterability and the possible codification of those movements.

Although it seems that there is a prizing of the emotive, individualized embodied performance, there is also an understanding that this individuality is one that is not exclusively internally motivated. Instead, it is gained through refinement and practice, learned from an external source. Even the embodied element of Yūri's enactment that becomes valorized is still the result of a practiced performance. Put differently, individualism itself seems to be a performance that is dependent on elements outside of the self while simultaneously acknowledging the specificity of that character. Consequently, the series appears heavily indebted to figurative acting's operations of constituting characters despite its embrace of the dynamics of embodied performance.

Across the series, the narrative regularly exposes the interconnection between embodied and figurative acting. For example, the "In Regards to Love: Eros" song and general program, along with the "Yūri on Ice" routine, are presented as individualized performances but are both repeated throughout each competition shown on-screen. Each version is slightly different, however, with certain changes made to the skating moves and the order. In such ways, the anime seems to narrativize the operations of figurative acting (the reiteration of codes with minor variation and citation) but still keeps it in tension with embodied acting (exhibiting an external expression of interiority through individualized movements) as Yūri's quest for high achievement in figure skating is coupled with his seeking confidence in himself.

Indeed, Yūri must struggle to refine his enactment of codified skating moves while also finding and refining his individuality through embodied performance. Notably, Yūri feels most comfortable with his family and friends in his hometown, where he almost exclusively performs through the figurative acting codes common in anime and where these form the base for his self-confidence. In consideration of this, the show can be seen as undercutting traditional notions of individualism: One is not individual because of some internal element expressed externally. On the contrary, individuality is something that is produced through cultivation and careful effort, just like learning figurative acting codes. Furthermore, the individualistic elements are only made possible through the high refinement of figurative acting moves. As such, *YOI* presents a conception of selfhood that, despite its embrace of embodied acting, acknowledges the broader interconnection of elements that composite the self and the linkages between internal and external.

Performing Selves

Given the general bend toward figurative acting's constitution of selfhood, it is no surprise that many of Yūri's problems alternate between stoic individualism and receding into his shell, followed by him overcoming the difficulty through an acknowledgment of those around him. Additionally, these challenges are surmounted through a practice of those externally learned (or rather, cited) elements, whether they be words or moments of support that are repeated or replayed, or actual movements and techniques that he reenacts. This is a common pattern in anime narratives, ranging from romance, to sports, to action anime genres (aspects of which are all visible in *YOI*). Indeed, the last lines of the series are: "There is a place that you can't reach unless you have a dream too big to take on by yourself. All things on ice are 'love.'"

With this in mind, the general sense of comradery that is present through-out the series can be seen as an expansion of the affection of the external and as an acknowledgment of the importance of others around you. This is not just people but animals (e.g., Victor's dog) as well as objects (e.g., foods, in particular, *katsudon* pork cutlets on rice), with the occasional identification with the object itself (e.g., Yūri exclaiming that he himself is the most delicious *katsudon*). In terms of human companions, Yūri goes from a loner to appreciating the support of his family and friends, and to recognizing his expanded social circle of other high-ranking international competitors in the figure skating world. This is also regularly discussed in the monologues of other figure skating characters, as they note the signifi-cance of their competition, how rivals and idols can be beneficial to them, thus helping to motivate or to strive forward. In some ways, because these are internal monologues, one might even say that these external rivals and idols are integral parts of the interiority of the characters.

But among these various relationships, it is clear that Yūri and Victor have a special bond. Their romantic relationship displays how they have each in turn spurred on the other and how there is a strong connection between them that is specific to these two characters. Moreover, the question of "will he, won't he" of Yūri's sports success and the "will they, won't they" sus-pense of their romantic relationship constitute the two central plots of the series, which are themselves intertwined as Victor is Yūri's coach. This sense of mutual constitution, their deepening interconnection with one another, assists Yūri in finding love, as well as getting over his slump and performing to a high level in figure skating.

It also points to how, despite the emphasis on repetition, there is still par-ticularity and distinction through the operations of figurative acting. This is achieved through the combination of select codes, and the frequency of some codes over others. For instance, Victor is a motivator, an idol, or a competitor of many of the other figure skaters, and Yurio specifically has the technical skill to perform Victor's moves. Indeed, he can do these so well that he wins the final competition, with Yūri taking second place. But there is a more frequently repeated combination and intensity of performances of Victor's own enactments by Yūri (of course, Yūri is the protagonist, so we see his moves the most often). In this manner, Victor affects many of the characters, but more so Yūri, who reiterates and engages with Victor in a specific way. As such, there is a certain particularity to Yūri and his rela-tionship to those codes.

In terms of how character personalities are created through figurative acting, it is important to note that Yurio is kind of a *tsundere* character. The broader understanding and classification of *tsundere* character types reveals how much fans implicitly grasp the operations of figurative acting. These characters are known for their alternation between *tsun* (haughtiness, feigning of indifference, or expressions of irritation) and *dere* (affection). Each have codified expressions, such as the furrowed eyebrows and a scowl for irritation constantly worn by Yurio, or the light blushing on the upper cheeks beneath the eyes for affection or embarrassment at the kindness of others, something Yurio only occasionally enacts. Even rarer are moments of Yurio smiling (Fig. 11.1b). The regular alternation between expressions that fall under the *tsun* and *dere* spectrum would then allow a character to be constituted as a *tsundere* type. Of course, what and who they react to is going to be different for each character, and Yurio's irritation and affection are directed at Yūri (and at others to a lesser extent) as his rival. In these ways, the specific combination and frequency of figurative acting codes is what constitutes a character's personality.

Challenging Performances

Just as the operations of figurative acting depend on both prior and future iterations of a code, *YOI* narrativizes the transmission of skating technique through the inclusion of diverse figure skating idols that characters emulate. Yūri sees Victor as his idol and Yūri himself is idolized by the younger skater Kenjirō Minami. Both younger idolizers perform the moves and wear the costumes of their idols. But it should be noted that, like figurative acting in anime in general, the approach is not a precise duplication. Rather, change occurs through repetitions where minor variation is stressed.

It is also important to consider the gendering of the competitions as all male. Here, the various versions of expressing love, and distinct takes on traditionally masculine and feminine approaches to such enactments are all couched in terms of equally valid ways for men to perform, especially in episode 8. In other words, these modes of expression are depicted as performances that must be learned, practiced, and then executed, and none of them are necessarily exhibited as the most correct or proper for men to enact – there can be a number of ways to perform. Taking into account that Yurio is a male *tsundere* despite the character type tending to be female, the show generally presents gender as a performance, one in which the binaries between masculine and feminine, or rather, the supposed exclusivity of feminine and masculine expressions, are regularly crossed, mixed, and matched in varying combinations. At the same time, *YOI*'s narrative places importance on the introspective self-discovery (Yūri's "coming out" regarding his homosexuality and talent as a figure skater). Yūri ultimately realizes a confidence in himself through his love for another person (Victor) and learns to express this externally in both romance and skating, blurring the boundaries of inside and outside. In these ways, gender performance in *YOI* resonates with the anime's approach to the balancing of embodied and figurative acting.

While embodied acting is usually praised as the standard for quality animation, in its extreme, such performances can be isolating and indecipherable or be an exhausting imposition to consistently produce singular individuality. Figurative acting requires different skills to effectively enact, necessitating practiced and exacting executions of the conventional codes in precise combination. As such, distinct from the production of individualism implicit in embodied acting, figurative performances open up potentials for conceptualizing an interrelated selfhood that accepts a diversity of external performances, as evidenced in its operations in anime's character acting that is built from conventional codes. Offering an alternative to the exclusivity and sharp interior-exterior divides of individualism, figurative acting maintains inclusive, but also restrictive, capacities. There is always the ability to include more codes and any performers who adhere to those codes. Yet there is a rigidity involved: each enactment of a code must stick very close to the prior iterations or risk illegibility. But such conventionality should not be dismissed as entirely negative, as it enables a sense of commonality through a shared repertory, and in the case of figurative acting, is the very means by which the performance mode operates. On a larger scale, the reliance on conventions is evident in the very media form of anime itself, citing them across genres, studios, and even nations in its transnational production, affording a mode of performance that links across multiple borders.[7]

Notes

1. These terms were first explored by Donald Crafton in Donald Crafton, *Shadow of a Mouse: Performance, Belief, and World-Making in Animation* (Berkeley: University of California Press, 2013). See also Stevie Suan, *Anime's Identity: Performativity and Form Beyond Japan* (Minneapolis: University of Minnesota Press, 2021).
2. To avoid confusion, I have used the nickname Yurio, which he acquires in the show.
3. Crafton, *Shadow of a Mouse*, 37–41.
4. Crafton, *Shadow of a Mouse*, 44.
5. Thomas Lamarre, *The Anime Machine: A Media Theory of Animation* (Minneapolis: University of Minnesota Press, 2009), 193–96.
6. Marc Steinberg, *Anime's Media Mix: Franchising Toys and Characters in Japan* (Minneapolis: University of Minnesota Press, 2012), 6.
7. See Suan, *Anime's Identity*.

PART VI

Genres

12

DEBORAH SHAMOON

Manga Genres
Demographics and Themes

In manga studies, genres are usually assigned based on the magazines where a title was first serialized, with these magazines grouped according to the demographic of the readers, and broken down by age and gender. At first glance this genre classification might appear contradictory as it ignores the fact that readers outside those demographics have always read titles not explicitly aimed at them. The manga genre is, however, more than just a marketing segment or a series of editorial guidelines. Understanding the parameters and meanings of manga genres explains not only specific narrative and aesthetic choices but also how manga narratives function socially for readers. In Japan, manga genres are primarily demographic, organized under the two large categories of *shōnen* (boys) and *shōjo* (girls). Thematic genres such as sports are treated as subgenres, although these classifications are sometimes lost or changed in translation and export outside the country. This chapter will provide an overview of these two main manga genres of *shōnen manga* and *shōjo manga*, as well as other genres defined by demographics. It will then present two examples of thematic genres that cross demographics: sports manga and *isekai* ("other world"), a newly emerged genre based on video game logic.

Manga genres based on demographics may seem hopelessly vague because so many readers are outside the target range. For example, the primary demographic of *Weekly Shōnen Jump* is boys ages 10–15, but the publisher Shueisha reported that in 2021 more than a quarter of the readers were twenty-five years or older, and a significant percentage of readers were female.[1] This a not a recent phenomenon since girls (*shōjo*) and women (*josei*) have always consumed media aimed at boys (*shōnen*) and young men (*seinen*). While the reverse is less common, there have always been male fans of *shōjo manga*. Why then the continued insistence on dividing manga into *shōnen* and *shōjo* categories?

Skepticism about the effectiveness of genre as an interpretive tool is hardly unique to contemporary manga, and it has long been debated in literary studies: "The fact that a work 'disobeys' its genre does not mean the genre does not exist."[2] The same can be said of readers. Despite their names, *shōjo* and *shōnen* genres are not predictive or prohibitive of potential readership; instead, they inform readers of the type of content they can expect in terms of both narrative and art style. For example, although the categorization of *shōnen* as "action titles for boys" and *shōjo* as "romance for girls" is overly broad, language use suggests that *shōnen* titles are focused on plot. *Shōjo* titles, by contrast, center on emotional relationships.[3] In other words, there are significant differences between most *shōnen* and *shōjo* titles based on how they address their target reader, even though we can also acknowledge that people outside that range have always been reading them.

The division of manga magazines into titles for boys and girls reflects gendered marketing in the publishing world in Japan in general and predates the development of the manga industry. Modern magazine publication in Japan began in the 1910s as printing technologies improved to allow for the cheap production of text and image. At the same time, increasing education and a rising middle class meant a larger readership with disposable income, including women, teens, and children, who for the first time could buy magazines designed for them. By the 1920s, magazines aimed at boys and girls in secondary school had emerged as key sites of cultural production. These magazines were all segregated by gender, which was clearly marked in the title, for example, *Shōnen Club* (1914–62) and *Shōjo Club* (1923–62). While these magazines originally serialized a mix of illustrated novels, poetry, essays, and comic strips, in the 1950s they shifted their content to feature *story-manga*, in response to the popularity of children's comics in *akahon* booklets, and graphic narratives exclusively published for rental shops (*kashihon'ya*), where books could be read in the shop for a small fee. The generic traits of *shōnen manga* and *shōjo manga* originated in boys and girls magazines of the prewar era, and although the medium changed from novels to manga, the practice of marketing the magazines according to the gender binary remains in place today.

Shōjo Manga

The evolution of contemporary manga genres from early twentieth-century magazines can be seen most clearly in *shōjo manga*. It has been stated with regard to literary genres, "Where do genres come from? Quite simply from other genres. A new genre is always the transformation of an earlier one, or of several: by inversion, by displacement, by combination."[4] *Shōjo manga* grew out of the combination of literary and artistic genres in girls magazines of the 1920s and 1930s.

Girls novels (*shōjo shōsetsu*), which were serialized in girls magazines such as *Shōjo no Tomo* (1908–55), had two main generic features: a distinct prose style, and plots about homosocial relationships between girls, instead of heterosexual romance. These novels developed from translations of English-language girls fiction, such as Louisa May Alcott's *Little Women*, combined with the homosocial nature of girls culture, epitomized by the all-female Takarazuka Revue.[5] The Takarazuka Revue, founded in 1914, showcases young women in male and female roles in musical theater and spectacular song and dance performance. Takarazuka, both in its performance practices and its deeply involved fandom, was perceived as a fantasy space only for girls.

The most popular girls novelist was Nobuko Yoshiya, known for a flowery prose style described as *hirahira* ("fluttering" or "trembling"), and marked by poetic language and the frequent use of ellipses.[6] Yoshiya was especially skilled at using feminine speech patterns in dialogue and narration to speak directly to girls in their own language. These novels were accompanied by "lyrical images" (*jojōga*), which also emphasized emotion. The genre of lyrical images developed from a confluence of commercial illustration and design with trends in fine art in the 1920s. It was a way to address girls directly through images that stressed dreamy, sentimental inner feelings through exaggerated eyes with many highlights. Jun'ichi Nakahara's illustrations, in particular, pushed the enlarged eye to the extreme. Moreover, his work showed careful attention to fashion, appealing to the anticipated interests of female readers.

Heterosexual relationships could not be portrayed in girls novels, as dating or even friendship with boys was forbidden for middle- and upper-class girls Instead, the novels, poetry, and other content in the magazines reflected the real social patterns in girls' secondary schools, depicting what was called S, or sister, relationships (*S kankei*). These were close, exclusive romantic relationships between two girls, patterned on heterosexual courtship, and coded as transitory, teenage relationships that girls were expected to give up upon graduation, followed by arranged marriage. S relationships were the dominant theme in girls novels, and illustrations in girls magazines abound in images of girls in pairs.[7]

In the 1950s and 1960s, the aesthetics of girls novels were carried over into newly emerging manga, even though stories of S relationships disappeared, as mixed gender schools and heterosexual dating became the norm. Artists such as Macoto Takahashi and Hideko Mizuno brought Nakahara's style of character design to *shōjo manga*, especially the careful focus on elaborate fashions, and the exaggerated eye with many highlights that reflected the interiority of the characters. Osamu Tezuka created a long-running hit with *Princess Knight* (*Ribon no kishi*, in *Shōjo Club*, 1953–56; *Nakayoshi*, 1963–66; *Shōjo Friend*, 1967–68) that combined the same kind of adventure story he produced for *shōnen manga* with the explicitly referenced gender switching of the Takarazuka Revue, where young women played male roles. The *Shōjo Club* version of *Princess Knight* (1953–56) does not feature *shōjo* aesthetics, but Tezuka altered his style with the success of his protégé Mizuno in her series *Silver Petals* (*Gin no hanabira*, in *Shōjo Club*, 1957–59).[8] By the late 1950s, this big-eye style had become synonymous with *shōjo manga*. In the 1970s, a group of young women called the Magnificent 49ers (*Hana no 24 nengumi*) made significant changes to the *shōjo manga* genre, innovating symbolic backgrounds and layered panels to represent the inner lives of the characters and using a fragmented, first-person prose style.[9] Titles such as *The Rose of Versailles* (*Berusaiyu no bara*, in *Margaret*, 1972–74) by Riyoko Ikeda highlight themes of gender switching and psychological complexity.

While *shōjo manga* from the 1950s to the present day include various thematic genres (e.g., sports, horror, and science fiction [sci-fi]), romance is the most prominent, particularly heterosexual romance, with stories that tend to reinforce patriarchal gender norms. The most common plot has been described as "the love trap" where an ordinary, clumsy girl is saved by the love of a princely boy.[10] This permits a girl, who lacks some normative aspects of idealized femininity, to achieve the reward of the fairy-tale princess, that is, being saved by the handsome prince. But this is a trap, as the girl must remain passive to allow the boy to save her. The love trap still remains the motivating narrative feature in many *shōjo manga* titles.

Boys love, or BL, is another thematic genre of *shōjo manga*. Moto Hagio in *The Heart of Thomas* (*Tōma no shinzō*, in *Shōjo Comic*, 1974) and Keiko Takemiya in *The Poem of the Wind and the Trees* (*Kaze to ki no uta*, in *Shōjo Comic*, 1976–81; in *Petit Flower*, 1981–84) refreshed the concept of the S relationship by switching the genders and changing the setting to European all-boys schools in the early twentieth century. Making the main characters boys instead of girls let the plot sidestep the issues of the love trap and the expectations of passivity and chastity in girls. The genre was called *shōnen'ai* (boys love) or *tanbi* (aestheticism), referring to the emphasis on the flowery language and yearning of girls novels, but newly infused with blatant eroticism. In the 1980s, male-male (m-m) pairings also emerged in self-published manga (*dōjinshi*). Minami Ozaki parlayed her success with fan fiction of the *shōnen manga Captain Tsubasa* (by Yōichi Takahashi, in *Weekly Shōnen Jump*, 1981–88) into professional publication with *Absolute Love 1989* (*Zetsuai 1989*, in *Margaret*, 1989–91). As in slash or m-m fanfic from the United States, *dōjinshi* reimagined mainstream narratives about male partnerships in erotic terms, as imagined by heterosexual female authors and readers. This form of fanfic quickly became ubiquitous in self-published manga, and freed from the restraints of professional publishing, many constituted erotica. The focus on explicit sex scenes rather than plot is reflected in the name of the genre, *yaoi*, a portmanteau of *yama nashi, ochi nashi, imi nashi* (no climax, no resolution, no meaning). As self-publishing evolved as a pathway to a professional manga career, the distinction between *yaoi* and *shōnen'ai* was less clear, and by the early 1990s the manga publishing industry began using the term BL to indicate all m-m content. While some fans insist on genre distinctions between BL and *yaoi*, the terms are often used interchangeably.

BL shares a number of generic features with *shōjo manga* in general, particularly in terms of character design and panel arrangement. In narrative terms, BL pairings usually follow the heteronormative binary, with the *seme* (top) depicted as stereotypically masculine, and the *uke* (receiver) as feminine in appearance and behaving in a more passive manner. The prominence of the *uke/seme* binary in the BL genre is one reason gay male critics in the 1990s accused creators of appropriating and misrepresenting gay culture. Recently, however, some BL titles have subverted or dispensed with the *uke/seme* trope, and some authors, such as Fumi Yoshinaga, have endeavored to represent gay male characters more realistically.[11]

Shōnen Manga

Shōnen manga magazines also developed out of magazines from the 1920s, although the narrative and aesthetic features did not carry over from illustrated novels for boys. The greatest single influence in the creation of *shōnen manga* in the 1950s was Osamu Tezuka. A self-taught artist, Tezuka developed his art style by copying American comics he read as a child, in particular *Mickey Mouse* comics by Floyd Gottfredson and the newspaper strip *Bringing Up Father* by George McManus.[12] He emphasized a blend of action and humor, in service of utopian sci-fi stories, most notably *Astro Boy* (*Tetsuwan Atomu*, in *Shōnen*, 1952–68).

Tezuka nurtured the careers of numerous young artists, even though he was famously competitive when their skills and popularity rivaled his own, none more so than Shōtarō Ishinomori. Like Tezuka, Ishinomori is best known for sci-fi, but he wrote in several genres. Early in his career, Ishinomori collaborated with Hideko Mizuno and incorporated some elements of her *shōjo manga* art style into *shōnen* titles, including the expressive eye and layered panels. It was common in the 1950s and 1960s for manga artists to write both *shōnen* and *shōjo* titles, and many of the expressive aesthetic traits of *shōjo* were useful in *shōnen* narratives. Ishinomori's best-known series, *Cyborg 009*, reflects this genre diversity: The first arc was published in *Weekly Shōnen King* in 1964, while later arcs crossed into *gekiga* published in Tezuka's experimental magazine *COM* in 1969, and *shōjo manga* published in *Shōjo Comic* in 1975.

The genre of *shōnen manga* is dominated by one magazine, *Weekly Shōnen Jump* (1968–), with a circulation more than double its nearest competitors, *Weekly Shōnen Magazine* and *Weekly Shōnen Sunday*. *Jump* has serialized some of the biggest *shōnen manga* hits, including Eiichirō Oda's *One Piece* (1997–) and Kiyoharu Gotouge's *Demon Slayer: Kimetsu no Yaiba* (2016–20). One reason for *Jump*'s success is its ruthless editorial policy based on reader feedback. Soliciting reader opinion has been an integral part of the Japanese publishing industry since the early twentieth century. Although all manga magazines use reader surveys to determine which series will be cut, *Jump* is quicker to cancel low performing titles.[13] This high-pressure environment makes the magazine particularly responsive to readers' tastes. Due to its dominance in the market, *Jump* tends to set the genre expectations for all other *shōnen manga* magazines.

Jump's editorial policy is summarized in the well-known motto of "friendship, effort, victory" (*yūjō, doryoku, shōri*), which editor Tadasu Nagano developed in the 1960s based on surveys of fourth- and fifth-grade boys.[14] While not every title in *Jump* contains these ideals, "friendship, effort, victory" is a major theme in many *shōnen manga* serials. Regardless of whether the setting is realistic or fantastic, whether the plot is organized around sports, martial arts, giant robots, or high school, the story mainly involves the male protagonist assembling a team of companions to help each other achieve their goal together. The protagonist is usually not the most skilled or powerful and often fails in the beginning, but with the support of his friends, continues to work hard toward his goal. As in *shōjo manga*, making the main character less than perfect encourages reader identification. The emphasis on teamwork and hard work reflects the values of the Japanese educational system and salaryman ethos. The concept of victory ensures a happy ending, but in long-running serialized narratives, the conclusion is continually deferred, and realizing a goal is often a stepping stone to the next story arc.

Gekiga

One result of Tezuka's success with young readers in the 1950s was that the word "manga" became synonymous with stories for young children, but in just a few years those children who grew up on *Astro Boy* reached their teen years and longed for more adult storytelling. In 1957, Yoshihiro Tatsumi, working with a group of like-minded artists, coined the term *gekiga* to label this emerging genre for adults and to distinguish it from manga for children in order to evade censorship. In 1959, Tatsumi and eight other artists formed the Gekiga Workshop (*Gekiga Kōbō*), wrote a manifesto, and sent it to publishers. They were primarily publishing for rental shops, and their work was influenced by film noir: gritty crime stories with tragic endings and a rough art style, heavy on dark and light contrasts. During the 1960s and 1970s, *gekiga* indicated hard-boiled action stories with a correspondingly unpolished aesthetic, in contrast to the smooth lines and exaggerated eyes of *shōnen manga*. Some *gekiga* also had an element of social protest, such as Tatsumi's short stories collected in English under the titles *The Push Man* and *Abandon the Old in Tokyo*.[15] The most overtly political was Sanpei Shirato, who leveraged his success with the series *Manual of Ninja Martial Arts: The Legend of Kagemaru* (*Ninja bugeichō: Kagemaru-den*, 1959–62) to start the manga magazine *Garo* (1964–2002) as an outlet for his next ninja story, *The Legend of Kamui* (*Kamui-den*, 1964–71). Shirato intended *Kamui* to serve as an alternative leftist textbook for elementary school boys, to educate them about communism and the roots of social inequality and protest in seventeenth-century Japan. *Kamui*'s portrayal of Marxist ideals soon gained popularity among young adults in the student protest movement, and within a year, *Garo* had shifted its target audience from children to adults. Through the 1960s, *Garo* became the main publication site for avant-garde and experimental manga, which emphasized individual expression of the artist. The best-known *Garo* artist is Yoshiharu Tsuge, who achieved cult status for short stories blending surrealism and autobiography.

Gekiga developed in two directions: One was avant-garde, politically engaged manga exemplified by *Garo*. The other was manga for young, mainly male adults (*seinen*), exemplified by *Big Comic*, founded in 1968. In its early years, *Big Comic* included contributions by *gekiga* artists, such as Shirato and Shigeru Mizuki, and *shōnen manga* artists, such as Tezuka and Ishinomori. *Big Comic* appeals to adult male readers with stories that are more realistic than typical *shōnen manga*, but still lean heavily on violent spectacle. The flagship series of *Big Comic* is *Golgo 13* (1968–) by former Gekiga Workshop member Takao Saitō. *Golgo 13* is about a sniper assassin named Duke Tōgō, a lone-wolf antihero, in contrast to the emphasis in *shōnen manga* on teamwork and male friendship. The character design of Duke Tōgō, with craggy features, a downturned mouth, and tiny eyes covered by massive eyebrows, signals his rugged, macho persona. Like many *gekiga* and *seinen manga* heroes, his character design is intended to evoke admiration rather than identification, to show stoicism rather than emotion.

The 1960s and 1970s were the heyday of *gekiga*. Tatsumi's intention had been to delineate two separate genres, manga for children and *gekiga* for adults, but instead the term manga expanded to refer to the medium in general. Unlike in the 1950s, today most people understand that manga can refer to a variety of genres for all ages from child to adult. This shift of perception obviated the need for *gekiga* as a category, and today the term *seinen manga* more commonly refers to the genre for adult male readers. *Shōjo manga* went through a similar maturation process, with a new genre, *josei manga*, emerging to address adult female readers. The art style of *josei manga* is very similar to *shōjo manga*, with aesthetics that appeal to female readers and reflect the emotions of the characters, but with stories that tend to be realistic portrayals of careers, relationships, and family life. The term *ladies comics* (shortened to *redikomi*) is sometimes used interchangeably with *josei manga*.

Thematic Genres: Sports and *Isekai*

While the demographic genres of *shōjo* and *shōnen* are the predominant categories in both manga marketing and manga studies, manga contains the same diversity of thematic genres as other media such as film and television, including instructional (*gakushū*) comics. Many of these thematic genres exist in both *shōjo* and *shōnen manga*, although with significant differences that reflect the larger demographic genre. A brief look at two examples – sports and *isekai* – will show how these genres are reconfigured for different audiences.

Sports manga is typically considered a *shōnen* genre. Some of the most popular *shōnen* titles are sports manga, such as Tatsuo Yoshida's *Speed Racer* (*Mach Go Go Go*, in *Shōnen Book*, 1966–68) about car racing, Mitsuru Adachi's *Touch* (in *Weekly Shōnen Sunday*, 1981–86) about baseball, and *Captain Tsubasa* about soccer. The concept of "friendship, effort, victory" is particularly compatible with sports manga, as the structure of team sports lends itself to stories of male friendship, working hard to increase skills, and repeated short- and long-term endeavors toward victory. There is significant overlap between sports and martial arts genres, in the way both present leveling up ability in a quantifiable hierarchy and effort through intense training. The generic structure of sports manga even appears as the motivating principle in titles beyond contemporary team sports. For example, although Masashi Kishimoto's *Naruto* (in *Weekly Shōnen Jump*, 1999–2014) is nominally about ninja in a fantasy setting, the organization of the ninja village and the protagonist's ambition to improve is essentially a sports manga story. Even Takehiko Inoue's *Vagabond* (in *Morning*,

1998–2015), the fictional retelling of the life of seventeenth-century swordsman Miyamoto Musashi, derives its central motivation from sports manga, with the hero struggling to perfect his swordsmanship through hard work, in contrast to the naturally talented Kojirō Sasaki. Inoue's reinterpretation of this historical rivalry in terms of sports manga is perhaps not surprising, as his previous hits are the basketball titles *Slam Dunk* (in *Weekly Shōnen Jump*, 1990–96) and *Buzzer Beater* (in *Monthly Shōnen Jump*, 1996–98).

Shōjo manga have always featured sports stories. Some of the biggest hits of the Magnificent 49ers were sports stories, such as Sumika Yamamoto's *Aim for the Ace!* (*Ace o nerae!*, in *Margaret*, 1973–80) about tennis. A more recent example is Mitsuba Takanashi's *Crimson Hero* (*Beni'iro Hero*, in *Bessatsu Margaret*, 2003–11) about volleyball. Even ballet, a major theme in *shōjo manga* since the 1950s, is often depicted as a sports story, with the heroine striving to improve and win competitions. This is also a way for *shōjo* narratives to evade the love trap. Ballet manga brings a fairy-tale aesthetic to contemporary stories,[16] but the competitive aspect of professional ballet additionally gives the girl protagonist a goal other than romance. In *Swan* by Kyōko Ariyoshi (in *Margaret*, 1976–81), for example, the main character Masumi is the weakest of eight aspiring dancers selected for special training. Like the protagonist of a *shōnen* sports manga, Masumi starts from a disadvantaged position and undergoes intense training. While there are romance subplots, the focus is on Masumi's career ambition, giving her greater agency than the typical *shōjo* heroine.

Although sports manga has been perennially popular for more than fifty years, *isekai* is a recently emerged genre that appears in both *shōjo* and *shōnen manga*. *Isekai* is typically about a male or female protagonist who is summoned to or is reborn into a fictional world. Many manga and anime series have some element of travel to a different world, but the *isekai* genre specifically relies on role-playing game structure and logic.[17] The dominant feature of *isekai* is a character transported from contemporary Japan into the world of a video game they know well. The popularity of the *isekai* genre reflects the gamification of fictional narratives – that is, the reading pleasure comes from the common fantasy of playing a video game and imagining your real self inhabiting the game. *Isekai* began in light novels, such as Reki Kawahara's series *Sword Art Online* (2002–8), which became a media franchise, including manga and anime.

Isekai is equally a means for examining new identities in both *shōnen* and *shōjo manga*. The gamic setting is governed by rigid but easily understood rules, with clearly defined paths and the ability to cheat. Part of the pleasure of the *isekai* genre is subverting the expected path of the gamic narrative, while remaining within the parameters of the fictional world. In *shōjo isekai*, the female protagonist is usually reborn in an *otome* game, or a romance novel in a fantasy eighteenth-century European setting.[18] This device utilizes the fairy-tale setting with *shōjo* aesthetics in the costumes but from the point of view of a contemporary girl who resists or rewrites the patriarchal expectations of that era. A number of *shōjo isekai* stories also recast the protagonist as a villain or a minor character in the fictional world, allowing her to play against type, redeem vilified character tropes, and question generic romance conventions. One example is *My Next Life as a Villainess: All Routes Lead to Doom! (Otome gūmu no hametsu furagu shika nai akuyaku reijō ni tensei shite shimatta ...)*, a light novel series by Satoru Yamaguchi, adapted for manga by Nami Hidaka in 2017. The *isekai* genre has become so overwhelmingly popular that several contests intended to locate new manga talent have banned it in an attempt to diversify content.

Genre remains an important tool for analyzing manga, even when, or especially when genre classifications are fluid. While readership of print magazines is declining in favor of online sources, recognizable features of *shōnen* and *shōjo* genres persist, as they are powerful means of addressing target audiences. But as the methods of distribution and the interests of readers change, so too will new genres continue to emerge.

Notes

1. Shueisha Media Guide 2021, https://adnavi.shueisha.co.jp/mediaguide/. A poll of high school students in 2021 found 19.4 percent of girls read *Weekly Shōnen Jump*, compared to only 6.9 percent who reported reading *shōjo manga* magazines *Ribon* and *Bessatsu Margaret*, https://research-platform.line.me/archives/37928113.html.

2. Tzvetan Todorov, "The Origins of Genres." In *Modern Genre Theory*, edited by David Duff (London: Longman, 2000), 196.

3. Giancarla Unser-Schutz, "Redefining Shōjo and Shōnen Manga through Language Patterns." In *Shōjo across Media: Exploring "Girl" Practices in Contemporary Japan*, edited by Jaqueline Berndt, Kazumi Nagaike, and Fusami Ogi (Cham: Palgrave Macmillan, 2019), 49–82.

4. Todorov, "The Origins of Genres," 197.

5. Hiromi Tsuchiya Dollase, *Age of Shōjo: The Emergence, Evolution, and Power of Japanese Girls' Magazine Fiction* (Albany: State University Press of New York, 2019); Makiko Yamanashi, *A History of the Takarazuka Revue since 1914: Modernity, Girls' Culture, Japan Pop* (Leiden: Brill, 2012).

6. Masuko Honda, "The Genealogy of Hirahira: The Liminality of the Girl." In *Girl Reading Girl in Japan*, edited and translated by Tomoko Aoyama and Barbara Hartley (New York: Routledge, 2012), 19–37.

7. For detailed discussion, see Deborah Shamoon, *Passionate Friendship: The Aesthetics of Girls' Culture* (Honolulu: University of Hawai'i Press, 2012).

8. Deborah Shamoon, "Fire!: Mizuno Hideko and the Development of 1960s Shōjo Manga," In *Routledge Handbook of Japanese Media*, edited by Fabienne Darling-Wolf (New York: Routledge, 2018), 69–85.

9. The Magnificent 49ers refers loosely to women manga artists born around 1949 who debuted in the early 1970s and brought greater psychological depth and aesthetic complexity to the *shōjo manga* genre.

10. Yukari Fujimoto, *Watashi no ibasho wa doko ni aru no? Shōjo manga ga utusu kokoro no katachi* (Tokyo: Gakuyō Shobō, 1998), 13–15.

11. Kazumi Nagaike, "Queer Readings of BL: Are Women 'Plunderers' of Gay Men?" In *International Perspectives on Shōjo and Shōjo Manga: The Influence of Girl Culture*, edited by Toku Masami (New York: Routledge, 2015), 64–73.

12. Ryan Holmberg, "Heirs of Gottfredson: Osamu Tezuka." In Floyd Gottfredson *Mickey Mouse Outwits the Phantom Blot, vol. 5, Walt Disney's Mickey Mouse* (Seattle: Fantagraphics, 2014), 280–85; Eike Exner, *Comics and the Origins of Manga: A Revisionist History* (New Brunswick: Rutgers University Press, 2022), 171.

13. Bryan Hikari Hartzheim, "Making of a Mangaka: Industrial Reflexivity and Shūeisha's Weekly Shōnen Jump," *Television & New Media,* 22, no. 5 (2021): 570–87.

14. Hartzheim, "Making of a Mangaka," 574.

15. Yoshihiro Tatsumi, *The Push Man and Other Stories*, translated by Yuji Oniki (Montreal: Drawn & Quarterly Publications, 2005); Yoshihiro Tatsumi, *Abandon the Old in Tokyo*, translated by Yuji Oniki (Montreal: Drawn & Quarterly Publications, 2006). Both are collections of short stories. "The Push Man" (*Oshi-ya*) and other stories were originally published in the magazine *Gekiga Young* in 1969. "Abandon the Old in Tokyo" (*Tōkyō no ubasuteyama*) was first published in *Weekly Shōnen Magazine* in 1970. Other stories in that collection were first published in *Garo*.

16. Masafumi Monden, "Layers of the Ethereal: A Cultural Investigation of Beauty, Girlhood, and Ballet in Japanese Shōjo Manga," *Fashion Theory,* 18, no. 3 (2014): 251–96.

17. Paul S. Price, "A Survey of the Story Elements of Isekai Manga," *Journal of Anime and Manga Studies,* 2 (2021): 57–91.

18. *Otome* ("maiden") game is a genre of dating sim video games aimed at girls and women, with the same aesthetic features as *shōjo manga* in the character design.

13

BRYAN HIKARI HARTZHEIM

Genre Networks and Anime Studios

Genres within anime range from the unique (robot, magical girl, slice of life) to the conventional (action, mystery, romance). Among them, science fiction (sci-fi) has historically been well represented since the earliest television series in the 1960s. There is seemingly far more sci-fi and fantasy anime than any other type, a fact that many critics and scholars have picked up on and written extensively about. But why is it that sci-fi has featured so prominently in anime?

Simple explanations for this phenomenon might include the fact that sci-fi was not only popular in anime, but in all types of media in Japan and elsewhere in the postwar period. As a medium not tethered to real people or locations, animation – from any country – has the capacity to portray fantastical sci-fi worlds and scenarios more easily and more affordably than live-action media. This alone, however, does not necessarily explain sci-fi's strong presence in anime. It is also important to look at the industrial, institutional, and communal networks that were a part of sci-fi before anime fandoms emerged in the 1970s and 1980s. Though genres function as textual and discursive categories,[1] genre networks direct and manage the creative energies of various anime producers.

This chapter advocates a studio-centered approach to genre research, using the well-known anime studio Gainax as a case study. Gainax became internationally celebrated in the mid-1990s with the smash hit *Neon Genesis Evangelion* (*Shinseiki Evangerion*, dir. Hideaki Anno, 1995–96), but the studio's growth during the "first anime boom" of the 1980s was much more precarious. Founded in 1984, Gainax could rely on Japan-based sci-fi networks formed in the 1970s for promotional marketing and professional labor. The studio's prehistory and survival is a turning point between the institutions of broad sci-fi fans and creators in the 1970s and anime and manga *otaku*, or superfans, in the 1980s.

Studying Studios

A studio-centered approach to genre draws from the "archival turn" that traces back to film studies toward the end of the twentieth century. Attention was directed to how Hollywood studios and producers – and not auteur directors – were responsible for the formation and popularization of genres such as the Western, romantic comedy, or gangster flick.[2] Similar types of analysis have been applied to the Japanese studio system, but this approach becomes problematic in the discussion of anime. The anime industry lacks the centralization and vertical integration of the classic studio system. Today, there are over 300 "studios" in Japan, although many of these are highly specialized and few are equipped to spearhead their own productions. Most creative labor in the anime industry is also employed contractually, meaning that the artistic personnel at a studio can be radically different from year to year, or even season to season. In this sense, the instability exhibited by Gainax throughout its history is not atypical of anime studios, around 40 percent of which still operate in the red according to recent estimates.[3]

Considering the anime studio's historical precarity, this chapter focuses on the two frenzied organizations that comprised Gainax before it was established as a production studio: the licensing store General Products and the production company Daicon Film. It examines the discourse of General Products' and Daicon Film's ongoing attempts to use sci-fi institutions and fandoms as a means of survival and expansion. An analysis of the political economy and business history of animation corporations such as the Walt Disney Company and DreamWorks demonstrates how Hollywood – and a struggling Disney corporation in the 1970s – incorporated new trends and adapted to changing social and economic conditions of twentieth-century America.[4] Correspondingly, research into Gainax's pre-studio business origins offers some understanding of how the anime industry integrated sci-fi institutions, and how it adapted to the rapidly changing social and economic conditions of 1980s Japan.

The Gainax Origin Story

Sci-fi purportedly emerged in prewar Japan as a literary genre heavily influenced by translations of Anglophone texts. It grew considerably in the postwar era with the circulation of niche magazines such as *Uchūjin* and *SF Magazine*, which helped to coalesce diverse readerships across the country.[5] By the 1970s, sci-fi had garnered extraordinary popular international attention through various films, TV shows, comics, and other mass entertainments. Sci-fi-themed stories and films simultaneously made inroads into other forms of mass culture in Japan, most notably manga, anime, and *tokusatsu*, a form of live-action television that emphasized practical special effects in weekly battles between futuristic superheroes and villains. Many of these shows appealed to producers as they targeted young male audiences with stories of action and spectacle that also served as advertisements for the toy products featured in the program. The end of the decade saw the making of TV programs with serial narratives focused on outer space and technology, such as *Space Battleship Yamato* (*Uchū senkan Yamato*, 1974–75) and *Mobile Suit Gundam* (*Kidō senshi Gandamu*, 1979–80), which were geared toward slightly older audiences. These series represented an expansion in Japanese sci-fi anime from a primarily child-oriented to a more adolescent audience that openly and passionately displayed its support through the purchase of record-breaking numbers of movie tickets, the collection of large amounts of plastic figures, and cosplay in public spaces.

In 1981, two prominent sci-fi fans – Toshio Okada and Yasuhiro Takeda – oversaw the organization of Daicon III, the 20th Japan SF Convention (Nihon SF Taikai), in their native Osaka Prefecture. The Japan SF Convention was an annual, geographically rotating event inspired by sci-fi conventions such as Worldcon. It hosted a range of activities from symposiums to parties to a marketplace selling books, fanzines, and other sci-fi-related goods.[6] Eager to create a festive atmosphere, Okada and Takeda commissioned Hiroyuki Yamaga, Hideaki Anno, and Takami Akai, three students from the Osaka University of Arts, to make a short animation for the convention's opening ceremonies. Yamaga, Anno, and Akai had no professional animation experience, and their budget was so small they were forced to use industrial sheet vinyl in place of animation cels.[7] Despite these limitations, together with several volunteer tracers and painters, they generated a work with startlingly sophisticated animation that freely borrowed from popular sci-fi films, anime, and *tokusatsu*.

Following the positive reception of this short film, the convention organizers and artists would go on to freelance at various production studios before creating a more ambitious and polished opening animation for Daicon IV in 1983. Following these two successful openings, the creators registered the trade name of Gainax for their production company.[8] Gainax's inaugural project was a feature-length animated film financed by the toy and media company Bandai about the first outer space launch in a fictional alternate world. This work, *Royal Space Force: The Wings of Honnêamise* (*Ōritsu uchūgun: Oneamisu no tsubasa*, 1987), was the most expensive Japanese animated film to date, although its takings at the box office were disappointing. These early ups and downs were characteristic of Gainax, which struggled to stay afloat with sporadic hits, and more frequent misses, before finally finding their footing in the mid-1990s with the phenomenon that was *Neon Genesis Evangelion*.

The Gainax origin story has been told and retold by critics, academics, the founders themselves, and even manga authors such as Kazuhiko Shimamoto, who dramatized the aforementioned events from his own perspective as a fellow student at Osaka University of Arts in the manga *Blue Blazes* (*Aoi honō*, 2007–). Some scholars emphasize the communal connections the creators developed and present the studio's accomplishments as a product of "the force of the personalities involved,"[9] while others have suggested that the origin story is also an effort of *otaku* self-publicity that obscures the significant "dysfunction that engendered Gainax's initial lack of success."[10] Such observations reflect how Gainax at its inception was a fledgling organization that relied heavily on the existing infrastructure provided by the Japan SF Convention. Gainax was celebrated as an anime studio and proof of the global spread of anime fandom, but it was not entirely dedicated to producing animation for much of its early history. Rather, it utilized the existing networks and institutions of sci-fi fan and creator culture to work on a series of products and platforms that strengthened the brand name of its creators. The following sections outline the two ways in which the Gainax founders tapped into this sci-fi culture for the marketing and production of its commodities – that is, through the promotional labor of General Products and the creative labor of Daicon Film.

General Products: Licensing and Promotion

Encouraged by the popularity of the convention's "dealer's room," which routinely sold out of merchandise, in 1982, Okada and Takeda founded General Products, a company specializing in the sale of licensed character and material goods. The lead schoolgirl heroine from the Daicon III and IV opening animations (OP) became the company's unofficial mascot; she inspired a flurry of fan-generated fiction and cosplay and featured in an array of products. One of the more innovative of these was arguably the first example of an OVA (original video animation), an anime film or short series in a direct-to-video format.[11] At the time, the Daicon III OP was considered something of a myth due to the fact that it was a one-time screening. Even though the work infringed on various copyrights through the use of unauthorized images and music, General Products sold hundreds of video cassette tape recordings of it for over 10,000 yen each. These sales helped to pay off the significant debts that had accumulated during the production of the Daicon III OP.[12]

General Products became a hub for licensed goods of popular sci-fi films, shows, and games in Japan. It specialized in the distribution of *dōjinshi*, or fan-made comics, and even commissioned its own original material from well-known manga creators, such as Hideo Azuma. General Products also popularized garage kits, or self-assembled polyresin model kits, that were popular at events like the Japan SF Convention. General Products partnered with companies including Tsuburaya, Toho, Bandai, and Enix to make merchandise based on monsters, robots, or weapons that appeared in franchises such as *Ultraman*, *Godzilla*, and *Dragon Quest*. These connections proved vital when attempting to create original anime productions under the Gainax label since Bandai would become the official sponsor for its first feature-length film.

The experience of General Products working with sci-fi conventions likewise assisted in the organization of fan initiatives that enabled the scouting of new talent and volunteers from its customer base. Before the company closed and incorporated into Gainax in 1992, it experimented with various fan-driven ventures. As the popularity for garage kits grew, the company organized Wonder Festival, a semiannual event with high-quality garage kits from popular sci-fi, anime, and game works. Wonder Festival continues to the present day, although under the auspices of a different company. In 1991, General Products also sponsored one of the first American anime conventions, AnimeCon, a spiritual predecessor to Anime Expo, the largest of its type in North America. Utilizing its experience in mounting the Japan SF Convention, the company mobilized volunteers and held multiple panel discussions and Q&As with industry staff, effectively doubling as a PR tool for its joint anime studio.

General Products importantly harnessed the promotional potential of sci-fi magazines. The success of *Space Battleship Yamato* resulted in a growing interest in anime from sci-fi fans and a broader viewership in the late 1970s. Coverage of *Yamato* and other anime began to appear more frequently in *SF Magazine* and subcultural periodicals such as *Gekkan Out*, which increasingly dealt with sci-fi developments in anime and manga. Dedicated anime magazines emerged and among them *Animec* played an integral role in advancing the works of Daicon Film before it was a commercial studio. *Animec* became known as a detail-oriented magazine that published extensive anime features and criticism. Its December 1981 issue, for example, dedicated a five-page spread to the Daicon III opening animation with over sixty shots and descriptions that functioned as a scene-by-scene synopsis just months after its single screening at the convention. The issue also had a three-page interview with the creators on the film's unusual construction with instructions in the margins of the page on how to contact the company to purchase VHS copies of the short film.

The partnership between General Products and *Animec* is an early example of the symbiotic relationship that evolved between the anime industry and subcultural journalism: General Products provided *Animec* with content in the form of interviews, columns, and original character designs, while the magazine became an outlet for the company to advertise its latest goods. Such content, penned by the organizers of Daicon III and IV opening animations, aided in downplaying the commercialism of General Products and emphasized that it was a group made by and for fans. Although General Products was eventually undone due to poor management and a string of failed projects, during its decade of activity it facilitated Gainax's animation production and distribution through leveraging the events, publications, and consumption patterns of sci-fi fandoms and communities.

Daicon Film: Technical Training and Labor Networks

The licensing and promotion of the Daicon III opening animation (OP) led to the anime industry's increased attention to the short film's three creators, Yamaga, Anno, and Akai. Yamaga and Anno moved to Tokyo at the invitation of Studio Nue, an animation company originally founded in 1972 by former members of the SF Central Art fan club for the express purpose of working on sci-fi art and animation. They worked on the TV anime series *Super Dimension Fortress Macross* (*Chōjikū yōsai Macross*, 1982–83), with Yamaga storyboarding and directing an episode and Anno serving as key animator on several others. This technical training was instrumental for both creators but especially for Anno, who was mentored by the experienced artists and animators at Studio Nue and coproducer Artland and who would spend nights perfecting key frames of explosions at his animation stand. Akai, on the other hand, opted to continue directing live-action *tokusatsu* films for Daicon Film, an enterprise formed in 1981 in the wake of Daicon III OP to make shorts in preparation for Daicon IV OP. These independent productions screened to small audiences and were sold through General Products' catalog. But Akai equally used the opportunity to experiment with live-action special effects and art design that would find its way into other animation productions, such as the heightened level of realism in the future design of the 1987 *Royal Space Force*.[13]

When it came time to produce the opening animation for Daicon IV two years later, the Daicon Film staff ballooned beyond the original three and its uncredited volunteers. Yamaga and Anno recruited several staff from Studio Nue and Artland, including Ichirō Itano, Mahiro Maeda, and Kazutaka Miyatake, who all had worked on *Macross*, to focus on animation and illustrations common within the sci-fi genre. Their special effects animation, otherworldly concept art, and detailed mechanical designs were incorporated into the Daicon IV OP, which referenced a cornucopia of sci-fi film and anime works and had its own highly polished animation action sequences that belied its amateur status.

The recruitment of the *Macross* animators to the Daicon films represents an early attempt at the highly porous but nonetheless specialized labor networks typical of animation production in Japan. As most animators are employed on a freelance basis, they frequently work on a variety of productions to make ends meet. In the course of animating for many different TV series or films, animators must become technically versatile, able to adjust their drawings to a variety of productions. But they also tend to specialize simultaneously in animation techniques to distinguish themselves and have their work become recognized within the industry and fan communities. In 1980s sci-fi anime, the most noticeable of these techniques often revolved around the animation of otherworldly special effects. Itano, for example, is well known for animating extremely complex ballistic missile sequences in which each projectile seems to have a trajectory of its own – the so-called Itano Circus. Such sequences are visible in the Daicon IV OP production and in *Royal Space Force*, for which many Studio Nue and Artland animators with expertise in designing and animating machines and special effects were recruited. As a result of this selective recruitment, the high level of technical animation on display in Daicon IV OP surpassed even that of most professional animation studios in Japan at the time.

An animator's ability to concentrate on certain types of animation becomes a kind of "figurative performance," or industry signature.[14] This was indeed the case for Anno. Following the Daicon IV OP premiere, Anno returned to Studio Nue to work on a feature film adaptation of *Macross*. He then worked on Hayao Miyazaki's *Nausicaä of the Valley of the Wind* (*Kaze no tani no Naushika*, 1984) at Studio Ghibli, where his reputation for special effects animation allowed him to key animate the giant biomechanical monster that appears at the end of the film. Anno's fluid animation of the giant and the realistic depiction of simultaneous frames of action became his signature technique in magazine profiles and Gainax promotional materials, such as a theatrical pamphlet for *Royal Space Force* in which Yamaga credited Anno for animating such explosive sequences in the film's climactic rocket launch.[15] Anno was recognized as the "author" of the brief, but spectacular, sequences in these films, and he became a celebrity-like figure despite not having the typical above-the-line position of director, writer, or producer. Such a privileging of Anno's animation by both fans and creators demonstrates a desire to "dehierarchize" the elements of production in order to decipher the animator's signature touch within the image.[16]

Anno's work on *Macross* engendered a sort of virtuous cycle. His professional network expanded, enabling him to invite others to contribute to his own studio's projects. This, in turn, led to other invitations to participate in their projects based on shared interests and technical skills. These professional associations demonstrate that sci-fi is not just a theme or set of signifiers, including robots and outer space, but also an organizing principle based on demand for specific technical labor skills. The practice continues to the present day, with directors and producers contacting particular animators for their ability to animate character expressions or action sequences. Such a close-knit network similarly exhibits another practice common today – namely, the "sweatshop conditions" due to tight scheduling and budget overruns. Many animators recruited for the Daicon IV OP would toil late into the night, packed into sauna-like rooms during the height of summer.[17] Daicon's crunch was not the first of its kind within the anime industry, and such a practice might be forgiven considering the amateur nature of the Daicon Film enterprise. But the custom of calling on colleagues to fill "gaps" in production would reappear in future Gainax productions, and it remains a common occurrence on short-staffed productions within the anime industry.

Combining Self-Promotion and Craft in Gainax

General Products and Daicon Film have thus far been discussed as separate entities, but despite their different activities there was also considerable overlap and tension between the two. This was certainly true in the case of the workforce, as divisions at Gainax were never clearly delineated, and staff were often engaged with multiple projects.[18] The loosely defined structure of the twin companies would become characteristic of Gainax's public image as a place where artists were given creative carte blanche. This can be seen in various aspects of the studio from the ways in which personnel would move between licensing, animation, or game development to its collaborative creative process in which a nominal director such as Yamaga would solicit ideas from all staff only to be overruled by strong opinions within departments.[19] Beyond the loose company structure, however, it is important to recognize that the diverse activities of General Products and Daicon Film reinforced one another. This reinforcement was facilitated by the fact that both groups drew from and relied upon established sci-fi networks and institutions, such as university clubs, niche magazines, hobby stores, and the large community of fan creators and fan critics that operated them. General Products employed the characters and publicity generated from the Daicon OPs to sell merchandise, and this resulted in increased exposure, promotion, and proceeds for Daicon Film from companies, including Studio Nue, to expand its production networks.

The Daicon III and IV conventions were also a turning point in the growth of sci-fi fandoms, as they began to diverge from the sci-fi institutions and organizations that had initially supported them. This shift in fan interest is evident in the covers of *Animec* from December 1981 and November 1983, which have features on the OP animations for Daicon III and Daicon IV, respectively. The former illustrates a detailed painting of a spaceship and space colony, articles titled "What is SF anime?" and an introduction to the horror manga creator Kazuo Umezu. The latter includes a spotlight on the robot anime *Aura Battler Dunbine* (*Seisenshi Dunbine*, 1983–84), but the magazine cover opts to focus on the fairy character Cham in various costumes and cute poses rather than any of the robots or heroes. Mirroring the outpouring of fan affection accorded to the attractive heroines in the Daicon shorts, *Macross*, and several other works with appealing female characters, the shift in visual emphasis of *Animec* is representative of a larger move in the public discourse of the 1980s away from the literary origins of sci-fi to the superfan interests of the emergent *otaku* (geek) culture connected to these productions.[20]

Similarly, we can read the changing strategies of Gainax as representing a new form of Japan's media mix, or multimedia franchises that revolve around characters. Characters have been at the center of anime since at least the time of Osamu Tezuka's *Astro Boy* (1963–), in which their licensing helped to finance the production of the series.[21] With Gainax, there is a recognition of the exploitative power of character images in licensing and commodities through the use of new distribution platforms, such as home video or gaming, which appeal directly to niche fan interests. In response to the financial disappointment and lack of merchandising opportunities of *Royal Space Force*, the studio created *Gunbuster* (*Toppu o neraé!*, 1987), an OVA that was designed as a parody of existing film and anime works with a large cast of perky female robot pilots. Unbeholden to a TV broadcaster's hopes for high ratings or to a sponsor's desire to sell toys to children, Gainax's parody appealed directly to adolescent and older male consumers who would purchase more expensive home video copies to support the series' production.

The same principle was at play with *Cybernetics Hi-School* (*Dennō gakuen*, 1989), a PC game developed by Gainax that cast the player in the role of a student at a high school staffed by lewd female teachers who stripped off their clothes when the player correctly answered quiz questions drawn from exclusive sci-fi and *otaku* knowledge. Such adult games already existed, but Gainax's innovations were the inclusion of "pretty graphics" and an irreverent attitude toward its own characters.[22] This can be seen, for example, in *Cybernetics Hi-School III* (1990), a sequel to the original based on the female characters of *Gunbuster*. Anno, who directed the OVA that originated the infamous "Gainax bounce," or animation of female characters' jiggling breasts, also storyboarded the game's characters in unabashedly scandalous poses. Such parodic works are more common among erotic fan fiction than its official creators, but they are not out of character with the fan producers of Gainax and General Products. By making an anime parody that it then parodied in ludic form, Gainax demonstrated a willingness to remove characters from their original context in order to allow fans to control and objectify them. This design ethos would lead to the creation of its most popular PC game, *Princess Maker* (1991), where a young girl is groomed into royalty by the parental figure player.

Despite pandering to *otaku* by positioning cute girls at the forefront of these works, *Gunbuster* and *Cybernetics Hi-School* are still replete with the sort of deep references to sci-fi culture that are so characteristic of the early Gainax companies. *Gunbuster* reflects the production networks of Daicon Film, as its animation and design staff are assembled from those who worked on the Daicon IV OP, with the addition of the popular character designer of *Macross*, Haruhiko Mikimoto. While ostensibly a parody of robot and sports anime, as well as the film *Top Gun*, *Gunbuster* is equally an homage to these works in its attention to detail in the designs, layouts, and animation that reference previous sci-fi robot works. Each episode, for example, is followed by a short animation "science lesson" that details the fictional physics behind the series' world; the first episode features a class on "ether cosmology" pioneered by the Nobel-award-winning physicist Dr. R. Tannhäuser, a clear reference to the Tannhäuser Gate in Ridley Scott's *Blade Runner* (1982). Moreover, from its second episode onward the OVA develops a startlingly dramatic sci-fi narrative that allegorizes the experiences of war and its traumatic consequences. The final two episodes of the series, in particular, borrow from Kihachi Okamoto's war and disaster films like *Battle of Okinawa* (*Gekidō no shōwashi: Okinawa kessen*, 1971) in their incorporation of onscreen captions, fatality statistics, and black and white cinematography to convey a docudrama sense of historical reality to the fictional setting. *Gunbuster*'s simultaneous display of cute characters and dense sci-fi references, images, and plots encapsulates the complementary activities of General Products and Daicon Film: self-promotion, sci-fi knowledge, and attractive female characters that referenced old networks and spoke directly to new ones. Such an approach would be reproduced in many other Gainax works including *Neon Genesis Evangelion*.

Conclusion

This chapter examined the origins of Gainax and how it was formed through, and benefited from, the many sci-fi networks existent in Japan in the late 1970s and early 1980s. Gainax became known as *the otaku* studio, in part for its celebration of these networks, but the studio was also applauded for its acknowledgment of an increasingly vocal anime-centered audience characterized by varied interests. This chapter has focused on the importance of sci-fi to the Gainax studio, yet the histories of anime, written by *otaku* audiences, frequently stress the influence of sci-fi on anime at the expense of other formative genres, studios, and audiences. As studios still play a major role in shaping labor and fan interest, it is important to acknowledge the contributions of other organizations and genres, and their effect on training creators and audiences, ranging from Toei Animation's production of the magical girl genre to Sunrise's innovation of the robot genre.[23] A studio-centered approach to genres can therefore continue to shed light on hitherto overlooked creators and audiences, as well as the ways in which their interaction fueled the production and persistence of other genres within the anime industry.

Notes

1. Rick Altman, "A Semantic/Syntactic Approach to Film Genre," *Cinema Journal*, 23, no. 3 (1984): 6–18.
2. Thomas Schatz, *The Genius of the System: Hollywood Filmmaking in the Studio Era* (New York: Metropolitan Books, 1988).
3. "'Anime seisaku gyōkai' dōkō chōsa 2022," *Teikoku Databank*, 12 August 2022, www.tdb.co.jp/report/watching/press/p220803.html.
4. See Douglas Gomery, "Disney's Business History: A Reinterpretation." In *Disney Discourse: Producing the Magic Kingdom*, edited by Eric Smoodin (New York: Routledge, 1994), 71–86; Rayna Denison, "How to Animate Your Franchise: DreamWorks Animation and the Franchising of How to Train Your Dragon." In *The Franchise Era: Managing Media in the Digital Economy*, edited by James Fleury, Bryan Hikari Hartzheim, and Stephen Mamber (Edinburgh: Edinburgh University Press, 2019), 158–78.
5. Takayuki Tatsumi, "Generations and Controversies: An Overview of Japanese Science Fiction, 1957–1997," *Science Fiction Studies*, 27, no. 1 (2000): 105.
6. Taimatsu Yoshimoto, *Otaku no kigen* (Tokyo: NTT Shuppan, 2009), 24–25.
7. Yasuhiro Takeda, *The Notenki Memoirs: Studio Gainax and the Men Who Created Evangelion* (Houston: ADV Manga, 2005), 50–51.
8. The name Gainax derives from the word *gaina*, which in the Yonago dialect of Tottori Prefecture (Yonago is Akai's hometown) means "big." The "x" was added at the end to make the company name sound more like a robot. See Takeda, *The Notenki Memoirs*, 90.
9. Ian Condry, *The Soul of Anime: Collaborative Creativity and Japan's Media Success Story* (Durham: Duke University Press, 2013), 133.

10. Rayna Denison, "Anime is (Not) Cult: Gainax and the Limits of Cult Cinema." In *The Routledge Companion to Cult Cinema*, edited by Ernest Mathijs and Jamie Sexton (London: Routledge, 2020), 124.

11. Jonathan Clements, *Anime: A History* (London: BFI Palgrave, 2013), 172.

12. Takeda, *The Notenki Memoirs*, 105.

13. Takami Akai and Hiroyuki Yamaga, *Director's Commentary on Royal Space Force: The Wings of Honnêamise DVD* (Chicago: Manga Entertainment, 2000).

14. Stevie Suan, *Anime's Identity: Performativity and Form Beyond Japan* (Minneapolis: University of Minnesota Press, 2021), 230.

15. Gainax/Bandai, *Ōritsu uchūgun: Oneamisu no tsubasa* [Movie Pamphlet] (Tokyo: Toho-Towa Shuppan, 1987), 22. In another interview in the booklet included in the 2007 DVD of the film, Yamaga states that even before he had decided on the film's story, he wanted to have an ending that would take advantage of Anno's ability to draw "shrapnel." See Hiroyuki Yamaga, "I Started from Utterly Breaking the 'Concept of Anime' That was within the Staff's Heads." In *Royal Space Force: Wings of Honnêamise* [Liner Notes] (Torrance: Bandai Visual, 2007), 6.

16. Thomas Lamarre, *The Anime Machine: A Media Theory of Animation* (Minneapolis: University of Minnesota Press, 2009), 145.

17. Takeda, *The Notenki Memoirs*, 77.

18. Toshio Okada, *Yuigon* (Tokyo: Chikuma Shobō, 2010), 217.

19. Akai and Yamaga, Director's Commentary.

20. Zoltan Kacsuk, "The Making of an Epoch-Making Anime: Understanding the Landmark Status of Neon Genesis Evangelion in Otaku Culture." In *Anime Studies: Media-Specific Approaches to Neon Genesis Evangelion*, edited by José Andrés Santiago Iglesias and Ana Soler Baena (Stockholm: Stockholm University Press, 2021), 215–46. Open Access.

21. Marc Steinberg, *Anime's Media Mix: Franchising Toys and Characters in Japan* (Minneapolis: University of Minnesota Press, 2012), 13–20.

22. Clements, *Anime*, 201.

23. See also Rayna Denison, *Studio Ghibli: An Industrial History* (London: Palgrave Macmillan, 2023), 6.

PART VII

Forms of Production

14

BON WON KOO

Manga Editors and Their Artists

Japan has the largest comics market in the world.[1] The fiscal year of 2020 alone witnessed the release of 12,939 new titles: 9,023 magazine issues and 3,916 collected paperback books (*tankōbon*), equating to around thirty-five new titles every day. Magazines have formed the backbone of this market since the late 1950s, and the republication of popular comics serials in bound *tankōbon* editions, so-called *komikkusu*, began in the late 1960s. Currently, eighty publishers account for the approximately ninety manga periodicals that run installments of roughly twenty serialized narratives each. Weekly serials generally result in the release of four *tankōbon* volumes every year and monthly serials in two. Some of these are categorized as books, but the majority are grouped in the same category as magazines: They can be returned to the publisher if not sold, and the turnover of new releases is faster than in the "book" category. This has helped manga to overcome booksellers' traditional prejudice against comics and to seize their own shelf space in stores. In 2018, magazines – and not just manga periodicals – constituted 25.3 percent of bookstores sales in Japan, with manga *tankōbon* at 16.6 percent.[2]

Japan has not always been a comics powerhouse, however. Until the 1990s, it was unimaginable that a manga publication like *Weekly Shōnen Jump* would exceed 6 million copies.[3] The all-time peak of magazine print runs was reached in 1995, but since then sales have witnessed a steady decline. The print run of *Weekly Shōnen Jump* slumped to 1.2 million copies by 2020, and the total circulation of magazines had dropped that year to 286.71 million from 1,594 million in 1995. Conversely, the return rate climbed from 18 to 43.2 percent – in other words, half of all printed magazines remained unsold. Decreased magazine sales do not necessarily indicate the crash of the Japanese comics market; rather, they mark a change in readers' purchasing patterns and medial preferences. In 2005, the magazine was overtaken commercially by the *tankōbon* format due to successful *Jump* series, including *Naruto* (1999–2014) by Masashi Kishimoto, *One Piece* (1997–) by Eiichirō Oda, and *Bleach* (2001–16) by Tite Kubo.

By the mid-2000s, the supremacy of *tankōbon* proved challenging to publishers, as there was a narrowing of readers' selection focus by then. Before that time, readers purchased a certain magazine issue because of a specific serial that had caught their attention, but while browsing the magazine they might also come across other manga. To compensate, publishers pursued new avenues of marketing, most notably enhanced franchising or the use of anime and film adaptations, to promote the initial graphic narrative. Yet overall sales continued to drop until 2014, when the statistics released by the Research Institute for Publications (Shuppan Kagaku Kenkyūsho) showed a slight annual increase in the manga market due to the inclusion of e-book sales. Digital comics were on the rise. In 2019, they overtook hard-copy manga publications – magazines and *tankōbon* books combined – which caused the manga market to exceed its 1995 peak in 2020.

One aspect of manga production that has remained constant in the magazine and e-book eras, and the focus of this chapter is the editor-in-charge. While not all manga pass through the hands of editors at major publishing houses – fan-produced *dōjinshi* and independent pieces being two examples – any discussion of Japan's extensive manga market must acknowledge their contribution. The principal task of editors is to sell comics, and so they strive to have artists (*mangaka*) create lucrative narratives, or they market existing works. Editors must motivate their *mangaka*, which is best achieved by allowing them artistic freedom. But as company employees, editors ultimately have to prioritize the commodity value of manga, sometimes at the expense of aesthetic considerations or sociopolitical relevance. They have to incentivize artists to create narratives that gel with the profile of their magazine or platform and the projected reader preferences. In manga magazines for elementary school girls such as *Ribon* and *Ciao*, for example, the illustration of characters with large eyes covering at least one third of the face is nonnegotiable. Manga magazines on BL (boys love) or TL (teens love) – the latter containing sexual content for older female readers – devote more than half of their pages to sex scenes. If a scene shows the protagonist entering the room of their love interest, the editor would ask the artist to picture the moment when the latter is changing clothes in order to provide a "service scene" (industry jargon referring to the exposure of body parts regardless of gender). This might suggest that editors actually hinder artistic freedom, but such scenes do well also in the noncorporate fan-cultural market. Derivative *dōjinshi* productions based on familiar characters are especially convenient as explanations about relationships are rendered superfluous in that fictional domain.

Ninety percent of all noncorporate publications are not economically viable and do not have to be, whereas for publishers, manga is a "service commodity." As editor Naoko Yamauchi succinctly observed: "Manga is just one way among many others of having an enjoyable time ... and we cannot lose out on providing entertainment of thirty minutes or an hour."[4] Osamu Tezuka, the legendary pioneer of graphic narratives in Japan, maintained that "manga is originally a sensual media ... with ridiculous contents."[5] Indeed, since the 1960s, manga has boasted a firm standing in the Japanese economy and society, not through compliance to mainstream norms or overcoming its reputation as low-brow culture by means of respectable content but rather by continuously offering captivating and commercially successful narratives. It is precisely this commercial power that afforded manga a position that could no longer be ignored.

Corporate Agent

Japan's comics culture relies on "the contentious relationship between editors and artists [which] is at once the crux and the crucible of manga production."[6] But "[i]t is difficult to discuss the work of editors because it is the editor's job to mask their own influence and facilitate the creativity of others"[7] – this applies equally to Japanese and non-Japanese settings despite significant differences in actual authority. The role of manga editors is multifaceted. They act as mediators between the primary creator, the publisher's sales department, wholesalers and retailers, journalists, casual readers, and fandoms. They coordinate the production process, ease the management burden of the *mangaka*, compile useful background material, and procure publications or tickets to performances and exhibitions organized by the same media corporation. They are also the strongest advocates for the *mangaka* in editorial meetings, where they seek to secure a place for their artists in the next magazine issue.

Once a serial has begun, the editor provides the best environment possible for the artist: introducing assistants, making arrangements for research-related interviews, organizing the schedule, and keeping track of deadlines. In the past, editors even ran personal errands for their artists, filling refrigerators or buying cigarettes in the middle of the night. Importantly, editors format and package the manga such that it resonates with potential readers. It is their responsibility, for example, to come up with sensational catchphrases and spectacular typography that appear on the frontispiece of magazine installments or the "belly-band" strip (*obi*) of *tankōbon* editions. They use any means available to generate attention, or what is now referred to as online "buzz" (*bazuru*), ranging from banner leaks to word-of-mouth recommendations and all kinds of ranking in manga criticism. Editors are generally in charge of a manga's lettering, including in the pre-digital era the actual pasting of typed words onto the manuscript pages and the selection of fonts, some of which are magazine-specific.

The relationship between magazine artists and editors has been likened, respectively, to that between subordinate and superior or blue-collar and white-collar workers. In the mid-1990s, during the boom of magazine sales, it was observed from an outside perspective that "[m]anga editors in large companies formed a distinctive and homogenous social group. All had graduated from a high-ranking university and succeeded in entering a prestigious publishing company immediately on graduation. Here they received social prestige and high monthly salaries. Most intended to remain in the company until they retired."[8]

In order to become an editor, an individual is required to take an "entrance examination" for a publishing company, and the traditional Big Three – Kodansha, Shogakukan, and Shueisha – are known for setting particularly difficult tests. It is also a fact that the generation of editors who drove the magazine boom in the mid-1990s had not initially sought out manga as a professional focus. Instead, they aimed for fashion magazines (in the case of Kodansha) or educational books (in the case of Shogakukan). Since the 2000s, however, universities have established programs in manga editing, and today even general job search sites advertise manga-specific editing positions.

East Asian circumstances are equally at play when dealing with hierarchies between artist and editor – namely, that these hierarchies rest on ranks related to age and social standing, such as senior versus junior or full-fledged member of society (*shakaijin*) versus apprentice, rather than on social class. Manga artists have often made their debut at a young age, without any formal education, whereas entrance into a media corporation has always required at least a bachelor's degree. Yet regardless of age, editors normally show respect for their artists' skills and address them with the honorific term, *sensei*.

The editor-in-charge system took hold in the heyday of manga magazines between the 1960s and the late 1990s. Unlike previously, when comics had been published in highly diverse book formats, the magazine format relied on serialization. This necessitated special efforts in securing "contents" to fill the issues. In the early days from the late 1950s to the late 1960s, magazine editors reached out to artists who had already proven themselves in other areas, such as rental comics (*kashihon manga*), and who were in such high demand that they always had several serials at different magazines running in tandem. Occasionally, they would even confine *mangaka* to a hotel room to hide them from rival magazines and to push them to draw the next installment for their magazine first.[9] Tezuka, for example, was well known for taking pleasure in editorial scuffles. In view of the fierce competition, a latecomer such as *Shōnen Jump* (launched in 1968) had to think of other strategies than the engagement of established artists. They shifted their focus to beginners, which was to change the role of editors in general, making it their main occupation to find and nurture talented newcomers.

While editors want their artists to create bestsellers, it is also their task to convince an artist to discontinue a serial that the editorial board finds lacking. Japanese publishers aim for works that achieve much more than just covering all related production costs. According to Takashi Nagasaki, editor-in-charge of the *mangaka* Naoki Urasawa, the million-sellers publishers envision are intended to appeal to an audience beyond the artist's fan base, which makes it harder for the artist to picture the readership they are expected to accommodate.[10] But it is not only editors who wish for commercial success. Artists, too, share the common goal of selling their work. The payment for a magazine serial barely allows artists to recoup production costs; it is only with the royalties for a *tankōbon* edition that they actually begin to earn money. The same applies to the publisher (although not necessarily with regard to webcomics because of the different initial costs). A *tankōbon* needs to sell a minimum of 20,000 copies to cover costs; profitability begins from the sale of 50,000 copies, reaching hit status with 100,000.

In order to sell that many and more, editors have to make sure that artists comply to the magazine's target and publication rhythm. *Weekly Shōnen Jump*, for example, requires ten (or more) original pages from scratch each week and concurrently the compilation of the related *tankōbon* volumes. Consequently, background drawings and finishing are allocated to assistants, whose instruction takes up time even if they are well trained. Artists also need to reserve time for their editor-in-charge, who checks the rough draft of each installment and might enforce changes dealing with the orientation of the narrative and the visual design. Story contents and layout are frequently revised as a result of these meetings. Ultimately no manga is published without the editor's approval. Corporate manga are thus in fact coproductions between artist and editor, which makes it difficult for auteurs to emerge.

After a first discussion of the story contents with the editor, the artist creates a layout sketch containing the dialogue lines, a rough panel breakdown, and abbreviated character images, that is, a *nēmu* (Fig. 14.1). The loanword *nēmu* (from the English *name*) dates back to the 1950s when these storyboards only consisted of words. The *nēmu* is checked by the editor. Artists – both newcomers and veterans – often lose sight of the reader's affective involvement, which is vital for corporate manga serials, and so they are generally asked to submit several subsequent revisions of their storyboard.[11]

Figure 14.1 Bon Won Koo, a page of a drawn storyboard (*nēmu*).

Editors usually prioritize how a character perceives a certain situation, over objectively introducing this situation up front. An example of editorial direction is illustrated in Figure 14.2a–c: First, we are shown an astronaut in space, without any pictorial runes (Fig. 14.2a). If flowers are scattered around the head, the character appears happy (Fig. 14.2b), but if the flowers are replaced by sweat drops, the character looks as if in crisis (Fig. 14.2c). Clearly, the situation can be conveyed without bringing any facial expression into play. If the next scene is to feature the astronaut looking out into space (Fig. 14.3a), the editor would probably ask the artist to place a close-up of the character (Fig. 14.3b) before an image of the vast universe – in other words, to present the agent of the gaze first in order to raise the tension and make the reader share the character's sensation.

A famous insider example of such editorial direction is a tear-jerking scene in volume 6 of Naoki Urasawa's *Pluto*,[12] which omits all tears until the last two panels. When the robots Gesicht and Astro Boy die, Gesicht's wife Helena meets Astro Boy's creator Dr. Tenma, who thus far has exhibited little affection for his substitute son. Helena is also a robot, but for the first time she has an indescribable feeling of loss. Tenma explains to her that

Figure 14.2a-c Bon Won Koo, example of a character's mental state specified by means of pictorial runes.

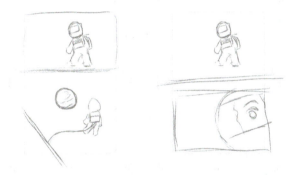

Figure 14.3a-b Bon Won Koo, example of panel sequence: (a) foregrounding the character's situation; (b) foregrounding the character's response to the situation.

humans cry at such moments and that it is acceptable to feign it. Eventually, Helena bursts into tears, as does Tenma. In actual fact, Helena had been emotional from the outset, but editor Nagasaki suggested to keep her subtly changing face tearless until the final two panels. Thanks to this suspension, the feigned looks real, and the sudden fit of weeping at the end conveys the intense sadness felt.[13]

Collaborator of the *Mangaka*

Approximately 6,000 people worked as *mangaka* in 2011.[14] One decade later, around 2,500 artists were active, as deducible from the number of manga releases given above, but this number does not include artists who work exclusively in the area of digital comics. Some of the artists have undergone self-study; most have graduated from one of the approximately 100 vocational schools and 22 art colleges and universities that offer programs.

While the majority of graduates do not ultimately produce magazine serials, they are nonetheless able to make a living, for example, by creating manga-style illustrations for light novels, textbooks and manuals in comics format, one-pagers for journals, and *yonkoma* comic strips for fashion magazines.

Those hoping to run a serialized narrative in a major magazine must convince an editor of their potential and then commit to a relationship of mutual trust – just as the characters do in the famous *Jump* series *Bakuman* (2008–12) by Tsugumi Ohba and Takeshi Obata.[15] Although there are several ways to debut as a *mangaka* in Japan, there is no way around an editor-in-charge. Traditionally, manga magazines require that manuscripts are brought in directly (*mochikomi*). Appointments are made by phone, and the editor who answers the call will then look over the manuscript and provide direct feedback. Meetings occasionally take place at manga-related events, such as the Comic Market (Comiket or Comike), where editorial departments have booths. The main purpose of the first manuscript is to demonstrate the potential of the artist to the editor and for the applicant to receive insider feedback regarding the type of story development, characters, and settings preferred by the respective magazine. This may prove useful for the applicant's future, even if the editor does not commit to publishing the work. Sometimes the applicant is encouraged to submit their manuscript to the magazine's next rookie award competition.

In the best-case scenario, the applicant is given the editor's contact information, but this does not guarantee anything. The editor might reject all subsequent revisions of the manuscript, or the artist might go elsewhere to work with another editor or another magazine. This is not surprising since an official relationship with the publisher would not have yet been established at this stage. While the "bringing in" of the manuscript represents the first informal step, the second is a formal entry, known as *tōkō*, to be reviewed by a number of editorial staff members at the same department. Most publishers organize manga contests, with major magazines holding and sponsoring monthly rookie awards and large-scale events once or twice a year. The submissions are evaluated and ranked within the editorial department. The winners receive prize money, merchandise, and, above all, a chance to debut their work. But non-winners, too, may be contacted by an editor, and many departments return the submitted manuscripts with practical feedback. It clearly makes a difference in the final ranking whether applicants already have an editor supporting them in editorial meetings.

In recent years, headhunting on the internet has become increasingly common via social media such as Pixiv, portals such as Shueisha's *Jump Rookie* and *MangaMee*, or Kodansha's *Days Neo*. Anyone can post, but unlike the *mochikomi* and *tōkō* noted above, there is no guarantee that editors will actually look over the posted manuscript. Webtoon platforms like Comico's *Challenge* or Line Manga's *Indies* also offer outlets for aspiring manga artists: Anyone can read these comics for free, including editors. This method of scouting for promising artists resembles practices focused on *dōjinshi* circles or personal websites, but with the added advantage of an already existing fan base for the artist in question. As Webtoons are usually free of charge in the beginning, editors prefer to promote extended serials from the outset over one-shots.

Very few artists are entrusted with a serial immediately after winning an award or having been scouted. In some cases, the first installment, or a prequel one-shot of a serial, is released to gauge reader response, often appearing in sister magazines that have the term *bessatsu*, or "separate volume," in their titles. But formal contracts are usually not signed when a serialization is decided upon. Unlike Webtoons, magazine serials regularly proceed based on verbal agreements. Payments are made on a page-by-page basis, ranging in 2021 from 5,000 to 10,000 yen for a *mangaka*'s first serial. The lack of a contract may seem detrimental, but many artists prefer the freedom of not being legally bound to a specific editor or magazine. Exceptions are *Weekly Shōnen Jump* and *Weekly Shōnen Magazine*, which have their artists enter into exclusive contracts, preventing them from working for other magazines during the contracted period. In return, artists receive a manuscript honorarium, a contract fee, and remuneration even after the conclusion of the serial. Most publishers will sign a formal contract with the artist when a manga under serialization is to be republished in the *tankōbon* format. For commercial purposes, the publisher is entrusted with the copyright for five years, which includes media-mix development, and the artist may expect 10 to 20 percent of *tankōbon* sales in return, while holding the original copyright. Yet, with the publication rights, the media corporation acquires a unique form of social control: "[I]nstead of controlling the copyright work as such, they manage the author and therefore influence the right holder."[16]

Compared to printed magazine serials, Webtoons are in color, and artists are paid not by page but by weekly installment – as of 2021 this was 50,000 yen for newcomers. One installment consists of sixty to ninety panels, which corresponds roughly to ten manuscript pages. Webtoons also differ from paper-based manga in that they are more frequently produced with a division of labor between key drawings, backgrounds and effects, coloring, and finishing. If Webtoons are produced within such a studio system, the involved parties have to be paid individually: the storyboard artist; the illustrator, who may also apply basic colors and effects; and the colorist. If an already popular webnovel is acquired up front, the storyboard artist receives around 30,000 yen per installment and the illustrator around 50,000–80,000 yen, as well as eventual royalties. Coloring is compensated hourly. An installment created by such a team of professionals is of higher quality and more costly than one by an individual artist who performs all tasks. If republished in the *tankōbon* format (which is less often the case than with print magazine serials), incentives are paid to artists (but not colorists) depending on the ultimate popularity.

Contracts are frequently concluded through agencies that take a 5 to 20 percent commission of the actual income. A *mangaka* may receive a guaranteed minimum of 200,000 yen a month for a weekly Webtoon serial from the agency. This is equivalent to a starting salary in Japan and provides more security than the actual clicks upon which the pay was dependent previously. If calculating the income per page, as is standard in print magazines, an average of thirty-two monthly pages at 5,000 yen would amount to 160,000 yen. Although assistants are not required for the production of thirty-two pages – an aspect that keeps the expenses lower than in a weekly magazine – the *mangaka*'s income is still poor. As a result, artists who work for monthlies often serve as assistants for more established colleagues until they can receive higher pay. If they manage to run a weekly serial with sixteen pages at 10,000 yen per page, their monthly income will be quite good. The hiring of assistants and the renting of a studio place comes from their overall income, however, frequently leaving them no more than 200,000 yen after taxes. This makes royalties from *tankōbon* and the incentives from e-book editions so vital.

Conclusion

Manga has used its commercial strength to secure a place in both national and global culture, an achievement made possible in great measure by the "invisible" editors. Their influence on manga narratives is difficult to quantify, and outside manga culture it is often viewed with suspicion. Foreign critics often blame editors (and editorial departments) for manga's restraint with regard to the representation of sociopolitical issues or mold-breaking aesthetic innovation. In fact, a number of recognizable political expressions in recent narratives and overt statements by artists related to imperial Japan and World War II – as well as nuclear power and the Fukushima nuclear-reactor disaster in 2011 – have caused a backlash in Japan and abroad that publishers feared would hamper business. *Oishinbo* (1983–) by Tetsu Kariya and Akira Hanesaki in 2014, *Attack on Titan* (*Shingeki no kyojin*, 2009–) by Hajime Isayama in 2013, and *My Hero Academia* (2014–) by Kōhei Horikoshi in 2020 are exemplary of this trend. As shown above, however, editors are more than corporate agents. They also serve as the *mangaka*'s manager or even collaborator. Moreover, they represent the audience of their specific magazine or platform. Shedding light on editors and their diversity therefore permits an examination of "comics as the product of cultural ecologies: the people, places, cultural practices and interactions that localize around specific publishers and imprints," and an acknowledgment of "other sources [than authorial intent or political representation] from which a work draws meaning."[17]

Corporate manga has foregrounded readership over authorship, and the latter has relied more on collaborative than on individual authorship, even if the legal practice continues to privilege the latter: "[D]espite the number of people involved in creating a Manga, both technically and creatively, authorship and with it the copyright remains focused on the Mangaka himself."[18] But things are changing. Traditionally, the majority of editors were male employees of media corporations[19] – even in the female manga genres – but since the 2000s more and more women have come to the fore, and a significant number of employees are leaving publishing houses to work independently. Recently, editors have become more visible because of the increased role of distribution. Some are in fact now credited as scenario authors, idea pitchers, and story coproducers, heralding perhaps a future when editorial creativity is afforded its due in manga studies.

Notes

1. In 2020, the Japanese market amounted to about 6.536 billion USD, followed by the US with 1.229 billion USD, China with 0.983 billion USD, and France with 0.286 billion USD. Korea Creative Content Agency, *2021 Cartoon Industry White Paper* (Najoo: KOCCA, 2021), 146–203.
2. Hiroshi Yamamori, *"Komikkusu" no media-shi* (Tokyo: Seikyūsha, 2019).
3. Shigeo Nishimura, *Manga no henshūjutsu* (Tokyo: Byakuya Shobō, 1999), 3. For an overview in English, see Enno and Jaqueline Berndt, "Magazines and Books: Changes in the Manga Market." In Jaqueline Berndt, *Manga: Medium, Kunst und Material/Manga: Medium, Art and Material*, Leipziger Ostasien-Studien 18 (Leipzig: Leipziger Universitätsverlag, 2015), 227–39.
4. Cited in Shunsuke Kimura, *Manga henshūsha* (Tokyo: Film Art-sha, 2015), 118. Translation from Japanese by the author.
5. Osamu Tezuka, *Denshi shosekiban Tezuka Osamu kōenshū* (Tokyo: Tezuka Production, 2014), Kindle, based on Osamu Tezuka, *Miraijin e no messēji* (Tokyo: Iwanami, 1986).
6. Jennifer Prough, *Straight from the Heart: Gender, Intimacy, and the Cultural Production of Shōjo Manga* (Honolulu: University of Hawai'i Press, 2011), 75; also Chapter 4, "Affective Labor: Gender, Generation, and Consumption in the Production of Shōjo Manga," 89–109.

7. Keith Friedlander, "The Editor, the Author Function, and the Social Function: A Methodological Survey," *Journal of Graphic Novels and Comics*, 9, no. 2 (2018): 159.
8. Sharon Kinsella, *Adult Manga: Culture & Power in Contemporary Japanese Society* (Honolulu: University of Hawai'i Press, 2000), 169.
9. Akira Maruyama, *Manga no kanzume: Tezuka Osamu to Tokiwa-sō no nakama tachi* (Tokyo: Horupu Shuppan, 1993), 24–40.
10. Takashi Nagasaki, "Manga henshūsha ga mita megahitto no hōsoku," *KINO*, 1 (2006): 13.
11. Tōru Ishii, *Manga henshūsha no tame no kyōkasho* (Tokyo: Kodansha, 2015), 112–13.
12. Naoki Urasawa and Takashi Nagasaki, *Pluto 6* (Tokyo: Shogakukan, 2008), 190.
13. Ken'ichirō Moteki, *NHK "Purofeshonaru" seisakuhan, Purofeshonaru: shigoto no ryūgi – Nagasaki Takashi, manga henshūsha, ai to kakugo no hitto mēkā* (Tokyo: NHK Shuppan, 2013), 13–14.
14. Last data collection conducted in 2011: http://dotplace.jp/archives/16322.
15. For the publisher's promotion activities related to "behind-the-scenes" programs, see Bryan Hikari Hartzheim, "Making of a Mangaka: Industrial Reflexivity and Shueisha's Weekly Shōnen Jump," *Television and New Media*, 22, no. 5 (2021): 570–87.
16. Simone Schroff, "An Alternative Universe? Authors as Copyright Owners – The Case of the Japanese Manga Industry," *Creative Industries Journal*, 12, no. 1 (2019): 144.
17. Friedlander, "The Editor, the Author Function, and the Social Function," 161–62.
18. Schroff, "An Alternative Universe?," 142.
19. Indicative of the traditional male dominance are the four editor interviews in *The Citi Exhibition Manga*, edited by Nicole Coolidge Rousmaniere and Matsuba Ryoko (London: Thames & Hudson, 2019), 84–99.

15

RENATO RIVERA RUSCA

Anime Production, Decentralized

Anime has achieved broad mainstream acceptance in the global media environment, and the increased interest in this field has uncovered many issues pertaining to its production, such as understaffed studios, overworked and underpaid animators, and contractions attributable to the COVID-19 pandemic. Recent advances in the digitalization of the production process allow for smoother interaction inside and outside of the main hub of production studios concentrated in the west of Tokyo in Koganei, Mitaka, Musashino, Nerima, and Suginami. As a result, it has become easier to establish regional bases and collaborate remotely. This chapter will examine several regional communities in Japan that have incorporated animation production facilities into their economic development plans in an attempt to attract both tourists and new residents and to reinvigorate local society.

In Japan, a typical animated project is first planned and advanced through a committee system that consists of several companies, each contributing to the production budget for a later return on their investment, with profits derived from royalties, merchandise and media sales, and license payments, among other things. While these companies might be in the "business" of anime, most are not involved in the actual production. This is the domain of the studios, the majority of which are hired by production committees to manage the medium-specific process of assembling the animation, and distinct from the overall multimedia packaging and dissemination of an intellectual property through its various incarnations. Due to the sheer number of required resources, it is virtually impossible for individual series or movies to be produced solely by a single animation studio. Instead, managing studios subcontract other studios to handle the diverse facets of the production. In turn, these studios usually commission freelancers to work on specific parts.

This rigidly managed production system gave rise to a complex patchwork of interlocking paperwork, comprising pencil-drawn layouts, keyframes, photography (compositing) timesheets, and other materials. Quick turnarounds from all parties concerned are vital. Therefore, studios until recently had to be located in close proximity to one another, so that tireless production assistants could hand-courier materials between them in large envelopes. In 2016, for example, there were 622 animation studios in Japan, of which 542 (87.1 percent) were based in the metropolitan area of Tokyo. In the city of Suginami alone there were 138 studios, a doubling from 70 in 2011 (the year of the last survey), and in Nerima it was 103, which may illustrate the geographically tight-knit nature of the studio network.[1]

While Tokyo's dominance sustains a growth in production houses, the spread across the archipelago is noteworthy, with Hokkaido witnessing an increase in anime studios from three to nine, Niigata from two to five, and Fukuoka from four to ten. Other areas have also emerged as new home bases for digital studios, including Akita, Tochigi, Wakayama, Aichi, and Okayama Prefectures.[2] Thus, the rise in digital production methods and the gradual shift away from pencil-on-paper materials have become a driving force in the industry's expansion into regional areas.

In actual fact, a majority of the newcomers are secondary facilities, such as Asahi Productions in Miyagi Prefecture, which receives work from its head office in Nerima, Tokyo. In many instances, the new production sites serve a specific function in the overall "assembly line," as opposed to the multidivisional studios that can handle all stages. One might focus on background art, another on compositing images, while a third deals with the actual animation process (sakuga).

The COVID-19 pandemic accelerated the shift to remote working in the animation industry. Initially, the greatest problem was the feasibility of vocal performance recording, which in Japan is rarely conducted in isolation – voice actors usually meet in the recording studio and play off each other's reactions. By contrast, sakuga artists were less impacted by the pandemic. Before then, it was still common for the sakuga division to use pencil and paper, with the materials digitized later and manipulated on computer at the coloring and compositing stages. This allowed freelance artists to work from home since no individual investment in technical equipment was required. During the pandemic the issue of digitization came to the fore, but progress was slow due to the lack of standardized software, as well as the persistent practice of physically taxiing envelopes from place to place around the city. As long as this practice continues, the possibility of working online remotely cannot be fully realized, thus the need for the existing process to be streamlined.

AsuraFilm, for example, a studio based in Asagaya in western Tokyo, has smaller divisions in Okayama and Ishikawa Prefectures, and even

Okinawa. The Okayama studio is located in the rural city of Ibara in a single-roomed refitted storage annex of a residential house that can accommodate around eight people. The space is used exclusively for the compositing stage of production – that is, the combination of the different layers, including character drawings, background art, and computer-generated elements. Compositing is now entirely digital, and therefore relatively few paper documents and materials require circulation. Thus, AsuraFilm can be involved concurrently in dozens of top-tier global titles, such as *Pokémon* (*Pocket Monster*, 1997–) and *SSSS. Gridman* (2018). But examples like this represent only small steps within the scope of the entire industry. In order to truly expand, companies in regional areas must go beyond serving as subcontracted entities and instead establish themselves as independent creative bases so as to make themselves eligible for licensing revenue. This necessitates capital as well as political support by the local communities.

A case in point is the animation studio Ekakiya, located in the city of Sōja in Okayama Prefecture. Formed in 2016 after the former Tezuka Productions and Studio Ghibli veteran staffer Miyoko Kobayashi had returned to her hometown to care for her father,[3] Ekakiya has become a viable, albeit small, remote studio that accepts contracts for hand-drawn work on anime, such as the series *JoJo's Bizarre Adventure: Diamond is Unbreakable* (*Jojo no kimyōna bōken: daiyamondo wa kudakenai*, 2016), and the movie *Weathering With You* (*Tenki no ko*, 2019). Although Ekakiya is independent and may not be a wholly owned subsidiary of a larger Tokyo-based corporation, it is nevertheless a studio primarily focused on subcontracted production work sourced from Tokyo. For that reason, it does not own intellectual property that can be licensed out.

Anime "Pilgrimages" and New Business Strategies

Anime viewers tend to travel to real-life locations known from anime in order to experience the respective storyworld. This phenomenon is labeled "sacred pilgrimage" (*seichi junrei*), and it can be traced to the 1970s and the *World Masterpiece Theater* (*Sekai meisaku gekijō*), which broadcasted series such as *Heidi, Girl of the Alps* (*Arupusu no shōjo Haiji*, 1974) and *A Dog of Flanders* (*Furandāsu no inu*, 1975). Their popularity led to increased overseas tourism to destinations like the Swiss Alps and Antwerp.[4] In recent years, the economic impact of anime pilgrimages in Japan has been examined in great depth[5] and is understood as cultivating a mutually beneficial relationship between normally urban-centric affluent consumers and more rural communities.

The recognition of such pilgrimages (and the profitability thereof) escalated following the successful collaboration of Washinomiya Shrine in Saitama with the production committee of the popular anime *Lucky Star* (2007). This resulted in sales of goods and merchandise, such as specially designed *ema* prayer tablets and *o-mamori* good-luck charms with the characters from the show. From 2008 onward, the Washinomiya Chamber of Commerce arranged for *Lucky Star* to be a permanent fixture, almost synonymous with the shrine in having objects such as a *mikoshi* – a palanquin housing sacred spirits carried during local festivals – featuring a *Lucky Star* design. This attracted 50,000 visitors to the festival that year.[6] The example of Washinomiya Shrine is evidence that the symbiosis between anime production committees and local governments could generate new possibilities for business models, and a working relationship between local communities and the entertainment sector.

While in many ways accidental and trial-and-error, the synergy in the strategy of local government and media companies joining forces to create a new brand of content-based tourism nevertheless represented a paradigm shift in the anime industry. This set in motion a trend that evolved into further interindustry collaborations. By the time of the release of the anime series *Lagrange: The Flower of Rin-ne* (*Rinne no raguranje*, 2011), this synergy had become almost second nature to the planning and launch of any new intellectual property. The futuristic setting of *Lagrange* featured considerable fictional state-of-the-art technology, and the mechanical designs were not handled in-house at a production studio, rather contracted to the automobile manufacturer Nissan. Furthermore, the story was set in the picturesque city of Kamogawa in Chiba Prefecture, which was little altered except for the insertion of a fictional sci-fi-styled robot base. The show is therefore a culmination of interindustry collaborations, so much so that brochures and tourist information for Kamogawa were distributed at the public premiere of the first episode held at the Nissan Global Headquarters in Yokohama. The region's official involvement with the production committee became even more intensified during production of the second season.

Such innovative strategies should not be viewed as an extra for both the tourism and anime industries. These types of collaborative models have become essential, not only for their profitability but also for the very survival of many of the communities and businesses concerned. The ongoing benefits of this formula are predicated on the repetition of a cycle – that is, the end user travels to the location where they stay and spend money, with producers continuing to cultivate demand by maintaining interest in the region through the hosting of events and generating more consumable content.

Anime as a Tool for Regional Revitalization

Even before the COVID-19 outbreak, the pilgrimage strategy as a pillar of both anime business and regional sustainability was already displaying certain weaknesses. For example, the long-term profitability of such pilgrimages is dependent on short-term visitors, and the anime that drives the flow of users in the first place is commercially focused on the affluent urban areas where young consumers reside. Promotion utilizes the popularity of preexistent intellectual property and relies on its established user base to generate revenue through tie-ins. A sustainable cycle of creation, however, requires an extended period before it can generate substantial results.

The "Manga Kingdom Tottori" is an example of inbound tourism, which capitalizes not on Tottori as a specific anime setting but rather on the fact that it is the hometown of famous creators. Tottori Prefecture has a reputation as being the home of manga artists such as Goshō Aoyama and Shigeru Mizuki, a fact that has been exploited to offset the impact of depopulation in the region and to maintain its status as a tourist destination for fans. This is achieved through an ongoing series of events and the promotion of attractions, including the rebranding of facilities and utilities, such as the "Detective Conan Sand Dunes Airport" and the "Detective Conan/Kitarō Train," and regular local events, most notably the Shigeru Mizuki Birthday Celebration and Detective Conan Festival. The prefecture has also organized annual manga and vocal performance competitions (the latter was mounted with online entries for the 2020 edition; it was canceled in 2021 due to COVID-19).

Another analogous example is the city of Ishinomaki in Miyagi Prefecture, birthplace of the famed manga artist Shōtarō Ishinomori and today the location of the Ishinomori Manga Museum. The area surrounding this unusual building and the path leading from it to the local train station are lined with images and life-size statues of manga characters to create the tourist attraction known as the "Ishinomaki Manga Road." The interior of the station features stained glasswork of characters from Ishinomori's work, and some of the trains running between there and Sendai are also decorated with Ishinomori manga designs. The local gift stores have an array of manga-related items, mostly unique to the area. Together, these kinds of operations serve to promote the respective region as a popular destination of inbound fan tourism.

In contrast, the city of Takahashi in Okayama Prefecture is attempting to rebrand itself by means of anime. It achieves this not by following the example of places like Tottori Prefecture or Ishinomaki but rather by establishing itself as a viable hub where creators can live, produce marketable contents, and contribute to the local economy through job creation, while at the same time nurturing the next generation of artists and producers. Moreover, a digitally based network ensures that business partners do not need to be in the same country, thereby taking advantage of the increased global demand for Japanese creative contents by forming international partnerships and aiming at an overseas audience. This is offset against the need to cater primarily to a shrinking domestic market.

In the case of Takahashi, three main actors have been engaged in a sustainable strategy: the local Kibi International University (KIU), the animation studio Machiken (short for Bitchū-Takahashi Machizukuri Kenkyūsho), and the local government. The university is a private institution that has a School of Animation Culture, where students learn the history and techniques of both Japanese and international animation. Machiken was established as part of a regional revitalization project, financed in part with local government subsidies for the first five years of operation, and devised primarily for international coproductions, not subcontracted projects from Tokyo-based studios. This aspect of globalization was touted as a major plus for the Machiken venture in an article by the local news media on the internship program for international students at KIU's Machiken studio.[7] Takahashi's Chamber of Commerce managed the general direction of Machiken and the funds of the company and its projects, while guaranteeing that the company's output remained its own property, thus contributing directly to the local economy.

The concept of pilgrimage is not new to Takahashi. Its historic architecture, in particular, the Fukiya district, its natural landscape, and its castle have made it a destination for dozens of live-action films, from the *Tora-san* series (*Otoko wa tsurai yo*, 1968–) to *The Battery* (2007), with the latest being the 2021 *Baragaki: Unbroken Samurai* (*Moeyo ken*). The city realized, however, that a reliance on tourism alone would not avert near-certain bankruptcy and a population downturn. Thus, in recent years, it has attempted to generate interest in Takahashi as a focal point for creative community activities.

As in Tottori and in many other regional areas in Japan, Takahashi has experienced depopulation, but the city witnesses a constant influx of young people entering KIU. The connection between Machiken and the university's School of Animation Culture was expected to help graduates secure employment in their area of study without having to relocate to Tokyo. By offering them a place to settle down, they would form the core of a new creative phase in the city's long-term planning. Yet many of the university's students and teaching staff commute from neighboring cities, such as Okayama and Sōja, that have more residential amenities and services. Moreover, many of the students in Takahashi are in fact international students who will most likely return to their home countries once their studies were completed.

A stronger network between the various cultural institutions in Takahashi might have manifested had they worked together toward a clear mutual goal and experienced the benefits to be gained from such collaboration. After all, Takahashi is also the home to the famous Kibi Kawakami Fureai Manga Museum, a rather unique space housing a vast collection of historic comics. Notably, this museum and Machiken have never collaborated on a community project or event – in contradistinction to the Hishio Center for Cultural Exchange in Maniwa described in the next section.

From Grassroots and Community-Focused Endeavors to Market Expansion

Government strategies concentrate on maximizing productivity by conjoining industry and community at an administration level incentivized by grants from public funds, but the potential for success also exists at a grassroots level – namely, a production environment based on craftsmanship and personal interrelations.

An example of the impact of grassroots initiatives is the city of Maniwa in Okayama Prefecture, where local town planners have organized the Katsuyama Animation Showcase (later rebranded as the Maniwa Animation Festival), a series of events aimed at the local population for the purposes of education and community-building.[8] At first glance it might resemble the efforts of Takahashi. Yet the key to its success lay in the wish to provide a space that young people can use as a sandbox for stimulating innovation and creativity through a community-oriented menu of fun and play, rather than a rigid system that appears task-based and profit-driven. Maniwa's pledge for inclusivity is evident in events such as the *Animation Mapping*, held every summer from 2013 to 2019, during which time the town was brought to life at night with the projection of animated works on the facades of the traditional buildings of the Katsuyama townscape.[9]

The driving creative force behind many of these events in Maniwa is the independent illustrator and animation auteur Taku Furukawa, who is today the chairman of the Japan Animation Association (Nihon Animation Kyōkai). He began his career in animation working at studio TCJ (Television Corporation of Japan Co., Ltd., today Eiken) in the 1960s. TCJ famously made its name producing an adaptation of Mitsuteru Yokoyama's popular manga *Iron Man No. 28* (*Tetsujin 28-gō*) in 1963 (adapted into English by Fred Ladd as *Gigantor* the next year), the same year that *Astro Boy* (*Tetsuwan Atom*) was launched as the first weekly thirty-minute episodic animated series by Osamu Tezuka's company Mushi Production. Furukawa's work has typically been seen on the film festival circuit, not on mainstream television, and he recalls how he gradually felt a dissonance between the requisites of an anime studio sustaining weekly televised broadcasts and his own artistic aspirations, in particular, after being inspired by a book of Saul Steinberg illustrations.[10] His long involvement in the animation festivals in Maniwa and the town's attempts to revitalize the community through participatory art activities calls to mind a grassroots spirit that does not appear to the same extent in Takahashi, despite the two being neighboring cities.

A New Contender

In January 2022, the Kōchi prefectural government stated that it would host a series of ventures with the goal of using anime to revitalize the local economies of smaller cities and towns and to alleviate some of the effects of depopulation.[11] Touting regional revitalization through a stimulus of the local economy, as well as alleviating the lack of human resources in the anime industry, the goals proposed in the Kōchi project seem almost identical to those envisioned by the city of Takahashi. The Kōchi initiative is of a larger scale, however, especially when considering that it encompasses the three cities of Kōchi, Nankoku, and Susaki, together with the Kōchi Shinyō Kinko Bank and the prefectural government.

During the press conference announcing the project, the chairperson of the Kōchi Shinyō Kinko Bank, Kurumi Yamazaki, noted that they would "solve the issues concerning the futures of both the anime industry and Kōchi through the power of creativity and digital technology,"[12] thus announcing the establishment of the anime production company Studio Eight Colors. Although similar to Machiken in the sense that it is a studio intended to boost the local economy, Eight Colors differs in its aims to function as a service provider for Tokyo-based productions, specifically for a process known as digital repair that involves the redrawing, retouching, and correcting of preexisting artwork and footage. Digital repair is easily and quickly performed remotely; it is particularly useful when quick turnaround times are crucial and the main studio is understaffed and overburdened. One can then assume that at least initially the Kōchi studio would need to rely on a Tokyo-based studio to receive commissions (similar to Ekakiya in Kurashiki). As part of this process, local staff would receive on-the-job training, eventually leading to greater projects. A plan to expand the network to encompass numerous regional studios has been suggested.

Eight Colors serves as a regional, independent studio, reliant on subcontracted work by Tokyo firms. Conversely, Machiken's original, and perhaps idealistic, ambition was to circumvent the Tokyo network from the start. Instead of taking on commissions, which would garner a short-term fee but no additional benefits other than possibly royalties, Machiken's goal was for the studio to develop and produce its own intellectual property. The vast majority of anime production companies operate on a work-for-hire basis, and Machiken's intention was to be one of the rare studios outside Tokyo that would own the copyright to their work, thereby ensuring longer term profits in licensing it to other players in various industries and markets. This was one of the key strengths of the Machiken plan, which, had it been successful, would have guaranteed a steady flow of revenue into the local economy through licensing deals alone. Yet despite the boldness of its plan, the studio closed prematurely after securing partnership deals for overseas coproductions. This was attributed to the inexperience of the risk-averse upper management in the development of creative work and the wariness of the stockholders once they realized that the initial investment would only begin to show returns after a number of years, as opposed to the minor but immediate profits from work outsourced from Tokyo. Added to this were record-breaking rains and floods in 2018 that caused the Takahashi River to breach its banks, which impacted the Machiken studio and necessitated the reapportioning of the city's funds to reconstruction efforts.

Conclusion

The cases of Ekakiya, Machiken, and more recently Eight Colors offer insightful observations into the increasing trend of "decentralized" animation production in areas such as Okayama and Kōchi prefectures. It is also important to focus on their corporate makeup, their position within the overall industry network, and how they approach their contributions to the local community. On the one hand, a startup grant drawing on public funds can secure an administrative budget controlled by upper management, but matters regarding the investment in the development of original intellectual property that will later reap rewards will almost always require outside capital. The latter played a role in Machiken's failure. On the other hand, a system based on outsourced work, which takes advantage of digital technology to work remotely from the head office, has proven successful thus far.

The culture, fandom, and consumption of animated film traditionally stems from a younger demographic, their organization leading to creative groups and circles that generate their own content and have the power to influence the current media zeitgeist. Efforts to stimulate this in a top-down fashion, such as a government-sanctioned regional revitalization program, would be fruitful if the community aspect was more deeply engaged than previously. The provision of spaces for families and residents of all ages to interact with each other through learning experiences and local recognition of the art of animation may be the key to implementing these endeavors. For example, more animation-oriented educational activities could be planned and promoted in the region at both an institutional and a grassroots level. This author has planned and conducted the latter in the form of a series of stop-motion animation workshops in Okayama, which were attended by participants of all ages.

With the majority of anime studios located in Tokyo, the surrounding areas are home to vocational colleges that over the years have expanded to form an industry of their own, diversifying from simple animation schools to institutions specializing in digital art and even courses in voice acting. Their popularity and growth are indicative of the decline of on-the-job training – seemingly a goal of the Kōchi venture – due to the insurmountable demand for content, studio workload, and tight schedules. A major hurdle for regional expansion, therefore, is the issue of training and human resource development in areas where the industry traditionally does not have a presence. Partnering with educational institutions could alleviate this problem. The Machiken project showed awareness of this, for example, in its partnership with the School of Animation Culture at KIU. It is hoped that further regional revitalization projects using animation will emerge, but it remains to be seen which will have the ability to sustain the management and growth of future joint ventures.

Notes

1. Ippan Shadan Hōjin Nihon Dōga Kyōkai, *Anime Sangyō Repōto 2020* (Tokyo: Ippan Shadan Hōjin Nihon Dōga Kyōkai 2020), appendix 4.
2. Ippan Shadan Hōjin Nihon Dōga Kyōkai, *Anime Sangyō Repōto 2020*, appendix 4.
3. "Kono sora no shita de: anime sutajio 'Ekakiya' Okayama-ken Sōja-shi," *Mainichi Shimbun*, December 27, 2018, https://video.mainichi.jp/detail/video/5983817220001.
4. "Shintō Kokusai Gakkai dai 22-kai seminā: 'Gendai no seichi: Wakamono bunka to Shintō' hōkoku," *Shintō forumu* (ISSA International Shinto Studies Association), 60 (January 1, 2020): 2–3.
5. Takeyoshi Yamamura, *Fukyū-ban: Anime manga de chiiki fukkō: machi no fan o umu kontentsu tsūrizumu kaihatsuhō* (Nanto: Paru Books, 2019); Toru Sakai, *Anime ga chihō o sukū!? "Seichi junrei" no keizai-teki kōka o kangaeru* (Tokyo: Wani Books, 2016).

6. "Washinomiya ni okeru machi okoshi no keii," *Kuki-shi shōkōkai Washinomiya shisho homepage*, www.wasimiya.org/history/2008.html.
7. "Nihon no anime o manabitai! Anime sutajio de intān hajimaru," *KSB 5ch (Setonaikai Broadcasting Corporation)*, September 3, 2018, https://news.ksb.co.jp/article/13836190.
8. Katsuyama Hishio Center for Cultural Exchange, list of past events, http://hishioarts.com/exhibition-events/current-exhibition/maniwa-eizo-college-2021/.
9. *Katsuyama Animation Festival 2012–2015 kirokushū* (Katsuyama: Katsuyama Bunka Ōraikan Hishio, 2016).
10. Makoto Kishikawa, ed., *Sekai ni hasshin! Creator no anime-jutsu* (Tokyo: Kinema Junpo 2005), 109.
11. "Kochi Seeks to Become Anime, Manga Hub as Remote Work Base," *Kyodo News*, January 29, 2022, https://english.kyodonews.net/news/2022/01/c3efe44fc0ed-kochi-seeks-to-become-anime-manga-hub-as-remote-work-base.html.
12. "Kōchi kara anime no ōgata project happyō, sangyō shūseki kara jinzai ikusei, ibento made," *Animation Business Journal*, January 24, 2022, http://animationbusiness.info/archives/12589.

PART VIII

Forms of Distribution

Power of Attorney

16

DALMA KÁLOVICS

Manga Media from Analog to Digital

Manga Market Now

One of the first facts most foreigners learn about manga is that Japanese
comics were initially published in phonebook-like magazines. The success
of the manga industry was indeed facilitated by this particular publication format assuming a central role in academic and fan discourse, but the
importance of the magazine in the development of manga is something of
a myth. Certainly, magazines were the driving force behind the domestic
Japanese manga market when it first peaked in 1995 with an estimated
sales of 586.4 billion yen, but subsequently magazines declined. Collected
paperbacks of manga (*tankōbon*) emerged in the late 1960s, establishing the
current magazine-to-paperback publishing system, and their significance
has grown ever since. Paperback sales eventually overtook those of magazines in 2005. At the same time, the new medium of digital comics began
its steep rise and topped overall print manga sales in 2019. Nevertheless,
the combined manga market was on a slight decline until 2017, with a
sudden increase of 12.82 percent in 2019 and 23.01 percent in 2020.[1] This
upturn was caused by the overwhelming success of *Demon Slayer: Kimetsu
no Yaiba* (2016–20), the product of both the power of franchising and the
COVID-19 pandemic. Overall, manga sales in 2020 of 612.6 billion yen
topped the 1995 record, proof that manga publishing can thrive even without magazines (Fig. 16.1).

Magazines have been the center of manga discourse for decades, but postwar manga has undergone numerous publishing formats, and these have
affected its visual and narrative structure beyond editorial choices or reader
expectations. Manga criticism usually regards the original site of publication as decisive; however, the materiality of (re)publishing formats matters
not just for usage but also on occasion for style. This chapter focuses on the
formats of story manga – comics with complex narratives and layouts – at
the expense of comic strips, or *yonkoma*, and so-called essay manga or their

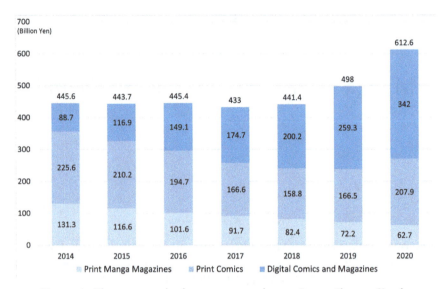

Figure 16.1 The manga market between 2014 and 2020. Source: Shuppan Kagaku Kenkyūsho, 2021.

predecessors. It refrains from including how manga functions, for instance, in a fashion magazine, or how gendered manga were presented in unisex educational magazines.

Akahon and Rental Books

In the immediate postwar era, children's magazines, the forerunners of manga magazines, featured only a few comics. The first manga-centric medium was the *akahon* (red-cover book), cheap, small booklets of sixteen to thirty-six pages characterized by low-quality printing, and often published by print shops, as well as candy and toy sellers, who hired amateur artists. A good portion of these were subject to rampant piracy,[2] but *akahon* also included quality productions by legitimate publishers, such as Osamu Tezuka's *The New Treasure Island* (*Shintakarajima*, 1947). *Akahon* became more expensive in the early 1950s and disappeared when readers turned to the more inexpensive rental comics. These were produced by minor publishers for rental stores (*kashihon'ya*), where books that normally would cost 130–150 yen to purchase could be rented nightly for 10 yen.[3] Rental publishers offered an opportunity for emerging artists. Big names like Takao Saitō and Gōseki Kojima honed their skills with rental publishers before moving on to mainstream magazines. Although rental publishers paid less than magazines, they nonetheless exercised less control over content. This gave birth to *gekiga* in the late 1950s – comics targeting a slightly older audience and having weightier narratives.[4]

Rental comics usually contained stand-alone narratives – an exception being the seventeen-volume *Manual of Ninja Martial Arts* (*Ninja bugeichō*, 1959–62) – as rental stores rarely offered every issue of a long series. In 1959, mainstream publishers debuted weekly children's magazines, and in order to provide a more regular content rental publishers also launched monthly anthologies with diverse thematic genres. While these adopted some magazine features, such as readers' columns and drawing competitions, a real-time dialogue with readers was less feasible due to unreliable circulation and a longer period of use. In addition, publication dates were not indicated.

Rental comics declined in the 1960s when higher living standards allowed children to purchase magazines and later book editions. Before the collecting of magazine serials in paperback became common, materials were occasionally reprinted for rental circulation. It was perhaps due to this practice that some rental publishers such as Wakagi Shobō participated in the boom of narrow-type paperbacks (*shinshoban*) in the late 1960s, enabling their survival for a few more years. Eventually mainstream publishers, such as Kodansha and Shueisha, secured copyrights to reprint their own magazine serials, and rental publishers exited the market. With this, magazines became the representative site of manga publishing for several decades,[5] and paperbacks their republishing media.

The Manga Magazine

Makeup and History

Distinct from rental manga, children's magazines issued by mainstream publishers were circulated in bookstores, at train stations, and since the 1970s in convenience stores. Although some magazines, such as *Omoshiro Book* or *Shōnen Shōjo Bōken Ō* in the early 1950s, sought to target both boys and girls, children's magazines since the prewar era have been divided into two principal demographic categories: *shōnen* for boys and *shōjo* for girls. Later, other demographics, such as *seinen* for young adult men and *josei* for adult women. Thematic genres were also introduced.

In the early 1950s, children's magazines had only 10 percent manga content, primarily in the form of short graphic stories, in addition to literary narratives, articles, and picture stories (*emonogatari*). Manga was closely interrelated with other contents: Themes in novels and articles often surfaced in manga and vice versa. By the end of the decade the manga content had risen to 30 percent, but in order to offer more, freebie manga booklets (*bessatsu furoku*) of thirty to one hundred pages in various formats were added to magazine issues. Booklets carried both stand-alone and serialized graphic narratives, frequently appearing with the magazine: The first eight pages of an installment would be printed in color in the magazine, to be continued in the booklet.

In the 1960s, monthly magazines temporarily lost ground to weeklies, such as *Weekly Shōnen Magazine* and *Weekly Margaret*, and while many ceased publication, new monthly sister magazines of weeklies were also launched. Monthlies from the 1950s, including *Nakayoshi* and *Ribon*, retained their mixed contents even though the ratio of manga grew to 70 percent by the late 1960s, and magazine length went from about 250 to more than 400 pages. By contrast, already in the mid-1960s, recently established sister magazines, such as *Bessatsu Margaret* and *Bessatsu Shōjo Friend*, were manga-centric with over 70 percent of graphic narratives. This eventually became the predominant format for manga magazines.

Whereas older manga monthlies issued mainly serials, the new sister magazines at first featured only short stories, frequently debuting fresh talent. With the practice of systematic paperback releases not yet institutionalized, "collected editions" (*sōshūhen*) of weekly serializations were common and rereleased materials in 50- to 100-page segments. This continued until the mid-1970s, but gradually disappeared with paperbacks becoming common. Due to railway transportation regulation for weeklies, which forbade materials without topicality, freebie booklets were limited to monthlies. With the growing portion of manga contents, however, they became redundant. Manga-centric sister magazines did not need them, and others replaced them with stationery during the 1970s.

Weekly children's magazines appeared in 1959 with *Weekly Shōnen Magazine* and *Weekly Shōnen Sunday*. This format was successful as it provided readers with weekly rather than monthly entertainment, and by 1967, *Weekly Shōnen Magazine* exceeded one million copies, as did *Weekly Margaret* in 1969 – a first for a *shōnen* and a *shōjo* magazine. Similar to monthlies, children's weeklies were initially general magazines. The ratio of manga in these increased from below 50 percent to 80 percent during the 1960s, and the magazine length also grew from 170–180 to 260–280 pages. Nowadays, manga content in any magazine falls between 85 and 95 percent, and the remaining pages are taken up by self-promotion and adaptations, readers' columns, talent awards, occasional media news, and interviews.

Shōnen/seinen weeklies are still popular, but *shōjo manga* weeklies have disappeared, with only a few biweeklies still in circulation, such as *Margaret* and *Hana to Yume*. Oft-cited, but disputed, reasons for this are that female readers like to take their time to read a magazine thoroughly, that they prefer slower, introspective narratives and that female artists – the majority of *shōjo manga* creators – favor more relaxed monthly schedules and slower narratives without the need to insert a cliff-hanger every twenty pages, as is common practice in weeklies.[6] But the different publishing frequency for the traditional gendered genres might be simply a matter of convention. After all, female readers have become a substantial financial force as consumers of *shōnen manga*, making up 20 percent of *Weekly Shōnen Jump*'s readership.[7] Moreover, female artists, such as Rumiko Takahashi, have been active in *shōnen* weeklies since the 1980s. Storytelling and consumption have changed significantly, especially with newer comics media. Webtoons (digital comics composed in long vertical strips mainly for smartphones), for instance, are released on a weekly or ten-day schedule regardless of gendered genre.

Materiality and Content

The place and time of publication affect visual style and narrative. Initially, manga media of different sizes had specific page layouts, presumably related to readability. Rental comics were originally published in B6 format (128 × 182 mm) hardcover books, but by the 1960s the A5 size with softcovers became the standard format;[8] these favored three tiers and relatively simple, grid-like paneling. Mainstream magazines were originally in A5, suitable for text-centric content, but with emphasis shifting to visuals, the format changed to B5 (182 × 257 mm) in the mid-1950s. These prioritized four-tier paneling, and their page layout varied in complexity according to genre and publication frequency.[9] During the 1960s different magazine formats and booklets had their own layout, but this diversity disappeared when the magazine-to-paperback system solidified in the 1970s. In the 2020s, the type of paneling is mostly determined by reader demographics, themes, and trends.

Rental publications released stand-alone narratives of 100–140 pages, and this gave artists the opportunity to develop the story as a whole and to unfold scenes at a slower pace. Conversely, serialized narratives need to end every installment with a cliff-hanger to motivate readers to purchase the next issue, and this requires tighter storytelling. Thus, the fifteen- to twenty-page installments in *Weekly Shōnen Jump*, such as *My Hero Academia* (*Boku no hīrō akademia*, 2014–), are very dynamic, whereas similar action narratives of thirty to fifty pages in the monthly *Jump SQ*, such as *Blue Exorcist* (*Ao no ekusoshisuto*, 2009–), can evolve at a more measured pace.

In time, and in line with increasingly complex stories, weeklies began to extend narratives to keep their readers hooked. Paperback publishing also favors lengthy series as greater profit can be made from them than from stand-alones. Successful weekly serializations tend to have long runs: *One Piece* (1997–) and *Detective Conan* (*Meitantei Konan*, 1994–), to name two, reached 100 volumes each in 2021. The tendency in *shōjo manga* is toward shorter series, but as the genre moved away from the "literary" trends of the 1970s to more prosaic narratives, popular series began to be stretched out. While publications over fifty volumes are rare, sports-themed *Chihayafuru* (2007–22) consists of fifty volumes and the fantasy adventure *Yona of the Dawn* (*Akatsuki no Yona*, 2009–) stood at thirty-nine in 2022.

The position of a serial in a magazine is relevant. Publishers use questionnaires to measure popularity. *Weekly Shōnen Jump* famously bases its lineup on these, placing popular titles in the front and discontinuing unpopular series prematurely. Other magazines take paperback sales and adaptations into consideration, resulting in even fewer in-demand titles being placed up front for promotion. The end of the magazine is generally reserved for something different, such as a short gag manga or, as was the case in the past, newcomer debuts. Taking it one step further, placement can also serve an unusual presentation of a narrative. *In this Corner of the World* (*Kono sekai no katasumi ni*, 2007–09), for example, was featured in the magazine *Manga Action* between the table of contents, which is usually on the last page of a magazine, and the inside back cover.[10]

Until the late 1960s manga were highly transient materials, and coupled with the initial image of low-quality entertainment, they have not been archived in libraries. The National Diet Library in Tokyo, for instance, has not collected *akahon* and rental manga through legal deposit, and previously the acquisition of magazine issues was incomplete and without freebie booklets. Rental comics used thick paper to ensure a degree of physical durability, but they were not meant to be collected. Cheap printing technologies resulted in low-quality products that were inexpensive to rent but too expensive to own. Magazines have been an ephemeral, throwaway format; however, demographics do influence certain differing characteristics. Children's magazines at the outset employed rough paper that resulted in subpar print quality, and while thinner silky paper was surprisingly cheaper, children preferred the rougher type because it made magazines look thicker and therefore promising more content.[11] *Seinen* magazines have been printed on thin paper since their emergence at the end of the 1960s, and *seinen* weeklies are the only type to be saddle-stitched.

Except for *seinen* magazines, which often have photographed bikini models on the covers, since the late 1960s manga magazines have featured manga characters. Both rental comics and children's magazines use colored ink, and magazines even employ colored paper inside, changing colors several times in a single issue. Printing with black ink has been reserved for magazines aimed at adults. The overall low quality of manga magazines has remained unaltered to the present day, with poor printing and unfortunate color combinations that impact the reading experience. In *seinen* weeklies, the verso of a page is normally visible through the thin paper, and over time ink will bleed through even in magazines with thick paper. These shortcomings of magazine materiality are one reason why readers rely on reprints for collecting (in addition to limited shelf space).

Republishing Formats

Before the beginning of the systematic republishing of magazine serials in paperback books in the late 1960s, only popular artists had their works released in a collected format, typically, but not exclusively, as rental books. The publisher Shueisha issued Osamu Tezuka's *Big X* (1963–66) in a format similar to magazines in 1965: It was B5-sized and had the same paper, ink, and print quality, but unlike the series' magazine *Shōnen Book* with its circa 300 pages per issue, each of its book volumes was only about 100 pages long. The release of magazine serials as rental books involved reformatting, as every medium had its own page layout. When a four-tier magazine manga was republished, the layout was changed to three tiers by cutting up manuscripts, rearranging panels on new manuscript sheets, and trimming or enlarging panels through additional drawing. While less common, similar editing occurred when a rental manga was published in a magazine, or booklet material was rereleased in the main magazine.[12] Reformatting materials disappeared, perhaps due to time restraints, when the mass-production of paperbacks started in the 1970s; it is now reemerging in the digital age.

Publishers reprinting magazine serials under their own label had a breakthrough with narrow B6-size (103 × 182 mm) comics (*shinshoban*). Eventually, however, the regular B6 format (128 × 182 mm) became standard, with the narrow type reserved for some *shōjo* and *shōnen manga* labels. But even without reformatted layouts, magazine and paperback editions deviate from each other. Color pages of the magazine are generally reproduced in monochrome, and frontispieces of weekly materials are usually not incorporated. Paperbacks frequently have bonus materials at the end of the book, including artist profiles and comments on the flaps. Initially, serials were not made with a paperback edition in mind, and the left-right position of the pages often shifted when repetitions and installment summaries were

Figure 16.2 Manga publishing formats (from left to right, top to bottom): manga magazine, rental comic book, narrow B6-size paperback, B6-size paperback, pocketbook, complete edition, collector edition.

removed, which broke up the original double-spreads. Redrawing a few panels for a new edition and filling the space of magazine advertisements with images has been common since the outset, both made easier with digital technologies.

The success of the paperback format occasioned a change in reading customs: Many readers opted to wait for the book edition instead of purchasing continuous magazine issues. Manga magazines – the initial site for publishing the "final form" of manga – became an intermediate stage toward the paperback. Consequently, it has become acceptable for artists to submit unfinished manuscripts for a magazine release because these could be corrected for the paperback edition. In 2021, the popular serials *Jujutsu Kaisen* (2018–) and *Blue Exorcist* both contained unfinished pages in some of their magazine issues. While a further indication of the transiency of the magazine medium, this practice also signals that magazines have lost their central position.

The paperback has been the most common type of collected edition, but there are several reprint formats for different purposes (Fig. 16.2). For instance, the handy A6-size pocketbooks (*bunkobon*) have better paper and printing than paperbacks and their unassuming covers appeal to adult readers. The downside is that details of the art can get lost in these tiny books. There are also high-quality complete editions (*kanzenban*) that occasionally have hardcovers. They are usually A5-sized with good paper and printing, have color pages and frontispieces, and may include previously uncollected episodes and bonus material. Likewise noteworthy are collector editions (*aizōban*), usually in A5; they are not always of the best quality and often lack color pages and bonus material. Some may even have up to 900 pages, and while such omnibus editions may save shelf space due to the reduced number of covers and their usually thinner paper for the pages, they are also difficult to handle. Further formats include inexpensive, easy to pick up and discard convenience-store editions (*conbiniban*) which are thick B6-size books without dust jackets and on low-quality paper; wide editions (*waido-ban*) that republish material in A5 or bigger formats; and new editions (*shinsōban*) in various formats that are distinguished by new covers and bonus materials. Notably, the content can be edited for later reeditions. Drastic changes are rare, but words and depictions deemed problematic may be changed, and earlier issues may be revised. An example of the latter is the placement of pages in the 2005 complete edition of *The Rose of Versailles* (*Berusaiyu no bara*, 1972–73).

Digital Comics

In the late 1990s, the established manga publishing system was challenged by the emergence of digital comics. After flip phones offered comics to "surf" panel by panel[13] – not unlike the Guided View currently employed by smartphone applications of American comics – larger smartphones displaying whole paneled pages became the standard. Currently, original and digitalized comics are available on big webportals and their smartphone applications, such as *Cmoa* and *Renta!*, but some publishers also maintain their own platforms, such as Hakusensha's *Manga Park*. Webportals still use the double-page spread as their default display setting, but this can be changed to a single-page layout with either horizontal or vertical scrolling, just like the smartphone default. Although the analog book format facilitated the double-page spread as the basic unit of manga's visual style, the composition of double-spreads might become irrelevant in the future as digital consumption becomes the norm.

Newly created print comics have digital editions, which are published on the same day or with a time lag. Occasionally, a privileged service initially releases the content exclusively. Portals continue to retain the original demographic categories, often with the addition of thematic genres as subcategories or tags. Print and digital versions may differ, with extra contents from under the dust jacket or flaps frequently not included in the digital version. The censorship of erotic content tends to be stricter online, but the level varies depending on the portal. Moreover, apps need to adhere to the content rules of Apple and Google to be featured in their stores, which likewise can lead to more stringent censorship.

Most print magazines have digital editions, and suspended publications sometimes move online. Overall, however, the need for the magazine format is diminishing. *Hana Yume Ai*, for example, was launched in 2018 in place of the suspended print magazine *Bessatsu Hana to Yume*, but aside from the magazine edition, installments can also be purchased separately. Furthermore, some publishers do not compile magazines; they simply launch a label and publish narratives chapter-wise, such as the boys love label *moment* by Shu-Cream, or they launch their own platform, such as Shueisha's *Shōnen Jump+*.

Once enough installments are available, chapter-wise released digital comics are collected as "digital paperbacks" with bonus material, and popular titles are republished in print. For the reader, single chapters are more expensive to purchase than the complete volume. Digital comics cost nearly the same as print comics, but while print comics cannot be discounted (causing the secondhand market to flourish), digital comics sites regularly offer discounts, and many maintain a rental subsite for a portion of their catalog, usually for half the price. Many portals, furthermore, have an "all-you-can-read" subscription for a fixed fee per month, similar to Amazon's Kindle Unlimited. Digital comics are reminiscent of rental manga, not just with regard to renting but also to other characteristics, such as the lack of publication date.

Besides digital comics that emulate traditional print layouts, smartphone-optimal webtoons with long vertical comic strips have been gaining popularity in Japan. The webtoon format originates in Korea, and while there are Japanese successes in this format, such as *ReLIFE* (2013–18), most webtoons are licensed from Korea, and to a lesser degree China, and offered by Japanese subsidiaries of Korean companies. In terms of their format, webtoons have revived the practice of layout reformatting. Some digital comics portals convert scrolls to traditional page layout, and sometimes webtoons are published in paperback. Traditional layouts might also be converted to a scrollable webtoon format. Turning scrolls into traditional layouts is difficult,[14] and there are various avenues in cases where the Japanese print edition cannot be produced by simply translating an already existent Korean print edition. For instance, the popular boys-love webtoon *Painter of the Night* (*Yahwacheop*, 2019–) was first printed in Taiwan in 2020, before it debuted online in Japanese with a different page layout and was released in print in 2021. It is noteworthy that the reading direction of the Taiwanese and Japanese versions varies, although the panels themselves remain unflipped. Japanese print editions of webtoons usually follow established Japanese paperback norms, and not the Korean standard of A5-sized books printed on heavy, glossy paper, to accommodate their domestic target audience.

Digital comics are portable. They do not take up space, and due to lower costs they have become popular for reviving out-of-print comics that would be unprofitable to reprint. They introduce a new set of issues, however, including the constant danger of technologies becoming obsolete. The resolution of image files might not be up to standard over time due to better display technologies. The printing standard of 400 dpi for traditional comics is presently not at risk, yet webtoon publishers generally use low-resolution materials. Comico, for example, only requires a minimum of 72 dpi from artists, which makes their materials look blurry on computer screens. Unlike print, however, mistakes can be corrected immediately in digital comics, which publishers may misuse. *The Cornered Mouse Dreams of Cheese* (*Kyūso wa chīzu no yume o miru*, 2004–06) and its sequel were originally published as mildly erotic ladies comics for mature readers, but the sexual content and some discriminatory language were reedited in anticipation of a live-action movie adaptation in 2020. Instead of releasing an additional all-age version, the existing digital edition was revised, thereby updating previously purchased digital copies without informing readers of this significant change beforehand. Such practices raise concerns regarding censorship, and the overwriting of materials makes research into certain periods of digital manga publishing a challenge, not to mention that the preservation and archiving of digital materials thus far remains an unresolved issue.

Franchising

Manga has leaned increasingly on franchising (or so-called media mix), particularly since the decline of magazines. The reliance on different media or commodities to reach a wider audience began in 1963 with *Astro Boy* (*Tetsuwan Atomu*), when Tezuka's manga of the same name became the first anime series with a continuing narrative, and the popularity of *Astro Boy* stickers in Marble Chocolates set a trend of character merchandising.[15] Manga is not always the origin of a franchise, however. There are instances of simultaneously developed transmedia storytelling in the 1960s, as seen in *Comet-san* (1967), which debuted a few weeks apart as a manga and a live-action television series. Eventually manga adaptations of anime and light novels have also become common.

Multimedia franchising is crucial for manga since today's children encounter other entertainment media before they become familiar with comics.[16] Coupled with declining birth rates, it has become difficult to recruit readers. In this regard, franchising has the power to win over consumers for manga beyond expectations, as the recent example of *Demon Slayer: Kimetsu no Yaiba* demonstrated. In 2019, the manga made a breakthrough with a high-quality anime series that spread beyond the usual audience by word of mouth and later through TV promotion. Its popularity was heightened in 2020 with an animated movie that became the highest-grossing film in Japan of all time. The *Demon Slayer* manga became the top-selling title in terms of volumes and series in 2020 and in the first half of 2021 in the Oricon ranking, overtaking longtime frontrunner *One Piece*. This success was further enhanced by spin-offs, novel adaptations, music, collaboration campaigns with different businesses, and character goods available not just in specialized stores but also in general souvenir shops. The power of franchising led to a revival of 1990s favorites in recent years with new anime adaptations and manga sequels, such as *Dragon Ball Super* (manga: 2015–, anime: 2015–18) or *Cardcaptor Sakura: Clear Card* (manga: 2016–24, anime: 2018). These revivals capitalize on the latest, more developed venues of merchandising to target older, grown-up fans in the hope of attracting new audiences.

Conclusion

Manga is deeply intertwined with materiality, as both physical dimensions and publishing customs have determined its visual and narrative forms. This has been largely ignored in manga criticism in favor of narrow semiotic considerations of the visual language of manga and representation-oriented analyses of single works. With the shift of manga publishing from magazines to paperbacks and from analog to digital, as well as the new scroll layout of webtoons, it is time for materiality to finally enter the field of vision.

Notes

1. Shuppan Kagaku Kenkyūsho, ed., *2021-ban shuppan shihyō nenpō* (Tokyo: Zenkoku Shuppan Kyōkai, 2021), 221.
2. Ryan Holmberg, "The Bottom of a Bottomless Barrel: Introducing Akahon Manga," *The Comics Journal*, January 5, 2012, www.tcj.com/the-bottom-of-a-bottomless-barrel-introducing-akahon-manga/.
3. Hidenori Miyake, "Kashihon manga no yutakana sekai: sengo no kashihon gyōkai to kashihon manga." In *Kashihon Manga RETURNS*, edited by Kashihon Manga Kenkyūkai (Tokyo: Poplar Publishing, 2006), 14–15.
4. Haruyuki Nakano, *Manga sangyōron* (Tokyo: Chikuma Shobō, 2007 [2004]), 59.
5. Hiroshi Yamamori, *"Komikkusu" no media-shi* (Tokyo: Seikyusha, 2019), 114.
6. Nakano, *Manga sangyōron*, 131–32.
7. Shueisha AD NAVI, "Shōnen komikku-shi seinen komikku-shi," *Shueisha Media Guide 2014*, https://web.archive.org/web/20140430025858/http://adnavi.shueisha.co.jp/mediaguide/2014/pdf/boys.pdf.
8. Kashihon Manga Kenkyūkai, ed., "Kashihon manga no zōhon," in *Kashihon Manga RETURNS* (Tokyo: Poplar Publishing, 2006), 129.

9. Dalma Kálovics, "Manga across Media: Style Adapting to Form in the 1950s and 1960s and in the Digital Age," *Mechademia*, 12, no. 2 (2020): 105–6.

10. Jaqueline Berndt, "Conjoined by Hand: Aesthetic Materiality in Kouno Fumiyo's Manga in This Corner of the World," *Mechademia*, 12, no. 2 (2020): 94.

11. Nobumasa Konagai, *Watashi no shōjo manga-shi* (Tokyo: Nishida Shoten, 2001), 74–75.

12. Kálovics, "Manga across Media," 106–8.

13. Sanae Ochiai, "Denshi shoseki to wa nani ka: keitai komikku/keitai shōsetsu kōsatsu," *Jōhō no kagaku to gijutsu,* 62, no. 6 (2012), https://doi.org/10.18919/jkg.62.6_248, 249.

14. Kálovics, "Manga across Media," 118–19.

15. Marc Steinberg, *Anime's Media Mix: Franchising Toys and Characters in Japan* (Minneapolis: University of Minnesota Press), 34–41.

16. Nakano, *Manga sangyōron*, 137.

17

DARIO LOLLI

Media Mix as Licensed Distribution

In 2019, the anime series *Mobile Suit Gundam* celebrated its fortieth birthday. The sci-fi saga, initially cocreated and directed by Yoshiyuki Tomino in 1979, rose to fame by pushing the boundaries of TV anime through a number of visual and conceptual innovations. The series departed from the then popular super robot genre by depicting a dramatic conflict between humans settling in space, with epic battles fought aboard mechanical mobile suits – that is, humanoid robots characterized by designer Kunio Ōkawara as "realistic" military machines. The pilots of these robots – special individuals gifted with advanced senses due to an evolutionary habituation to life in space – are called "newtype" in the series, a keyword that became so popular among fans that it was later adopted as the title of one of Japan's first monthly anime magazines. In the wake of this early creative output, the fictional world of *Mobile Suit Gundam* evolved over the next four decades across numerous new series and transmedia adaptations to become an extremely prolific, long-running anime franchise. *Gundam* is therefore an outstanding example of what in Japanese marketing is known as media mix, a multimedia franchise often developed in-house by a large media conglomerate and based on specialized consumption by anime enthusiasts.[1] It is no surprise that the fortieth anniversary of this flagship anime series was publicly celebrated with special initiatives involving the entire Bandai Namco corporate group, one of Japan's biggest entertainment conglomerates and the owner of Sunrise Studio where *Gundam* is made.

In the same year, *Gundam* and the expression "newtype" featured in a number of popular consumer products with no apparent relation to the anime industry. Georgia Newtype, for example, was a limited-edition canned coffee produced by Georgia, a brand owned by the Coca-Cola Company's Japanese subsidiary, under license from the anime production company Sunrise. Exclusively distributed across Japan through automated vending machines, Georgia Newtype was launched to commemorate the fortieth anniversary of *Mobile Suit Gundam* through a specially designed

226

can depicting four characters from the anime series (Fig. 17.1). As such, it was part of a broader lineup of original products meant to reassert the enduring standing of this series on the market through an anniversary campaign based on numerous "collaborations" with other popular brands.

In an era awash with digital content and delivery platforms, anniversaries of notable anime series have come to function as the perfect anchoring points for what we might call extended anime distribution – that is, the authorized proliferation of content and characters well beyond a mediamix system exclusively attending to niche or subcultural consumption. According to some observers, value creation at the present time is shifting from a logic mostly based on scarcity and usefulness to one based on sensation, feeling, and meaningful selection. Bestselling author and consultant Shū Yamaguchi, for example, has advanced this argument through an incidental reference to *Mobile Suit Gundam*. In a book about management and work style, Yamaguchi describes "newtype" as individuals and

Figure 17.1 Georgia Newtype displayed in a Japanese vending machine. Every "commemorative" can come with two designs, each portraying a random *Gundam* character. When four cans with different designs are placed together, two on the side and two on top, they reproduce a still from the anime series. Photo by Dario Lolli.

organizations able to navigate a world characterized by great material afflu-
ence, mobility, and information.[2] According to him, it is vital to not just
market goods but to enthuse new and existing audiences through immersive
"experience economies" that can ensure deeper and more lucrative forms
of consumer engagement over time.[3] Owing to its proven capacity to generate strong feelings and affective attachments among different audience
groups, anime has been profoundly invested in these broader changes. In a
Japanese market characterized by overflowing digital content, narrow audience segments, and reduced birth rates, content derived from anime series is
no longer exclusively developed to promote the specialist publications and
collectible merchandise historically associated with fans and *otaku* subcultures. Rather, it is exploited more and more to add value to products and
services in unprecedented commercial spheres, including drinks, tourism,
and urban requalification.

What does it mean to distribute anime in this way? What can we learn
from dispersed and processual licensing practices? By taking the *Mobile
Suit Gundam*'s fortieth anniversary as a formal case for analysis, this chapter will illustrate the close links between the contemporary anime industry
and the fast-growing licensing sector – the business of intellectual property extension. Through a focus on this anniversary campaign and some
of its licensed products, it will be possible to establish an empirical middle
ground, identifying a series of apparently unrelated phenomena that are
nonetheless connected to the emergence of digital channels, the aging of
anime series, and the changing demographics of their consumers. A closer
look at an anniversary campaign based on extended anime distribution will
open up a window to the ordinary processes by which the proliferation of
anime on-screen and off is routinely and contingently produced in the context of Japan's ever-changing mediascape.

"Beyond": *Gundam* at Forty

The *Mobile Suit Gundam*'s fortieth anniversary was founded as a corporate project controlled by the large media conglomerate Bandai Namco
through two of its subsidiary firms: the anime studio Sunrise and the advertising agency Sōtsū, both of which play a central role in the franchising and
licensing of *Gundam*-related materials. The campaign was formally named
Beyond, using an English word to explicitly mark the goal of addressing
a wide audience through crossover initiatives aimed at transcending "the
boundaries of individual *Gundam* series as well as national and generational
borders."[4] In line with this concept, the project revolved around the release
of five new anime series and films that were distributed through television

or digital platforms. These were basically sequels and spin-offs targeting the different audience segments already covered by the *Gundam* franchise. For example, older fans of the first anime series could watch its spin-off *Mobile Suit Gundam: The Origin – The Advent of the Red Comet* (2019) at a typical late-night slot on the national public broadcaster NHK, while the series *Gundam Build Divers Re: Rise* (2020), aimed at a younger audience of kids, was entirely distributed online through the official *Gundam* YouTube channel. Cutting across different delivery platforms, the anniversary functioned as a sort of organizing principle, providing renewed currency and heightened visibility to a vast media mix often composed by niche or loosely interrelated anime series.

The symbolic function of the anniversary, however, was not merely organizational. In order to function as expected, it had to be implemented visually by means of a logo, an easily recognizable instrument able to mark all the special products developed for this campaign and to link them together. This was especially useful for communication purposes, as it permitted the aggregation of all the information about the anniversary under a single website connected with Sunrise, the official *Gundam* fan club, and other corporate initiatives. The logo was specifically designed in the form of a badge reminiscent of the militaristic setting of the series, while the numeral zero in 40 was subtly stylized to recreate one of the anime's most iconic scenes: director Tomino's signature view of the sunlight peeking out from behind planet Earth.[5] As this example illustrates, anniversary campaigns such as Beyond are not just generic marketing instruments that are arbitrarily applied to anime. Rather, they are the contingent results of economic and creative intermediation premised on the very possibility of drawing from all the texts, designs, and sounds of an existing anime series – its entire history or cultural footprint – through the management of its intellectual properties.

The creative management of immaterial assets such as anime series did not appear overnight as a result of digitization processes. The very rise of entertainment animation in the early twentieth century was accompanied by various legal regulations concerning characters and objects on-screen. Although initially exogenous to animation production, these regulations soon became intertwined with the ability of the new medium to endow creatures and things with movement, animating them and bringing them to "life."[6] This established a parallel of sorts between animation as an industrial technique for the production of moving characters and the juridical personalities of these very characters as legal entities manageable in a fashion similar to celebrities or enterprises. The management of animated characters as intellectual properties has thus developed in different countries and over an extended period of time. In postwar Japan, it eventually consolidated around a sophisticated system of niche or specialized consumption centered around anime and involving manga, magazines, music, video games, toys, and more. Since the 1980s, this nexus of transmedia serialization came to be known in Japanese advertising and marketing circles as the media mix.

Anniversary campaigns such as Beyond, however, are meant to do more than just reproduce this successful model of transmedia serialization. Their scope is not only one of consolidating niche market segments but also of establishing meaningful bonds with new and existing consumers through the very mobilization of anime's cultural footprint. In principle, these types of anniversaries can be understood as attempts at anticipating the festive mobilization of affectionate fans and at discretely soliciting (and channeling) orchestrated consumptive goals. In order to be more effective and spark heightened moments of consumer engagement, such campaigns equally involve partnerships with companies in different and often unexpected industrial sectors as a way to generate buzz from surprised social media users and draw the attention of even broader audience groups, especially those who are labeled by brand managers as "digitally distracted consumers."[7] As such, anniversary campaigns entail a vast array of creative, legal, and economic agents, and can easily take years of invisible planning and networking before coming to fruition. Nevertheless, their organization is by no means untraceable. The professional practice that presides over their off-the-radar, cross-sector arrangements is known as licensing, or the extension of another party's intellectual property into new categories of goods, promotions, or events.

Licensing *Gundam*: Georgia Newtype and the Gundam Factory Yokohama

Licensing, the legal practice of organizing intellectual property rights, is an industrial sector that has been growing steadily worldwide. Thanks to the presence of an affluent consumer base and globally successful contents industries (*kontentsu sangyō*), licensing in Japan is advanced and boasts sector-specific trade associations, such as the Character Brand Licensing Association or the Japan Merchandising Rights Association. In addition, Japan features regularly, alongside the United States and the United Kingdom, as one of the top three largest global markets for licensed products.[8]

The Japanese media sector has typically resorted to licensing for the production of the cheap merchandise needed to support the development of media-mix series, including the plastic model kits of *Mobile Suit Gundam* (known as *gunpla*) that have made the fortune of Japanese toy maker Bandai, now part of the multinational entertainment group Bandai Namco. What is particularly interesting about this practice today, however, is its adaptation to an ever-shrinking, but proportionally more affluent, consumer demographic. Indeed, although the Japanese local market cannot boast the growth rates of neighboring countries, such as China, the per capita expenditure of Japanese consumers remains comparatively higher.[9] This means that, as the Japanese population continues to age while its birth rates drop, licensing products are increasingly repositioned to involve those categories of older consumers having high disposable income and affective bonds with long-lived anime series but who do not necessarily fall into the subcultural category of anime enthusiasts. Anime anniversaries represent an excellent instrument to engage simultaneously with them and with younger consumer groups through the launch of crossover initiatives in unprecedented industrial domains. The collaboration between Sunrise and Coca-Cola in the development and marketing of the canned coffee Georgia Newtype is especially illustrative of this trend.

Ready-to-drink canned coffee, marketed in Japan since the late 1960s, is a popular and ordinary product widely distributed throughout the country thanks to a tight network of convenience stores and automated vending machines. This easily available energizing drink is commonly associated with short refreshing breaks, be they on the streets or at the workplace. Coffee consumption tends to be preferred by Japanese men, but the All Japan Coffee Association records that consumption is rising consistently in professional men and women in the forty to fifty-nine age group.[10] This data closely corresponds with the predominantly male, now middle-aged, demographic that first encountered *Mobile Suit Gundam* as children and teenagers. Designing Georgia Newtype cans as unusual, commemorative, and eminently collectible objects allows for attracting interest not only from these committed coffee drinkers but also from less relevant coffee demographics, such as young anime audiences.

Such licensing partnerships are nonetheless far from infallible. Although they are routinely encouraged through professional conventions and trade shows, the nature of their cross-industry initiatives is often contingent and experimental, even for their own makers.[11] Furthermore, the economic effectiveness of such programs can vary consistently. Even so, licensing partnerships are increasingly sought after, as they promise to bring a number of additional benefits to the subscribing organizations. In fact, the cooperative interaction established between the intellectual property owner or licensor (e.g., Sunrise/Bandai Namco) and the licensee (e.g., the coffee brand Georgia/ the Coca-Cola Company) usually presupposes mutual benefits that easily exceed the aforementioned advantage of engaging with the partner's existing consumer base. Bandai Namco, for example, was able to manufacture suitable products for the *Gundam* anniversary – Georgia Newtype and other series of commemorative cans – without investing economic resources in coffee production and distribution facilities.

Less evident is what kind of additional benefit the Coca-Cola Company might have gained from partnering with a popular anime studio. Very often manufacturers enter into licensing agreements to extend the range of their already existing distribution channels, as larger wholesalers and retailers are more likely to distribute products branded with well-known intellectual properties. Yet with its ownership of "around 980,000 of Japan's 2.5 million beverage vending machines," the Coca-Cola Company was already in control of possibly the country's strongest distribution infrastructure.[12] In other words, the real advantage in acquiring the license of *Mobile Suit Gundam* has to be understood less in quantitative than in qualitative terms, less as a matter of vending machine numbers than one of exclusive access.

Indeed, one of the flagship events of the entire *Gundam* Beyond campaign was the opening of a temporary entertainment complex on Yokohama's Yamashita pier that was designed and operated by Bandai Namco to stay until March 2024. Besides interactive exhibitions, official shops, and a planned conference room for workshops and presentations, the site boasts a full-scale 18 m high moving Gundam as its main attraction. Designed well before the dramatic outbreak of the COVID-19 pandemic, the Gundam Factory Yokohama (GFY) was initially created to take advantage of both the fortieth anniversary of *Gundam* and the inflow of international tourists expected for the 2020 Olympic Games in nearby Tokyo. While these ambitious plans had to confront the harsh reality of the global pandemic, including the implementation of social distancing and the postponement of the site's opening to December 2020, the GFY's press launch was widely relayed through Japanese and foreign sources.

Inside the complex, which reproduces immersive architectures designed in consultation with *Gundam* creator Yoshiyuki Tomino, active audience engagement is a key aspect. In the "themed" environment of the GFY, the cultural footprint of the series has been translated accurately into an affective ambience whose design engages the visitors at a cognitive and noncognitive sensorial level, making them feel as if they are inhabiting the "real" world of popular anime characters. This is made explicit by the site's promotional material, in which two young women are photographed sightseeing and taking selfies at the top of the panoramic Gundam-Dock Tower.[13] The "coming to life" typical of animation is here given a new twist through immersive architecture and design practices based on protected intellectual properties.

In the context of this highly affective entertainment complex, the licensing agreement with Bandai Namco provided the Coca-Cola Company's

Japanese subsidiary with an opportunity to figure as the site's official "drink partner." This granted it the exclusive right to distribute Georgia coffee and other drink products on the premises. Visitors can not only enjoy drinking Coca-Cola in the official café with a vista of the moving Gundam but they can also purchase special edition canned coffee at a Gundam-shaped vending machine capable of reproducing the voices of the series' popular characters. In the interaction with this unusual vending machine, visual, aural, olfactory, gustatory, and tactile stimuli are unleashed simultaneously through an affective experience solicited by licensed design. Although the sale of coffee and entry tickets is a central goal for both partners, this temporary collaboration is equally a means of surreptitiously addressing consumers at the level of the body, establishing the conditions for a positive sensorial association with both Georgia coffee and *Mobile Suit Gundam*. While there is no guarantee that consumers will remain faithful to these products, this kind of experiential engagement is usually seen as reaching further than conventional advertising, as it establishes nonconscious "links of image and perception" capable of adding new meanings, or the creation of a personal "narrative," to future consumer exchanges with the companies.[14]

Through the Bandai Namco/Coca-Cola partnership, it is easy to see how cross-industry licensing agreements contribute to the growing proliferation of anime in the contemporary lived environment. These agreements frequently prey on the practical ordinariness of digital forms of engagement, including user-generated content like selfie shots, to mark their distinctiveness and to ensure their success. By mobilizing anime's cultural footprint, extended distribution brings into play complex design economies that increasingly overlap with tourism as well as the eventful and affective nature of everyday sensorial experiences.

"Mediatizing" Commercial Streets: The *Gundam* Manhole Project

Down in the streets, away from the imposing Gundam statue facing Yokohama's pier, is another unusual design object developed as part of *Gundam*'s fortieth anniversary. Although this object is not available for consumption, even here one of its implicit functions is subtle sensorial address. This artifact is nothing more than a humble manhole cover, the lid that hides access to basic underground infrastructures, such as sewers and gas pipelines.

The Gundam Manhole Project (GMP) was launched by Sunrise and its affiliated advertising agency Sōtsū as an initiative extended to Japanese municipalities and local governments willing to include these objects among their tourist promotion resources (Fig. 17.2).

Figure 17.2 An outcome of the Gundam Manhole Project. Along with other covers from
different anime franchises, it paves the way to the Kadokawa Culture Museum
in Tokorozawa. Notice the corporate marks of Sōtsū and Sunrise
at its top. Photo by Jaqueline Berndt.

According to the project's instruction notes, the rights to install covers
depicting some of the series' most iconic characters – Amuro, Char, and
their respective mobile suits – are granted for free upon presentation of a
convincing expression of interest.[15] Certain conditions, however, have to
be met before any formal agreement. For example, the covers and their
frames must be installed exclusively on pedestrian streets with the total costs
borne by the recipient. Moreover, these covers are only made in standard
and unmodifiable designs, thus ruling out the possible inclusion of local
heritage elements alongside the fictional *Gundam* universe. From Sunrise's
perspective, this choice may be seen as an attempt at protecting some pro-
prietary assets from unwanted associations with objects and sites that, for
whatever reason, might prove inconsistent with the narrative or aesthetic
content of its flagship series. Potential inconsistencies can damage the value
of intellectual properties by attracting popular criticism and disaffection, so
strict limits are imposed on their licensed use. These measures are a further
reminder of the contingent and project-based nature of anime licensing, as
well as the active role attributed to the public at the moment of reception.

Once installed in pedestrian streets these eye-catching covers promise to
merge with everyday urban experiences, subtly aestheticizing or "mediatiz-
ing" them.[16] They participate with other urban furniture in the "production
of locality," an ordinary and collective place-making practice articulated by
heterogeneous networks of local inhabitants, visitors, and other human and

nonhuman agents, such as city councils and tourist websites.[17] Strategically placed in commercial pedestrian areas, these manhole covers contribute to the forging of image and perception associations aimed at facilitating consumption. They address passers-by through a kinesthetic experience enhanced by a meaningful narrative.

What we are calling "narrative" has to be understood less in terms of a direct reference to some textual content from the anime series than as a shared and unstructured affectivity evoked by the unusual presence of Gundam on the streets – quite literally, what we have previously named the anime's cultural footprint. Indeed, while locals and visitors might provide different accounts of this mediatized urban narrative, its collective articulation and dissemination through everyday discourses, brochures, television programs, and online sources still fulfills two complementary objectives. On the one hand, this collective articulation brings more Japanese visitors to off-the-radar local municipalities, thereby requalifying them as tourist attractions. On the other, it establishes – especially in the eyes of international anime enthusiasts – a commodified image of Japan as a country in which media culture and entertainment possess a constant and tangible presence, even in remote areas.

Exploiting the cultural significance of *Gundam*'s anniversary, the Beyond initiative responds to the need of experimenting with new distribution strategies able to transcend niche segmentation and anime's domestic consumption. At the same time, it can be seen as part of a broader model of national and urban requalification that increasingly mobilizes not only cultural, natural, and architectural heritage but also intellectual properties of previously stigmatized anime as legitimated sources of economic valorization.[18] In fact, the GMP fits particularly well into the Japanese government's ongoing aspiration to foster domestic and international tourism through public-private partnerships based on audiovisual intellectual properties.[19] As such, this initiative can be taken as a further sign of broader demographic shifts in anime consumption, which are slowly reorienting distribution toward older and nonregular local consumers or previously secondary foreign audiences.

Conclusion

Today, anime distribution appears as a dispersed and processual phenomenon that can take as many forms as there are infinitely divisible intellectual property rights. In this respect, the formal and informal distribution of anime through digital infrastructures, increasingly organized in the form of streaming and video-on-demand platforms, is just one of its multifarious manifestations.[20] Instead of attempting a panoramic overview of all its possible forms, the focus here has been on some current distribution strategies through the lenses of the fortieth anniversary of *Mobile Suit Gundam*. Such a perspective allows us to reflect on the distribution of anime across products and services not usually associated with its consumption – a phenomenon named extended anime distribution above. By mapping formal exchanges based on intellectual properties, it has been highlighted how licensing strategies have been developed in response to a profitable, yet constantly aging and globalizing, Japanese anime market. The simultaneous televisual and digital distribution of *Gundam*'s new series, the commercialization of Georgia Newtype, the opening of the Gundam Factory Yokohama, and the launching of the Gundam Manhole Project have all been considered as different instances of apparently unrelated transformations that have occurred in recent years across the Japanese mediascape.

In retrospect, it has been particularly fitting to analyze these emerging trends through reference to *Mobile Suit Gundam*, a series that in the early 1980s was accidentally rescued from oblivion precisely because of a licensing deal. Surprising as it may sound today, the airing of the first *Gundam* anime series, in its dramatically and narratively complex form, failed to meet the interest of its ideal target audience of children to the point that it was canceled prematurely.[21] Taking advantage of this situation, toy maker Bandai – at that time only a modest licensee from Sunrise – secured the rights of the series' mechanical designs to produce plastic model kits, which were then presented to a slightly older audience of teenagers and young men. The contingent repositioning of these models on the market triggered an unexpected series of commercial successes and industrial acquisitions, which eventually turned *Gundam* into an exceptionally long-running media mix and Bandai Namco into one of the world's largest entertainment companies.

As the latest development in this lengthy corporate history, the Beyond anniversary was structured around a much wider network of cross-industry initiatives stretching anime distribution from digital channels to official cafés, live events, tourist attractions, and more. Rather than an arbitrary marketing tool straightforwardly pushed upon consumers, this campaign was entirely premised on the idea of an active and shifting audience, whose changing taste and behavior had to be researched, debated, and possibly anticipated by countless creative professionals, brand managers, and consultants.[22] The Beyond campaign appears simultaneously as a routinized and risk-averse, highly experimental and collaborative management practice.

Campaigns such as *Gundam* Beyond play a crucial role in the mediatization of everyday life, deploying design-intensive, affective, and experiential economies able to encourage more spending from aging or casual consumers. Moreover, they also address Japanese tourists and international anime enthusiasts more regularly. Over time, this extended distribution has emerged as a contingent answer to a series of technological transformations that have slightly altered the morphology of the lucrative anime market of the late twentieth century. While it might be incorrect to disentangle these interconnected processes, taking their result as the dawn of a radical "newtype" era,[23] *Gundam*'s fortieth anniversary is a powerful testament to the fact that it is not just anime series that change and age over time but also their audiences and the whole media environment around them.

Notes

1. Marc Steinberg, *Anime's Media Mix: Franchising Toys and Characters in Japan* (Minneapolis: University of Minnesota Press, 2012).
2. Shū Yamaguchi, *Nyūtaipu no jidai: shinjidai o ikinuku nijūyon no shikō, kōdō shōshiki* (Tokyo: Diamond-sha, 2019).
3. B. Joseph Pine and James H. Gilmore, *The Experience Economy* (Boston: Harvard Business Review Press, 2011).
4. "'Kidō Senshi Gandamu 40-shūnen purojekuto shidō!' 5 sakuhin no tenkai kettei & LUNA SEA ni yoru tēma-kyoku happyō!," 2018, www.gundam.info/news/hot-topics/news_hot-topics_20181121_12.html.
5. See the campaign's official website, http://gundam40th.net/.
6. Thomas Lamarre, "Coming to Life: Cartoon Animals and Natural Philosophy." In *Pervasive Animation*, edited by Suzanne Buchan (New York: Routledge, 2013), 134.
7. Martin Hayward, "How Brands Can Reach Out to the Digitally Distracted Consumer," *Campaign*, 2015, www.campaignlive.co.uk/article/brands-reach-digitally-distracted-consumer/1362283?utm_source=website&utm_medium=social.
8. Greg Battersby and Danny Simon, *The New and Complete Business of Licensing: The Essential Guide to Monetizing Intellectual Property* (Westport: Kent Press, 2018).
9. Anon., "A Look at the Market," *License Global*, special issue *LEJ Preview 2017* (March 2017): 9, www.licenseglobal.com/magazine/lej-preview-2017
10. The All Japan Coffee Association, "Coffee Market in Japan," 2012, 7, http://coffee.ajca.or.jp/wp-content/uploads/2012/07/coffee_market_in_japan.pdf.
11. Dario Lolli, "Infrastructures for Media 'Extension': Licensing Trade Expos and the Production of Media Distribution," *Media, Culture & Society*, 44, no. 2 (2022): 210–29, https://doi.org/10.1177/01634437211037003.
12. The Coca-Cola Company, "Coca-Cola Ready-to-Drink Coffee Market in Japan," 2017, www.coca-colacompany.com/news/coca-cola-ready-to-drink-coffee-market-in-japan.
13. See https://gundam-factory.net/howtoenjoy/.
14. Celia Lury, *Cultural Rights: Technology, Legality and Personality* (London: Routledge, 1993), 87. "The more effectively an experience engages the senses, the more memorable it will be," Pine and Gilmore, *The Experience Economy*, 88.

15. Kidō senshi Gandamu 40-shūnen purojekuto kōshiki saito, "Gandamu man-hōru," n.d., https://g-manhole.net/
16. Nick Couldry and Andreas Hepp, "Conceptualizing Mediatization: Contexts, Traditions, Arguments," *Communication Theory*, 23, no. 3 (2013): 191–202.
17. Arjun Appadurai, *Modernity at Large: Cultural Dimensions of Globalization* (Minneapolis: University of Minnesota Press, 1996), 178; see also Guy Julier, "Urban Designscapes and the Production of Aesthetic Consent," *Urban Studies*, 42, no. 5–6 (2005): 869–87.
18. Takeshi Matsui, "Nation Branding through Stigmatized Popular Culture: The 'Cool Japan' Craze among Central Ministries in Japan," *Hitotsubashi Journal of Commerce and Management*, 48, no. 1 (2014): 81–97.
19. Takayoshi Yamamura, "Contents Tourism and Local Community Response: Lucky Star and Collaborative Anime-Induced Tourism in Washimiya," *Japan Forum*, 27, no. 1 (2015): 61–62.
20. Marc Steinberg, *The Platform Economy: How Japan Transformed the Consumer Internet* (Minneapolis: University of Minnesota Press, 2019); Rayna Denison, "Anime's Distribution Worlds: Formal and Information Distribution in the Analogue and Digital Eras," *Routledge Handbook of Japanese Media* (New York: Routledge, 2018).
21. Ian Condry, *The Soul of Anime: Collaborative Creativity and Japan's Media Success Story* (Durham: Duke University Press, 2013), 123–25.
22. Condry, *The Soul of Anime*. See also Lolli, "Infrastructures for Media 'Extension'."
23. Yamaguchi, *Nyūtaipu no jidai*.

PART IX

Forms of Use

18

PATRICK W. GALBRAITH

Manga Readerships, Imaginative Agency, and the "Erotic Barrier"

Manga Markets and Readers

In 2021, the Japanese manga market was evaluated at 675.9 billion yen.[1] With booming digital sales due to COVID-19, the combined digital and paper market was estimated to be the "largest in history."[2] The rise of digital production and distribution and stand-alone manga publications has generated ongoing changes in the field, but the postwar model centering on print magazines still casts a long shadow. In this model, manga narratives would be initiated and gain a following through serialization in weekly or monthly magazines. If readers of the magazine supported the work, often gauged by surveys and letters, a serial could continue for years or even decades. Production of such long-form serials had major effects on the lives of artists; the successful among them became wealthy celebrities and idols for readers. The path to walk in their footsteps was laid out by magazines. It was conventional to learn to draw at a young age by copying art and submitting it to reader pages and, as one advanced and grew, to editors. With the intimacy of magazine and manga communication, the line between readership and fandom, consumer and producer, could be almost nonexistent.

In the second half of the twentieth century, the extremely robust Japanese manga market was divided by target age and gender. Strong stylistic and thematic differences were refined and reproduced through core publishers, magazines, and editorial boards. The four primary publication categories of manga are for boys (*shōnen manga*), girls (*shōjo manga*), youth (*seinen manga*), and women (*josei manga*). Of the four categories, magazines publishing manga for boys boast the highest circulation numbers and greatest cultural impact. In the traditional model, it was entirely possible for readers to start young and mature with magazines, including transitioning to those targeting older readers; it was equally possible to stay a loyal reader of particular magazines, gender/genre categories, and artists over a lifetime. The important thing about the manga market as it formed in Japan was that readers did not need to graduate from manga, which was fully established as a mature medium by the 1980s. Not only was manga big business, not only did it make its producers money, but it also supported artists with relative creative freedom to tell a wide range of stories. Moreover, it provided readers with choices and opportunities to develop their own imaginative agency.

Following on from the lack of age and gender limits on readership in Japan, it should come as little surprise that there is also content categorized as "adult" (*seijin muke manga*) and "ladies comics" (*redīsu komikku*), which can to some extent be taken as the sexually explicit corollaries of manga for "youth" and "women," respectively. Their sale is at times restricted to those aged eighteen and older. In practice, these age restrictions are not always enforced, and sexual content percolates to varying degrees into other categories. Themes and depictions that may strike readers outside Japan as very mature appear in manga categorized as for boys and girls, for example. Likewise, there is nothing stopping boys and girls from reaching for publications categorized as for older readers, with the (at least supposed) exception of age-restricted content.

This flies in the face of the deep-rooted notion that children should be shielded from mature content, which had a devastating effect on comics in North America. In *Seduction of the Innocent*, originally published in 1954 amid concern about juvenile delinquency, psychiatrist Fredric Wertham summarized the position – by then having spread to various corners of the United States via the popular press, educators, and religious organizations – that comic books should be regulated to avoid "social harm."[3] The rising tide of critics successfully pressured US publishers to establish – also in 1954 – the Comics Code Authority. This authority cut objectionable content such as violence and sex from what was to be a medium for children, after disastrous publicity generated by hearings on comics convened by the Senate Subcommittee on Juvenile Delinquency.

Such was not the case in Japan. Manga has seen constant efforts to expand the horizons of the medium with regard to representation and readership. A dramatic core example is provided by Osamu Tezuka, a postwar pioneer who folded ideas from world literature, film, and theater into his comics for children, in the process winning the hearts of millions and inspiring generations of disciples and rivals. As early as 1949, some of Tezuka's manga were already being deemed inappropriately mature, but he pressed on. In doing so, Tezuka and others established manga as a compelling and crucial form of popular culture before the spread of television. When it did come, television complemented, rather than competed with, manga in print. By adapting his hit manga *Astro Boy* (1952–68) into Japan's first weekly televised anime series in 1963, which included marketing tie-ups and toys,

Tezuka created synergy between comics, animation, and merchandise featuring characters. The result was increased manga sales and anime ratings; it also inspired consumption of related material forms and products, further invigorating the franchise. This strategy quickly permeated the entire industry. As such, the expanded manga market has generated appealing content, exposed more and more people to it, and coaxed them into its embrace.

Meanwhile, a new wave of comics artists, inspired by Tezuka but feeling that he was not mature enough, challenged him in the 1960s with their alternative *gekiga*, a type of graphic narrative that pushed boundaries with gritty sociopolitical commentary and spectacular violence appealing to young adults. Even as Tokyo's youth ordinances can be traced back to this moment and fears about manga and crime, artists and publishers did not bend to pressure. If what was prohibited by the Comics Code Authority in the United States made its way into Underground Comix in the 1960s, then *gekiga* at that time was not only adopted as counterculture but also proliferated rapidly. It opened new markets and potentials for expression and was integrated back into the mainstream by the late 1960s and early 1970s. From the late 1960s into the 1970s, comics for boys and girls tested the limits of sexual expression. Successive booms in sexually explicit adult manga in the 1970s, 1980s, and 1990s accelerated and amplified this tendency, and niche magazines incubated eccentric and unique talent.[4] Sexually explicit ladies comics drew attention with the founding of magazines such as *Be Love* and *Lady's Comic You* in 1980 and 1982, respectively. Further confusing for people who see comics as childish and distinct from mature content is the cute cartoony style that spread from Tezuka and manga for boys and girls to become the industry standard, irrespective of serious stories and depictions of violence and sex.

As manga readership, anime viewership, and the intense interest and investment characteristic of fandom continued to converge in the 1970s, clubs and conventions brought manga and anime enthusiasts together to share and sell original and derivative works. Some sought out professional debuts, others were just fans of particular series, characters, or creators. Spot-sales events for *dōjinshi*, or material published and distributed outside of traditional commercial channels, began to flourish. Certain forms evolved from here, most notably *yaoi* (works pairing male characters) and *lolicon* (works centering on cute girl characters). The flow of artists from *dōjinshi* to professional status impacted the manga industry as a whole.

For the most part, manga artists and publishers did not aggressively pursue legal action for copyright infringement. This allowed the poaching and reproduction of character images in *dōjinshi*, and drove fan participation in the largest spot-sales event, the Comic Market, to incredible heights. When

Figure 18.1 Catalog for Comic Market 97, held over four days in December 2019.

founded in December 1975, the Comic Market attracted thirty-two sellers and 700 participants, but in December 2019 over 32,000 sellers and 750,000 people attended the event over the course of four days (Fig. 18.1).[5] By one estimate, eight million magazines were sold. If we average the price at 500 yen each, four billion yen changed hands.

There are by now dedicated *dōjinshi* shops, some owned by companies publicly listed on the Japanese stock exchange. The streak of incredible growth was finally disrupted by the COVID-19 pandemic. Due to restrictions on in-person gatherings, 2020 will be remembered as the first in forty-five years not to have a physical convening of the Comic Market.

Manga as a whole has been impacted by an insistence on freedom of expression in this alternative sphere of production. Typically, the only prohibitions are that one cannot directly copy existing work and must abide by Japanese laws concerning obscenity. This does not in any way exclude the use of established characters, as demonstrated by the phenomenon of *yaoi* being supercharged by the female fandom surrounding *Captain Tsubasa* (by Yōichi Takahashi, in *Weekly Shōnen Jump*, 1981–88), ostensibly a sports manga and anime for boys, and *lolicon* emerging from male fandom surrounding cute girl characters in manga and anime for girls.[6] The forms here are fundamentally hybrid, or the result of manga and anime enthusiasts crossing gender/genre lines and collaborating. The result is work that pushes boundaries, often sexual, as in explicit pairings of male characters in *yaoi* and explicit sex with and between cute girl characters in *lolicon*. Indeed, between 20 and 30 percent of all the content is sexually explicit, and much of the bestselling *dōjinshi* at the Comic Market and beyond involve such expression. Through the process of "playing gender" and "playing sex/uality,"[7] fan content such as *yaoi* and *lolicon* spread into the mainstream from the late 1970s onward, most notably in the commercial forms of boys love (BL) and *bishōjo* (cute girls) works in the 1990s. In sum, *dōjinshi* culture feeds back into the manga machine by promoting serials and characters, cultivating new ideas and talent, and reenergizing the affective connections of fans. At the same time, with this broader field of manga readership, consumption, and use in frame, we can clearly see how women read manga for boys, men read manga for girls, and all of this shapes manga production that caters to and encourages fan engagement with magazines, serials, and characters.

An example will help ground this discussion and bring all the previous points about manga readership into focus. Consider *Weekly Shōnen Jump*, launched in 1968, which is the most popular manga magazine in Japan. While sales have suffered from the shrinking population and from competition with digital devices, at a high point in the mid-1990s, an estimated 40 percent of all publications in Japan were manga. In that decade, *Weekly Shōnen Jump* circulated over 6.5 million copies and reported a total readership of 18 million people. Manga serialized in its pages, such as *Dragon Ball* (1984–95), were adapted into anime that became television staples and cultural touchstones for generations of fans. Although its title informs that it is a magazine categorized as for boys, *Weekly Shōnen Jump*'s circulation and readership numbers indicate that its reach is not limited to that age or gender group.

Looking into the pages of *Weekly Shōnen Jump* reveals much about manga readership today. It first stands out that manga artists and readers are not easily contained by commercial content categories (Fig. 18.2).

For example, *Food Wars! Shokugeki no Soma,* serialized in *Weekly Shōnen Jump* from 2012 to 2019, features art by Shun Saeki, who professionally debuted drawing comics for adults – that is, sexually explicit comics categorized as "for adults." The magazine also publishes works like *To Love Ru* (2006–09), which includes scenes directly employing adult manga innovations such as "naughty tentacles." Small wonder, then, that

Figure 18.2 Cover of *Weekly Shōnen Jump* featuring *Food Wars! Shokugeki no Soma*.

Weekly Shōnen Jump appeals not only to the boys who in theory it targets but equally to the adults who make up the statistical majority of its readership. Furthermore, serials focused on attractive male characters, especially sports and adventure franchises, draw female readers, who are now a key (if not always acknowledged) demographic for *Weekly Shōnen Jump* and similar magazines.[8] At the Comic Market, where over half of those coming to buy and sell *dōjinshi* are women,[9] the genre designation "Jump" is all but synonymous with pairing male characters in romantic and sexual relationships. The desires of these fans are reflected in the pages of the commercial magazines that cater to them, even as these magazines increasingly adopt affective and erotic styles from fanworks, and fans debut and work as professional artists.

Despite regular forecasts of imminent doom (in the face of record sales), the manga juggernaut continues to chug along. This was demonstrated by *Demon Slayer: Kimetsu no Yaiba*, a manga serialized in *Weekly Shōnen Jump* from 2016 to 2020. After a relatively low-key run in its first years, when it was overshadowed by longer-running flagships of the magazine, the series had its major break with an anime adaptation in 2019. The twenty-six episodes of the TV anime series became a smash hit, driving sales of collected trade paperback volumes of *Demon Slayer*. By the end of 2020, it was reported that the series held the top twenty-two spots for individual manga volume sales. Moreover, an animated movie extending the story of the animated series had the biggest box office opening in Japanese film history and, again, by the end of 2020, had become the highest-grossing Japanese film of all time. It is all the more shocking because the *Demon Slayer* movie broke these records amid a global pandemic limiting public gatherings.

The case of *Demon Slayer* illuminates not only the power of the expanded manga market, but also the potential fame and fortune available to a diverse range of creators. Born in 1989 and debuting professionally in 2013, *Demon Slayer* creator Koyoharu Gotouge – identified by a *Weekly Shōnen Jump* employee as female but not confirmed publicly – was young and a relative newcomer when they smashed records and reaped rewards. Climbing to the top of the pyramid, let alone so rapidly, is obviously rare, but the base of that pyramid is broad and offers many others routes up. According to an industry survey of the market in 2003, of the 291 manga magazines published at the time, only 23, or 8 percent of the total number, were categorized as for boys.[10] (The number of manga magazines was 266 by 2007 and continues to drop steadily. Recall that the relatively small percentage represented by manga magazines for boys has always had the largest print runs and circulation.) Beyond that are countless other categories of magazines, and female artists dominate magazines dedicated to manga for girls and women, BL, and ladies comics. As Gotouge's work in *Weekly Shōnen Jump* suggests, women are similarly dispersed across other categories. This is not merely a matter of representation and earning a living, although it is that, too. The diverse plethora of manga magazines open possibilities for mature expression by and for women and minorities. This is all the truer further down the pyramid with *dōjinshi* and their supporting conventions and communities. There are abundant chances to learn and participate. So it is that manga provides readers with choices and opportunities to develop their own imaginative agency, if not also to become creators themselves.

Challenges for Manga (Studies)

With anime's increased accessibility throughout the world via streaming services such as Netflix, Crunchyroll, and Amazon, and major investments being made in this sector to secure distribution rights and original content, the established pattern of manga readership, consumption, and use is facing new challenges. One of these concerns *dōjinshi*, or the alternative sphere of manga production, and a renegotiation of copyright.[11] During the COVID-19 pandemic, with *dōjinshi* events being canceled, and online events and sales rising, erotic *dōjinshi* were particularly hard hit. High-profile anime releases have been marked by production companies asking fans to refrain from using their characters, sometimes with threats of legal action. One of these came with the highly anticipated concluding chapter of the *Neon Genesis Evangelion* animated film series. As global hype gained momentum, the right holders released guidelines against fanworks that are for so-called pornographic purposes. This is not entirely new, as editors at *Weekly Shōnen Jump* once decried the fan output of *dōjinshi* during the *Captain Tsubasa* boom as a "pornographic sham," but the frequency and firmness of these statements comes against a specific backdrop.

While anime franchises such as *Neon Genesis Evangelion* arguably exploited the appeal of characters to encourage fan engagement up to and including *dōjinshi*,[12] international distribution and exposure seem to call for tighter control of intellectual property. Damage to character images has been part of legal arguments and crackdowns from large corporations such as Nintendo – infamously litigious and bringing the hammer down in the Japanese context for Pokémon *dōjinshi* – but it was long assumed that manga publishers and anime studios would more or less play along with fans. Online distribution and increasing profits from expensive products exceeding the typical print magazines sold at conventions have become an issue. Furthermore, *dōjinshi* face challenges with globalization of the market and competing copyright regimes, as demonstrated by negotiations around the proposed Trans-Pacific Partnership Agreement in the late 2010s. Ironically, the problem may also have been exacerbated by spot-sales events for *dōjinshi* being forced online during COVID-19. Visibility of the products and sales, long an absolutely open secret, demanded action.

Rather than copyright issues, much of the debate surrounding manga in global circulation and reception has been on sexual content and its regulation. To combat the scourge of child abuse, laws against child pornography have been evolving since the 1970s, and these have morphed into legal actions against adult comics, cartoons, and computer/console games from Japan. Countries such as Canada, the United Kingdom, and Australia have been among the most proactive in pursuing laws that would ban certain types of cartoon images, most notably sexual expression featuring cute manga and anime characters, and punish people for possession. There are consequences here, including not only arrests and prosecutions, but also scrutiny of all manga expression as a threat to children and women, and suspicion of its readership, consumption, and use as somehow influencing or inspiring sexual abuse and crime. The consensus appears to be building: In a report published in 2016, the United Nations Committee for the

Elimination of Discrimination Against Women advocates for new regulations based on its conclusion that "pornography, video games and animation products such as manga promote sexual violence against women and girls."[13] Notice how "manga," employed inaccurately, becomes equivalent to pornography and deemed harmful.

Much of the anger directed at Japan is based on the assumption that it does not regulate content, despite decades of struggle in the country about whether or not manga is "harmful" (yūgai). In fact, not long after Tezuka's manga was running afoul of parents (see above), a movement against harmful publications in Japan saw manga being burned in school yards in the 1950s. This mirrors the movement against comic books in the United States (leading to the key publication by Wertham), which also came with public incineration of offending content. (Reports have it that book burnings, with all their symbolic power, are still occurring in parts of North America.[14]) The pressure to get manga off of shelves and out of children's hands in Japan has mostly followed from the intuition that comics disrupt education, if not also provide a bad education that corrupts kids and turns them stupid, perverted, and/or criminal. In this way, the problem observed overseas of protecting children from predators transforms into protecting children from their own prurient interests and potential downfall. Closer to the Western model was the movement against harmful comics in Japan in the 1990s, when the target of regulatory concern morphed into adults and issues such as "the commodification of sex." Laws were passed, and by the time that manga underwent its first obscenity trial, which reached the Supreme Court of Japan in 2008, judges were inserting their own opinions about adult perverts, pedophiles, and predators; as one researcher puts it, the goal became the protection of children from adults with their own suspect "interests."[15] It thus became possible for high-ranking politicians such as Shintarō Ishihara, then Governor of Tokyo, to say that, "There are after all perverts in the world. Unfortunate people with messed up DNA. ... A man can't marry a 7- or 8-year-old girl or rape an innocent child, but somehow this should be allowed if the stories are drawings? Such things serve no purpose. I think that there is harm and not a single benefit from them." Worried about the "harmful environment" (yūgai kankyō), which twists desires, Masatada Tsuchiya, a senior member of the ruling Liberal Democratic Party at the national level, added that, "Human barriers are lowered by seeing over and over again manga, anime, and games depicting the rape and group assault of girl-children, which leads to crime."[16]

All of this in turn invigorates the movement for free speech and against censorship in Japan. For example, when a library was found to stock

thousands of novels dedicated to BL with manga-style covers and illustrations, staff removed the offending books, only for feminists to demand
an explanation for what made these books "harmful." When the library
could not answer, they returned the books to the shelves. This was taken
as an example of arbitrary enforcement based on concerns from those
with normative bias, which derailed what might have been a produc-
tive discussion. While one might, for example, raise legitimate concerns
about depictions of force and sexual violence in BL (and more broadly
adult manga and ladies comics) as "love rape,"[17] instead this was buried
under an overstretched and underexplained notion of "harm." Likewise,
the seemingly commonsense discourse leaning toward new regulation for
the protection of children espoused by Ishihara, Tsuchiya, and others
has been perceived as a power grab by conservatives who want to dictate
what sort of sex and fantasy is "good."[18] Indeed, Ishihara's call in Tokyo
to merely zone material that might be outright banned in other parts of
the world was met with a wall of resistance from manga artists and publishers, lawyers, and concerned citizens. Artists from all the generations
of manga, representing everything from Tezuka-style eroticism and girls
comics to *gekiga* and ladies comics, stood shoulder to shoulder to con-
demn the bid for censorship of any kind. They confessed to personally not
liking the content blasted by Ishihara, but on principle supported manga
expression in all its diversity. Many wondered once the door was open
to censorship if the target would not expand from "obvious" offend-
ers to more generally erotic content, which is exactly what happened
when Ishihara's ordinance passed in Tokyo and BL bore the brunt of the
board's efforts to designate and zone out of sight more and more comics
deemed "harmful."[19]

Rather than tuning into these ongoing debates in Japan, which often
go unnoticed due to linguistic barriers, widespread ignorance and unease
about manga and its readership can undergird movement for outright
bans abroad. In 2020, Australian activists investigating manga for sale in
bookstores found what they glossed as Astro Boy and Pokémon next to
titles that meet the definition of "child exploitation material." This reached
the offices of Stirling Griff, then a senator in Australia (but defeated in
2022), who singled out *Eromanga Sensei* (2014–21; Fig. 18.3). Serialized
in *Dengeki Daioh*, a magazine that walks a tightrope between manga for
boys and youth, online databases tag the content of *Eromanga Sensei* as
"love comedy," "home drama," and "industry." The story is about a pair
of step-siblings who struggle with their feelings for each other as they collaborate to produce "light novels;" the brother (age 15) writes, while his sister (age 12) provides character illustrations. Although not sexually explicit,

Figure 18.3 Cover of the first trade paperback in the *Eromanga Sensei* series.

Eromanga Sensei plays with eroticism in its art, namely in depictions of characters, their relations, and their work.

Despite its relatively mainstream positioning in Japan, Griff told journalists that the contents were "so disturbing I won't, I just can't, describe them."[20] Griff's name appeared in the news again in October 2020, when it was reported that Australian authorities were cracking down on the importation of sexually explicit comics from Japan. (Given the free flow of content on the internet, this was more or less a symbolic move.)

In addition to legislative and legal actions against such content, private companies and distributors have also taken matters into their own hands. In July 2020, it was reported that the *Eromanga Sensei* manga was among the many works delisted from Amazon Kindle. This occurred only on the English-language site – the original releases were still available for purchase in Japanese on the Japanese-language site – and the reasons for many of the delistings remains unclear. This is not the first time that works have disappeared from Amazon without warning, and it has also happened in Japan. In July 2013, for example, forty-six sexually explicit manga for adults suddenly vanished from Amazon Japan's e-book marketplace for causes unknown.[21] Certain publishers, serials, and keywords seem to have been targeted for violation of some standard, be it Japanese or global, but many found troubling the vague process of deliberation and denial of an opportunity to appeal.[22]

Now more than ever, manga scholars, researchers, and experts are called to lean in, rather than shy away from, serious debates about manga readership, consumption, and use. There continues nonetheless to be a paucity in discourse. To begin with, manga studies in Japan has historically tended to avoid eroticism, especially as it relates to explicit sexual expression for adult men. This dearth in the literature is a problem, as it is the content in question that is most often associated with current perceived dangers and calls for regulation. The limited Japanese-language texts on the topic that do exist are seldom translated into English or introduced into academic discussions, let alone policymaking circles. At the same time, the negative reception and backlash from abroad influences Japanese politicians, who are emboldened to crack down on content that they find disturbing for whatever reason. Seen against the tightening regulations and erasure of certain images, manga scholars and the general public alike may hear about controversial content but understand increasingly little about what they are supposed to be discussing.

A major challenge for manga studies, then, is resistance to manga-style sexual expression, "the erotic barrier," which has at its core "a negative response to the erotic."[23] The barrier can be further built up by opposition to particular forms of erotic expression, for example, *lolicon*, which thereby discourages seeking out situated knowledge. The consequences include a fundamentally biased and inaccurate view. The content of adult manga is often unknown and understudied. Critics in Japan have argued it is akin to "dark matter," or the missing mass that is necessary for us to understand how things work.[24] There is a general lack of appreciation for the deep and complex entanglement of sexual expression in manga, which has led eroticism to "spread thinly and broadly across the entire manga world."[25] This is how it becomes possible to go from an encounter with *Eromanga Sensei* to a backlash against sexually explicit manga for adults. Simultaneously, all of this content is pushed into the category of "child pornography" or "abuse material," which effectively makes it impossible to study without preconceived hostility. At best, there is a sense that it is inappropriate to research and analyze it as an integral facet of manga expression.

Even when considering explicit sexual expression, there are myriad assumptions about readership, consumption, and use. Many seem surprised by the insider estimate that around 30 percent of the artists producing manga categorized as for adults are women.[26] The number is much higher if we take into account artists in categories that are erotic and even explicit but principally targeted to women and typically not counted in these estimates. In the industry survey cited above, these categories would be BL and ladies comics, published in a combined sixty-six magazines as opposed to the fifty-six magazines listed as "adult oriented."[27] There is also "teens love," which rose in manga for girls from the 1990s and siphoned sexual expression from ladies comics. And, as suggested by pen-names such as Kengo Yonekura, Sōji Unite, and Naizō Kudara, it is not always evident that the artist is in fact a woman. Artists can appear male or female, both or neither; inclusivity, fluidity, and freedom of expression attract a wide range of artists, as well as a diverse readership, which of course includes women. Factoring in that the bulk of *dōjinshi* producers are women, and that much of this content is sexual expression featuring established characters, women are arguably the majority of erotic manga artists in Japan. This makes clear that assumptions about manga readership, consumption, and use need to be balanced with empirical work and grounded analysis. The point holds beyond sexually explicit content to manga as a whole.

Conclusion

To advance manga studies, it is necessary to question how and why scholars and critics insist on the term "manga," which can function as a marker of difference and discourage dialogue with the burgeoning international field of comics studies. Even on a charged topic such as sexual expression, it is not as if erotic comics do not exist outside of Japan, even in the United States before and after the Comics Code crackdown. It is moreover unlikely that erotic and taboo-busting images in imported magazines did not impact the expansion of sexual expression in manga from the late 1960s into the 1970s. Suffice to mention the influence of "Western pin-ups" on Gō Nagai's *Shameless School* (*Harenchi gakuen*, 1968–72), serialized in *Weekly Shōnen Jump*, but the currents run deep and strong.[28] Below-the-belt expressions are a hidden factor not only in comics and animation around the world but also in dialogue with Japan and vice versa. There is a legacy of exchange here, even on expressions that seem somehow fundamentally "manga" or "Japanese," for example, "naughty tentacles."[29] The difference in Japan is, one, the scale of production and readership, and two, the history of resisting regulation, which allowed for an expanded and open culture of imaginary sex in public. The past, present, and future of this culture offer exciting opportunities for comics studies in Japan and beyond.

Notes

1. Ken'ichi Amano, "'Kusa no ne' oshi no manga atsuku," *Nihon Keizai Shimbun*, June 25, 2022, www.nikkei.com/article/DGKKZO62059300V20C22A6 KNTP00/. For more, see Julien Bouvard, "Turning the Page: Reading Manga in the Pandemic Age." In *The Coronavirus Pandemic in Japanese Literature and Popular Culture*, edited by Mina Qiao (London: Routledge, 2023), 112–24.
2. Amano, "'Kusa no ne.'"
3. Fredric Wertham, *Seduction of the Innocent* (Laurel: Main Road Books, 2004), 330. See also 334–35.
4. Kaoru Nagayama, *Erotic Comics in Japan: An Introduction to Eromanga* (Amsterdam: Amsterdam University Press, 2020), 65–68.
5. Yūta Onda, "'Komikku māketto 97' raijō ninzū 75-man nin, natsu komi ni tsuzuki komike shijō saita o kōshin," *Kai-You*, December 31, 2019, https://kai-you.net/article/70630.
6. Patrick W. Galbraith, *Otaku and the Struggle for Imagination in Japan* (Durham: Duke University Press, 2019), 25–55.
7. Yukari Fujimoto, *Watashi no ibasho wa doko ni aru no? Shōjo manga ga utsusu kokoro no katachi* (Tokyo: Gakuyō Shobō, 1998), 196.
8. Jessica Bauwens-Sugimoto, "Queering Black Jack: A Look at How Manga Adapts to Changing Reading Demographics," *Orientaliska Studier*, 147 (2016): 114–18. Open Access.
9. Comic Market Preparations Committee, "What Is the Comic Market?," *The Official Comic Market Site*, February 25, 2008, www.comiket.co.jp/info-a/WhatIsEng080225.pdf.
10. Keiko Kawamata, "Nihon no kontentsu sangyō no genjō," *Kyōto manejimento rebyū*, 7 (2005): 129.
11. Takumi Furusato, "Derivative Content and Property Rights: How Does Fanfiction Work in the Anime and Manga Industry?," *Anime News Network*, March 12, 2021, www.animenewsnetwork.com/feature/2021-03-12/derivative-content-and-property-rights-how-does-fanfiction-work-in-the-anime-and-manga-industry/.170398.
12. Hiroki Azuma, *Otaku: Japan's Database Animals* (Minneapolis: University of Minnesota Press, 2009), 37–38.
13. United Nations, "Concluding Observations on the Combined Seventh and Eighth Periodic Reports of Japan," *Committee on the Elimination of Discrimination against Women*, March 10, 2016, https://digitallibrary.un.org/record/833895?ln=en.
14. Free Speech Project, "Can It Happen Here? The Return of Book Banning and Burning in the United States," Georgetown University, 2023, https://freespeechproject.georgetown.edu/can-it-happen-here-the-return-of-book-banning-and-burning-in-the-united-states/.
15. Kirsten Cather, *The Art of Censorship in Postwar Japan* (Honolulu: University of Hawai'i Press, 2012), 270.
16. Patrick W. Galbraith, *The Ethics of Affect: Lines and Life in a Tokyo Neighborhood* (Stockholm: University of Stockholm Press, 2021), 66, 99.
17. Nagayama, *Erotic Comics in Japan*, 175–77.

18. Mark McLelland, "Thought Policing or the Protection of Youth? Debate in Japan Over the 'Non-Existent Youth Bill'," *International Journal of Comic Art*, 13 (2011): 362.

19. Nagayama, *Erotic Comics in Japan*, 19–20.

20. Matt Coughlan, "Senator Calls for Child Abuse Anime Review," *The Canberra Times*, February 26, 2020, www.canberratimes.com.au/story/6650325/senator-calls-for-child-abuse-anime-review/?fbclid=IwAR0GvtfLloj1cxtD6F GL2aJ2LnYifD4cQNjwdNZw9A-oy5Y-8jl_jSjZAeA.

21. Nagayama, *Erotic Comics in Japan*, 258.

22. Nagayama, *Erotic Comics in Japan*, 258.

23. Nagayama, *Erotic Comics in Japan*, 41.

24. Rito Kimi, *Eromanga hyōgen shi* (Tokyo: Ōta Shuppan, 2017), 7.

25. Nagayama, *Erotic Comics in Japan*, 111.

26. Nagayama, *Erotic Comics in Japan*, 27.

27. Kawamata, "Nihon no kontentsu," 129.

28. Nagayama, *Erotic Comics in Japan*, 141–44, 204–5, 219.

29. Kimi, *Eromanga*, 133–42. See also Bobby Derie, *Sex and the Cthulhu Mythos* (New York: Hippocampus Press, 2014), 142–52.

19

AKIKO SUGAWA-SHIMADA

Anime Fandom in Japan and Beyond

Various media platforms, including movie theaters, television, specialized magazines, and the internet have nurtured anime fandom. It is manifest in practices such as the publication of fanzines (*dōjinshi*) and the communication with other fans face-to-face or through posts in magazines, blogs, and on social media. Through these mediums, fans not only consume their favorite anime, but they also produce derivative works or perform cosplay. Defining anime broadly as popular animated films and television series, this chapter traces anime fandoms since the late 1950s, focusing on the media platforms and "anime booms." The phenomenon of the anime boom signifies a trend resulting from a new style and composition of anime with significant impacts that expand the audience.[1] Four anime booms have been identified by critics: The first and second correspond to *Astro Boy* (*Tetsuwan Atom*, 1963–66) and *Space Battleship Yamato* (*Uchū senkan Yamato*, TV 1974–75; movie 1977), respectively. The third anime boom from the mid-1990s to the early 2000s was spearheaded by the TV anime *Neon Genesis Evangelion* (*Shinseiki Evangerion*, 1995–96) and the Studio Ghibli movie *Princess Mononoke* (*Mononokehime*, 1997), while the fourth is represented by *Demon Slayer: Kimetsu no Yaiba* (2019–), and *Jujutsu Kaisen* (2020–).

Anime not only involves the actual works; it is also dependent on the participation of audiences and especially fan audiences. This chapter traces how fan audiences have developed since the postwar period in terms of the physical venues and the digital platforms that have enabled them to interact with one another. Fan activities range from the publication of fanzines to the practice of cosplay, from visits (or pilgrimages) to anime locations to the production of fan-sub videos, music videos, and even video games that utilize material from anime.

Anime and Anime Fandom: The Late 1950s to the 1970s

In 1956, Hiroshi Ōkawa established Tōei Dōga (from 1998 onward, Toei Animation) with the aim of becoming the "Disney of the East." They

256

produced the first full-length color animated film, *Panda and the Magic Serpent* (*Hakujaden*, also *Legend of the White Serpent*, 1958). In his youth, Hayao Miyazaki was moved by the movie's heroine, and this experience prompted him to enter Tōei Dōga in 1963 where he met Isao Takahata. Even though the primary medium for watching anime in the 1960s was gradually shifting from movies in cinemas to series aired on television, Miyazaki would turn exclusively to the creation of animated movies after making several TV anime series at Tōei Dōga and Telecom Animation Film. In 1985, together with his closest collaborators (Takahata and Toshio Suzuki), he set up Studio Ghibli for that purpose.

In the 1960s, animated movies and TV series primarily targeted children, and these gave rise to what Japanese critics consider the first anime boom, which began in 1963 with the TV anime series, *Astro Boy* (dir. Osamu Tezuka). It was also represented by *Gigantor* (*Tetsujin 28-gō*, dir. Yonehiko Watanabe, 1963–65), and *Eighth Man* (dir. Haruyuki Kawashima, 1963–64) in addition to Tōei Dōga's *Wolf Boy Ken* (*Ōkami shōnen Ken*, dir. Sadao Tsukioka, 1963–65). These series appealed to children, their parents, and young adults, as can be deduced from the first official fan-club magazine, *Tetsuwan Atomu Club*, issued by its animation studio Mushi Production (1966–68). During this formative phase, fan clubs were run by anime studios for the purpose of promotion and to accommodate viewers' demands. Over time, fan clubs changed to fan-driven associations, but adult anime fans did not enter the public sphere until the late 1970s with the arrival of the second anime boom that was led by *Space Battleship Yamato*.

First broadcast on television in 1974–75, this sci-fi franchise was modeled on Japan's largest battleship during World War II, and it only became popular following the release of the movie in 1977. On the eve of its premiere, throngs of young adults lined up in front of Tokyo's movie theaters. The media reported this as a surprising development, sarcastically noting that even adults were now into anime.[2] It may be more accurate to say that *Space Battleship Yamato* in fact owed its success to both sci-fi enthusiasts and anime fans, who appreciated what made the viewing of the tale worthy to an adult audience – that is, the elaborate settings and the intriguing storyline. Other sci-fi TV anime that were massive hits in the late 1970s and have since grown into extensive franchises include *Galaxy Express 999* (*Ginga tetsudō 999*, dir. Nobutaka Nishizawa, 1978–81) and *Mobile Suit Gundam* (*Kidō senshi Gandamu*, dir. Yoshiyuki Tomino, 1979–80). They also made voice actors stars. Concerts and fan events held by voice actors attracted young anime audiences, and specialized fan communities were formed.

In the 1970s, the fans themselves organized numerous anime fan clubs. They circulated their peer-produced publications of manga, novels, and illustrations (i.e., *dōjinshi* fanzines), selling them at the Comic Market, which began in 1975. It is notable that even then this subculture was not exclusively male. Young women were also into anime, and they preferred to issue fanzines about series that featured hunk characters (*ikemen*), such as *Triton of the Sea* (*Umi no Toriton*, dir. Yoshiyuki Tomino, 1972) and *Science Ninja Team Gatchaman* (*Kagaku ninja tai Gatchaman*, dir. Hisayuki Toriumi, 1972–74). Concurrently, cosplay emerged as a new practice (initially called "costume play"). Fan-culture legend has it that dressing up as one's favorite character from sci-fi novels and films began in 1978 at the 17th Japan SF Convention when the critic Mari Kotani, inspired by a convention held in the United States, appeared in the attire of Tavia, the protagonist of Edgar Rice Burroughs' *A Fighting Man of Mars* (1931), and was mistaken by attendees as the title character from *Triton of the Sea*. Subsequently, female fans participated in conventions in costumes and props of their favorite anime characters.[3] In actual fact, female fans outnumbered male fans during this period, as sewing and makeup (then believed to be the domain of women) were required skills to assemble costumes and props.

Clearly, fans are not just consumers of anime texts. They also engage in creative activities as "produsers,"[4] which can lead to copyright infringement. Although a new Japanese Copyright Act was enacted in 1971, control was not strict enough to damage peer publications and cosplay. Fan activities were even promoted by commercial magazines such as *Anime Parody Comics* (later renamed *Ani-paro Comics*, 1982–93), which presented critical and humorous remakes of anime (so-called parodies) in the form of amateur manga.[5] Often fans of media contents in the broadest sense, anime produsers have played an important role in establishing anime-related convergence culture since the 1990s, when multimedia franchising gained momentum with the rise of the internet.[6]

Another noteworthy fan practice is anime-induced "contents tourism" (*kontentsu tsūrizumu*). In 1974, the year-long TV anime *Heidi, Girl of the Alps* (*Arupusu no shōjo Haiji*) – a series based on Johanna Spyri's 1881 children's book *Heidi* – strongly impressed child audiences with its realistic background images, storyline, and characters. It was the first TV anime for which its creators, including Isao Takahata and Hayao Miyazaki, went location hunting in Europe.[7] Their overseas experiences added realistic heft to a fantasy world, which in turn enticed its audience to travel to the anime's sites in Switzerland.[8] This became a trend that continued until the early 2000s with the annual TV anime series, later called *World Masterpiece Theater* (*Sekai meisaku gekijō*, or WMT). For instance, the Cathedral of Our Lady in Antwerp, Belgium, in the WMT's *A Dog of*

Flanders (Furandāsu no inu, 1975), still has a constant stream of Japanese visitors who were moved by this TV anime.

Anime and Anime Fandom: The 1980s to the 1990s

The year 1984 saw the release of three animated feature films that would become tremendous hits: *Nausicaä of the Valley of the Wind (Kaze no tani no Naushika,* dir. Hayao Miyazaki), *Urusei Yatsura 2: Beautiful Dreamer* (dir. Mamoru Oshii), and *Super Dimension Fortress Macross: Do You Remember My Love? (Chōjikū yōsai Makurosu: ai oboete imasu ka?,* dir. Noboru Ishiguro and Shōji Kawamori). These works set the tone for the subsequently prevailing style of animated movies. *Nausicaä,* for example, resulted from the collaboration between Hayao Miyazaki as director and Isao Takahata as producer. As noted above, Miyazaki and Takahata founded Studio Ghibli in 1985, which distinguished itself from other Japanese animation studios because it did not foreground TV anime series adapted from manga. Although the first animated movie produced under the Studio Ghibli brand was *Laputa: Castle in the Sky (Tenkū no shiro Rapyuta,* 1985), Ghibli fandom was already forming with the opening of *Nausicaä* the previous year. It was further sustained by the biennial release of new productions and nationwide PR campaigns, including a tie-up with Nihon Television Network, the only network that broadcasts Ghibli's past movies almost every summer.[9] Studio Ghibli once closed its production sector due to Miyazaki's retirement in 2014. He announced the resumption of production, however, and a new production department was set up in 2017. The year 2023 saw the release of his movie *The Boy and the Heron (Kimitachi wa dō ikiru ka).*

In addition to the emphasis on original movies, adaptations of TV anime series for auteurist films are significant. Noteworthy in this regard is Mamoru Oshii's *Beautiful Dreamer* mentioned above. It rested on the popular TV anime *Urusei yatsura* (1981–86), in turn an adaptation of Rumiko Takahashi's manga of the same name. Oshii was the first chief director of the TV anime, and his directing techniques, such as the unusual camerawork otherwise difficult to achieve with hand-drawn animation, was already applauded by fans. Oshii later directed *Patlabor: The Movie (Kidō keisatsu Patoreibā,* 1989), along with the related TV series (1989–90) and the films *Ghost in the Shell (Kōkaku kidōtai,* 1995) and *Ghost in the Shell 2: Innocence* (2004). Different from the majority of TV anime, these works appealed to domestic and international audiences alike.

The 1980s also witnessed a distinctive change in fan practices. The expansion of the Comic Market, as well as the development of printing technology, led to an increase in peer publishing. Several information magazines dedicated to anime were launched against this backdrop, pioneered by *Animage* (Tokuma Shoten, 1978) and followed by *Animedia* (Gakken Plus, 1981) and *Newtype* (Kadokawa, 1986).[10] They often featured detailed information on an anime's setting, storyboard, animation staff, and voice actors.[11] Fans could participate in supporting anime culture by submitting letters to the readers column. These anime magazines thus served as platforms for fans to gain in-depth knowledge, express their opinions, and interact with other fans.

Women's fanzine activities experienced a boom in the 1980s, with the most prevalent topics being anime parodies (narratives that used existing anime works), and the love between beautiful boy characters (boys love, or *yaoi*). Equivalent to slash fiction in the United States, the latter type interprets friendship and rivalry between boy characters in anime and manga as homosexual romance. An early case was the soccer anime *Captain Tsubasa* (1983–86) based on Yōichi Takahashi's manga. Popular pairings in this anime included those between the titular character, Tsubasa Ōzora, and his rival Kojirō Hyūga, or between Tsubasa and his teammate Tarō Misaki. These fan fictions actually infringed upon existing copyrights, but the originating artists and authors mostly remained silent, in part because derivative fan production became an indicator of a work's popularity. Manga fanzines continued to thrive, and the Comic Market eventually recorded its largest ever attendance of 750,000 people in winter 2019, prior to the outbreak of the COVID-19 pandemic.

In the 1990s, Japanese TV anime came to be acknowledged by audiences without much previous exposure to the medium, not only in Japan but worldwide. The multimedia franchising system known as media mix – a distinctive strategy in the marketing of popular-cultural, anime-centered products – was vital in this regard. Typical of its global success were *Pretty Guardian Sailor Moon* (*Bishōjo senshi Sērā Mūn*, 1992–97) and *Pokémon* (*Poketto Monsutā*, 1997–). *Pokémon* was adapted from the role-playing game and trading cards by Pokémon Co. Ltd. and the *Pocket Monster* series by Nintendo (1996–). Kids in the United States and elsewhere became involved through the Game Boy device.[12] From there they reached out and connected to other media, including anime and manga. Media-mix strategies thus made anime a site for viewing and for "experiencing" a whole storyworld transmedially.

Besides its popular games and trading cards, Pokémon is known to the Japanese public because of the "Pokémon Shock."[13] On December 16, 1997, around 680 children across Japan who were watching the TV anime *Pokémon* passed out and were hospitalized due to photosensitive seizures caused by the intense flashing on-screen. In response to this incident, the

Japan Commercial Broadcasters Association established guidelines in 1998, reminding anime broadcasters that they must act responsibly regarding the use of bright red flashes and sudden scene changes with high contrast.[14] In line with these guidelines, a warning began to appear at the beginning of children's anime programs in the form of an oral announcement and on-screen text: "When you watch TV anime, please try not to approach the screen and keep the room well illuminated."[15] After being taken off the air for a period, the TV anime *Pokémon* resumed on April 16, 1998; it has seen many continuations since then.

Another phenomenal work of the 1990s, *Pretty Guardian Sailor Moon*, became widely known among the Japanese public due to its popularity as anime and the dissemination of the related toys and multimedia adaptations. The anime series and subsequent movies were produced by Tōei Animation in line with its media-mix strategy. Drawing on a one-shot manga, *Code Name is Sailor V* (*Kōdo nēmu wa Sērā V*, 1991), artist Naoko Takeuchi and anime studio staff at Tōei conceptualized and plotted the anime narrative of *Sailor Moon*, which combines "fighting girls" with romance. At the suggestion of studio staff, sailor uniforms were adopted for the anime, and Takeuchi's love for Tōei's "Super Squadron" (*sūpā sentai*) action meta-series, featuring live-action and special effects (the source for the American *Power Rangers*), also came into play. Concurrent with the airing of the anime, Takeuchi published a serial of *Sailor Moon* in the girls manga magazine *Nakayoshi*; her cute, strong girl warriors immediately appealed to girls, young men, and adult women. The serial was soon adapted into a series of stage musicals (1993–2005) by the toy company Bandai and a live-action drama (2003) produced by Tōei. The *Musical Sailor Moon* series can be seen as an early successful example of what is now known as a 2.5-D musical, designating stage adaptations of anime, manga, and video games. It was remade in 2013 and continued until 2017 to celebrate the 25th anniversary of the *Sailor Moon* franchise.

Sailor Moon fans engage in cosplay, fan fiction, and contents tourism.[16] This is not limited to women; men dressed as Sailor Scouts also partake in cross-play at cosplay events. Fanzine creators have used the *Sailor Moon* characters to picture female-female relationships in a way similar to male-male romance in boys love. In *Sailor* Moon, this inclination to *yuri* (literally "lily") comes to the fore in the relationship between the high school classmates Haruka/Amara (Sailor Uranus) and Michiru/Michelle (Sailor Neptune).[17] Haruka/Amara is a tall, short-haired girl who approaches Usagi/Serena (Sailor Moon), and Usagi/Serena at first mistakes her for a boy. In the dubbed American TV version of *Sailor Moon*, the character settings of Haruka/Amara and Michiru/Michelle were changed into cousins;

nevertheless, their relationship prompted fans to create *yuri,* or slash fiction (same-sex romantic pairings have traditionally been indicated in English with the "/" sign and therefore called slash fiction, whereas the multiplication sign has been used for Japan-related boys-love and girls-love couplings). In addition, friendship among other Sailor Warriors was reinterpreted as a *yuri* relationship, one of the popular pairings being that between Usagi/ Serena and Rei/Raye (Sailor Mars) who are always arguing in the anime and precisely for that reason understood as being in love.

The locations that *Sailor Moon* was modeled on have attracted fans, making the serial representative of anime-induced contents tourism. For example, fans traced the fictional Hikawa ("Fire River") Shrine where Rei/Raye lives and works as a Shinto medium (*miko*) to two actual shrines in Azabu, Tokyo – that is, Hikawa ("Ice River") Shrine and Akasaka Hikawa Shrine. Both attract hordes of fans during the first shrine visit of the new year.[18] Fans' theater tourism to see *Sailor Moon* musicals on stage could likewise be included as a fan practice in contents tourism.[19] The *Musical Sailor Moon* series was performed at several different theaters, and fans flocked to these venues to consume the *Sailor Moon* storyworld.

During the 1990s fans began to watch anime while at the same time interacting with other fans online, as typified by the massive hit TV anime, *Neon Genesis Evangelion* (1995–96). The first series of this sci-fi anime was set in 2015 after most of humankind has been annihilated by a fatal explosion called the Second Impact. It became a social phenomenon in mid-1990s Japan, not only because of the unexpected storyline, the bizarre camerawork, and the actions of the characters but equally due to the traumatic experiences of the characters in relation to their family members, an aspect that resonated with viewers in their twenties and thirties. *Evangelion* fans with access to an online communication service exchanged critical opinions, possible answers for unexplained parts of the narrative, and expressions of their affection for characters – mainly female characters such as Rei Ayanami and Asuka Sōryū Langley – with the airing of every episode. This practice of simultaneous viewing and sharing among fans was more easily facilitated with the establishment of internet platforms such as 2-Channel in 1999. From that time onward, anime-related fan activities have drastically expanded to assume international scope via X (formerly Twitter), YouTube, and Instagram.

Diverse Anime Produsage Worldwide since the 2000s

Transnational fan produsage has become livelier since the early 2000s with the emergence of video-sharing sites and social media. Two of the most influential platforms for interactive fan practices are Nico Nico Dōga and YouTube. The first is a broadly used Japanese video-sharing service with a worldwide name value that was launched in 2006 by the telecommunications and media company Dwango. It offers a site where anime fans can interact with one another by posting comments and playful jargon onto uploaded anime videos (fans upload anime videos recorded from TV and retrieved from DVDs, even though this is illegal). Two of the most intriguing forms of creative produsage by anime fans are video posts in the categories of "Me Dancing To" (*odottemita*) and "Mishearing Parodies" (*soramimi parodi*). "Me Dancing To" posts are, as the name suggests, video clips that show fans dancing to songs and music. "Me Dancing to *Sunny Sunny Happiness*" (*Hare hare yukai*), the ending song from the TV anime *The Melancholy of Haruhi Suzumiya* (*Suzumiya Haruhi no yūutsu*, first season, 2006) is regarded as a pioneer in this genre. Fans paid careful attention to the way the moves of the characters precisely match the rhythm of the song. Some fans attempted to copy the dance routine, filming it and posting their videos on Nico Nico and YouTube. Such videos enjoyed even more popularity with the arrival of Vocaloid software (2007) and the 3D computer-generated dance of *The Idol M@ster*, a game for forming female idol singers (2007).[20]

One of the most successful "Mishearing Parody" videos relating to anime is the *Prince of Tennis Musical* (*Myūjikaru tenisu no ōjisama*, 2003–). This work, nicknamed *Tenimyu* (a portmanteau of the Japanese Anglicism for "tennis" and "musical"), is a stage performance adapted from *Prince of Tennis* (manga by Takeshi Konomi, 1999–2008; anime, 2001–05). Young and promising, albeit inexperienced, actors were selected through auditions using what is commonly known as the *"tenimyu* method." Their slurred speech and poor singing skills created opportunities for fans to mock and support them at the same time. In *Tenimyu* Mishearing Parody videos, fans insert subtitles retrieved from DVDs, which are meaningless or irrelevant to the actual lines because fans/users simply play on words for their entertainment value. These fan videos have been uploaded to Nico Nico, where other fans can post their reactions to the funny subtitles.

Fan videos uploaded to Nico Nico were often transmitted to YouTube, which began its service in Japan in 2007. From an international perspective, YouTube's most significant contribution to anime fandom is that it functions as a site for foreign fans to learn about Japanese anime productions otherwise unavailable in their own countries. The illegal uploading of anime videos by fans usually occurs in three steps. First, anime videos recorded from TV without subtitles are uploaded soon after the broadcast; these are "raw" videos. Next, fans translate raw videos into their own languages and add subtitles; these are "fan-subs" (i.e., versions subtitled by fans). Finally, the fan-sub videos are annotated with pop-up comments that explain Japanese customs and culture to non-Japanese viewers. On the one hand, such fan-sub videos adversely impacted the sales of anime DVD packages. On the other, these illegal uploads led to the popularity of Japanese anime among an audience who had no prior knowledge of this media form. But fan-sub videos have gradually decreased as many anime subscription video on demand and transactional video on demand services such as Crunchyroll, Amazon Prime, Netflix, and others deliver subtitled anime with little time lag from their initial broadcasting in Japan. TV Tokyo, for instance, was quick to team up with Crunchyroll in 2009 to air *Naruto* (dir. Hayato Date; broadcast in Japan 2002–07).

In 2021, fan-made videos using animation have witnessed increased momentum. Before this time, the majority of derivative fanwork appeared in print, primarily as manga and novels, because amateurs found manga easier to make than animation (exceptions included edited music videos that made illegal use of materials). One fan-made video game uploaded to YouTube thanks to the development of the PS4 creative software Dream Universe was based on the TV anime *World Trigger* (2014–22), a sci-fi tale adapted from a manga by Daisuke Ashihara in which young soldiers of the governmental defense organization, Border, are trained to fight against intruders called Neighbor.[21] The animated movements and the actions of the characters were of a quality that did not suggest an amateur creator. Since many fans of *World Trigger* had long hungered for the release of related video games, this fan-made video game immediately attracted enormous attention.

Conclusion

Fans have enthusiastically consumed and produced anime. In the formative period of the 1960s and 1970s, anime studios offered fan-club magazines. Gradually, peer-produced publications came to the fore, facilitated by the increasing number of venues where fanzines could be sold, purchased, and exchanged. In the 1980s, publishing companies issued magazines specializing in anime, most notably *Animage*, *Animedia*, and *Newtype*. Thus, fans relied on commercial magazines and peer publications to access detailed information about anime and related contents such as merchandising goods, toys, anime songs, stage productions, and voice actor performances. Fans created anime parodies, as well as boys love and girls love stories, using anime/manga/game characters, but the problem of copyright infringement remained. Fan produsage has supported the anime industry and promoted anime culture by seeking out the locations of their favorite anime. This spawned contents tourism, or "anime pilgrimages," as the new practice came to be known in the 2000s.

The internet and social media have facilitated the dissemination of anime and other contents produced through media mix on an international scope. Furthermore, they serve as platforms for fans to interact with each other domestically and globally. But new technologies and digital platforms are not the only factors determining fan produsage. It is how fans utilize those platforms and technologies that assist us in understanding anime as its own independent culture.

Notes

1. Nobuyuki Tsugata, *Shinban animēshon-gaku nyūmon* (Tokyo: Heibonsha, 2017), 83. Translation by the author. For a summary of Tsugata's discussion of "anime booms," see Zoltan Kacsuk, "The Making of an Epoch-Making Anime: Understanding the Landmark Status of Neon Genesis Evangelion in Otaku Culture." In *Anime Studies: Media-Specific Approaches to Neon Genesis Evangelion*, edited by José Andrés Santiago Iglesias and Ana Soler Baena (Stockholm: Stockholm University Press, 2021), 227–29. Open Access.
2. Yūsuke Nakagawa, *Sabukaru bokkōshi: subete wa 1970 nendai kara hajimatta* (Tokyo: Kadokawa, 2018), 235.
3. Frenchy Lunning, *Cosplay: The Fictional Mode of Existence* (Minneapolis: University of Minnesota Press, 2022), 47.
4. Axel Bruns suggests "The Distinctions between Producers and Users of Content Have Faded into Comparative Insignificance." In *Blogs, Wikipedia, Second Life, and Beyond: From Production to Produsage* (New York: Peter Lang Publishing, 2008), 2.
5. Takanaka Shimotsuki, "Niji sōsaku." In *Animēshon bunka 55 no kīwādo*, edited by Akiko Sugawa [sic!] and Miyuki Yonemura (Kyoto: Minerva Shobō, 2019), 236–39.
6. See Henry Jenkins, *Convergence Culture: Where Old and New Media Collide* (New York: New York University Press, 2006) for a general discussion.
7. Takayoshi Yamamura, "Travelling Heidi: International Contents Tourism Induced by Japanese Anime." In *Contents Tourism and Pop Culture Fandom: Transcultural Tourist Experiences*, edited by Takayoshi Yamamura and Philip Seaton (Bristol: Channel View Publications, 2020), 62–81.
8. Kaori Chiba, *Arupusu no shōjo Haiji no sekai* (Tokyo: Kyūryūdō, 2008).
9. James Rendell, "Bridge Builders, World Makers: Transcultural Studio Ghibli Fan Crafting" in "Special Edition Editorial: Introducing *Studio Ghibli*," edited by Rayna Denison and James Rendell, *East Asian Journal of Popular Culture*, 4, no. 1 (2018): 116–38.
10. Renato Rivera Rusca, "The Changing Role of Manga and Anime Magazines in the Japanese Animation Industry." In *Manga Vision: Cultural and Communicative Perspectives*, edited by Sarah Pasfield-Neofitou and Cathy Sell (Clayton: Monash University Publishing, 2016), 52–69, www.doabooks.org/doab?func=search&uiLanguage=en&template=&query=manga+vision.

11. See Minori Ishida, "Voice Actresses Rising: The Multilayered Stardom of Megumi Ogata in the 1990s." In *Anime Studies: Media-Specific Approaches to Neon Genesis Evangelion*, edited by José Andrés Santiago, Iglesias, and Ana Soler Baena (Stockholm: Stockholm University Press, 2021), 111–34. Open Access.

12. Ann Allison, *Millennial Monsters: Japanese Toys and Global Imagination* (Berkeley: University of California Press, 2006), Kindle, 196–97.

13. Thomas Lamarre, *The Anime Ecology: A Genealogy of Television, Animation, and Game Media* (Minneapolis: University of Minnesota Press, 2018), 33–37.

14. The Japan Commercial Broadcasters Association, "Animēshon nado no eizō shuhō ni kansuru gaidorain," 1998/2006, www.j-ba.or.jp/category/broadcasting/jba101033.

15. Lamarre, *The Anime Ecology*, 34.

16. Emerald King, "Sakura ga meijiru – Unlocking the Shōjo Wardrobe: Cosplay, Manga, 2.5D Space." In *Shōjo across Media: Exploring "Girl" Practices in Contemporary Japan*, edited by Jaqueline Berndt, Kazumi Nagaike, and Fusami Ogi (New York: Palgrave Macmillan, 2019), 233–60.

17. Here, the original Japanese name appears on the left and the English dubbed name on the right. On queerness caused by Haruka's voice, see Minori Ishida, "Voice Actresses Rising," 125–26.

18. Takeshi Okamoto, *Anime seichi junrei no kankō shakaigaku: kontentsu tsūrizumu no media komyunikēshon bunseki* (Tokyo: Hōritsu Bunkasha, 2018), 80.

19. Akiko Sugawa-Shimada, "The 2.5-Dimensional Theatre as a Communication Site: Non-site-Specific Theatre Tourism." In *Contents Tourism and Pop Culture Fandom: Transnational Tourist Experiences*, edited by Takayoshi Yamamura and Philip Seaton (Bristol: Channel View Publications, 2020), 128–43.

20. Masahiro Koyama, "Tōkō dōga," in *Animēshon bunka 55 no kīwādo*, ed. Akiko Sugawa [sic!] and Miyuki Yonemura (Kyoto: Minerva Shobō, 2019), 240–43.

21. The tutorial video of this game (made by shin sa) is available at www.youtube.com/watch?v=AHK1DfchAuA.

FURTHER READING

Abbott, Michael, and Charles Forceville. "Visual Representation of Emotion in Manga: 'Loss of control' Is 'Loss of Hands' in *Azumanga Daioh* Volume 4," *Language and Literature*, 20.2 (2011): 91–112.

Allison, Ann. *Permitted and Prohibited Desires*. Berkeley: University of California Press, 2000.

Annett, Sandra. *Anime Fan Communities*. New York: Palgrave Macmillan, 2014.

Antononoka, Olga. "Shōjo Manga beyond Shōjo Manga: The 'Female Mode of Address' in *Kabukumon*." In *Shōjo across Media: Exploring "Girl" Practices in Contemporary Japan*, edited by Jaqueline Berndt, Kazumi Nagaike, and Fusami Ogi. Cham, Switzerland: Palgrave Macmillan, 2019, 83–105.

Aoki, Deb, David, Brothers Christopher Butcher, and Chip Zdarsky/Steven Murray. *Mangasplaining* (2023), www.mangasplaining.com

Bauwens-Sugimoto, Jessica. "Queering Black Jack: A Look at How Manga Adapts to Changing Reading Demographics," *Orientaliska Studier*, 147 (2016): 111–42. Open Access.

Bauwens-Sugimoto, Jessica. "Expressing Visceral Female Subjectivity in Women's Manga: Double Standards, Censorship, and Staying Ahead of the Game," *International Journal of Comic Art*, 23.2 (2021): 359–66.

Beaty, Bart. "Jirō Taniguchi: France's Mangaka." In *Comics Studies Here and Now*, edited by Frederick L. Aldama. New York: Routledge, 2018, 144–60.

Berndt, Jaqueline. *"SKIM as GIRL*: Reading a Japanese North American Graphic Novel through Manga Lenses." In *Drawing New Color Lines: Transnational Asian American Graphic Narratives*, edited by Monica Chiu. Hong Kong: Hong Kong University Press, 2014, 257–78.

Berndt, Jaqueline. "Anime in Academia: Representative Object, Media Form, and Japanese Studies," *Arts*, 7.4 (2018): 56. Open Access.

Berndt, Jaqueline. "Manga, An Affective Form of Comics." In *The Cambridge Companion to Comics*, edited by Maaheen Ahmed. Cambridge: Cambridge University Press, 2023, 82–101.

Bolton, Christopher. *Interpreting Anime*. Minneapolis: University of Minnesota Press, 2018.

Booth, Paul, and Rebecca Williams, eds. *A Fan Studies Primer*. Iowa City: The University of Iowa Press, 2021.

Brown, Stephen T., ed. *Cinema Anime: Critical Engagements with Japanese Animation*. London: Palgrave Macmillan, 2006.

Casiello, Catlin. "Drawing Sex: Pages, Bodies, and Sighs in Japanese Eromanga," *punctum*, 7.2 (2021): 97–121. Open Access.

Clements, Jonathan. *Anime: A History*. London: Bloomsbury, 2013.

Cohn, Neil. *The Visual Language of Comics: Introduction to the Structure and Cognition of Sequential Images*. London: Bloomsbury, 2013.

Condry, Ian. *The Soul of Anime: Collaborative Creativity and Japan's Media Success Story*. Durham: Duke University Press, 2013.

Dale, Joshua Paul, et al. *The Aesthetics and Affects of Cuteness*. New York: Routledge, 2016.

Denison, Rayna. *Anime: A Critical Introduction. Film Genres*. London and New York: Bloomsbury Academic, 2015.

Denison, Rayna. "Anime's Distribution Worlds: Formal and Information Distribution in the Analogue and Digital Eras." In *Routledge Handbook of Japanese Media*, edited by Fabienne Darling-Wolf. New York: Routledge, 2018, 578–601.

Denison, Rayna. "Transmedial Relations – Manga at the Movies: Adaptation and Intertextuality." In *The Japanese Cinema Book*, edited by Hideaki Fujiki and Alastair Phillips. London: Bloomsbury, 2020, 203–13.

Denison, Rayna. "Media Mix: Theorizing and Historicizing Japanese Franchising." In *Handbook of Japanese Media and Popular Culture in Transition*, edited by Forum Mithani and Griseldis Kirsch. Amsterdam: Amsterdam University Press, 2022, 107–123.

Denison, Rayna. *Studio Ghibli: An Industrial History*. Cham, Switzerland: Palgrave/Springer, 2023.

Fanasca, Marta. "Tales of Lilies and Girls' Love. The Depiction of Female/Female Relationships in Yuri Manga." In *Tracing Pathways. Interdisciplinary Studies on Modern and Contemporary East Asia*, edited by Diego Cucinelli and Andrea Scibetta. Florence, Italy: Firenze University Press, 2020, 51–66. Open Access.

Fanasca, Marta. "Attack on Normativity: A Queer Reading of *Shingeki no Kyojin* (Attack on Titan)," *East Asian Journal of Popular Culture*, 7.2 (2021): 255–70.

Foster, Michael Dylan. "The Otherworlds of Mizuki Shigeru," *Mechademia*, 3.1 (2008): 8–28.

Freedman, Alisa, and Toby Slade, eds. *Introducing Japanese Popular Culture*. New York: Routledge, 2017.

Fukushima, Yoshiko. *Manga Discourse in Japanese Theater: The Location of Noda Hideki's Yume no Yuminsha*. London: Kegan Paul, 2003.

Galbraith, Patrick W., Thiam Huat Kam, and Björn-Ole Kamm, eds. *Debating Otaku in Contemporary Japan*. London: Bloomsbury, 2015.

Gedin, David. "Format Codings in Comics: The Elusive Art of Punctuation," *Inks: The Journal of the Comics Studies Society*, 3.3 (2019): 298–314.

Gray, Maggie, and Ian Horton, eds. *Seeing Comics through Art History: Alternative Approaches to the Form*. London: Palgrave Macmillan, 2022.

Greenwood, Forrest. "The Girl at the Center of the World: Gender, Genre, and Remediation in *Bishōjo* Media Works," *Mechademia*, 9 (2014): 237–52.

Groensteen, Thierry. *L'Univers des manga. Une introduction à la bande dessinée japonaise*. Tournai: Casterman, 1991.

Groensteen, Thierry. *Comics and Narration*, transl. Anne Miller. Jackson: University Press of Mississippi, 2013.

Hartzheim, Bryan Hikari. "The Affordances of Omaké in Gotouge Koyoharu's Kimetsu no Yaiba," *Transcommunication* (Waseda University), 8.2 (2021): 159–70. Open Access.

Hemmann, Kathryn. *Manga Cultures and the Female Gaze*. London: Palgrave Macmillan, 2020.

Holmberg, Ryan. "What Was Alternative Manga" (article series), *The Comics Journal*, 2011. www.tcj.com/?s=ryan+holmberg+alternative+manga

Holmberg, Ryan. "Garo Magazine and Alternative Manga." In *The Citi Exhibition Manga*, edited by Nicole Coolidge Rousmaniere and Matsuba Ryoko. London: Thames & Hudson, 2019, 316–19.

Hori, Hikari. *Promiscuous Media: Film and Visual Culture in Imperial Japan 1926–1945*. Ithaca: Cornell University Press, 2018.

Imamura, Taihei. "Japanese Cartoon Films," transl. Thomas Lamarre. *Mechademia*, 9 (2014): 107–24.

Ishida, Minori. "Voice Actresses Rising: The Multilayered Stardom of Megumi Ogata in the 1990s." In *Anime Studies: Media-Specific Approaches to Neon Genesis Evangelion*, edited by José Andrés Santiago Iglesias and Ana Soler Baena. Stockholm: Stockholm University Press, 2021, 111–34. Open Access.

Ishida, Minori, and Joon Yang Kim. *Gurōbaru anime ron: shintai, ākaibu, toransunashonaru*. Tokyo: Seidosha, 2022.

Israelson, Per. "The Vortex of the Weird: Systemic Feedback and Environmental Individuation in the Media Ecology of Ito Junji's Horror Comics," *Orientaliska Studier*, 156 (2018): 151–75. Open Access.

Iwashita, Hōsei. *Shōjo manga no hyōgen kikō: hirakareta manga hyōgenshi to Tezuka Osamu*. Tokyo: NTT Shuppan, 2013.

Jackson, Reginald. "Dying in Two Dimensions: Genji emaki and the Wages of Depth Perception," *Mechademia*, 7 (2012): 150–72.

Kacsuk, Zoltan. "Re-Examining the 'What is Manga' Problematic: The Tension and Interrelationship between the 'Style' versus 'Made in Japan' Positions," *Arts*, 7, 26 (2018): no pag. Open Access.

Kacsuk, Zoltan. "Using Fan-Compiled Metadata for Anime, Manga and Video Game Research Revisiting Azuma's 'Otaku: Japan's Database Animals' Twenty Years On." In *Japan's Contemporary Media Culture between Local and Global*, edited by Martin Roth, Hiroshi Yoshida, and Martin Picard. Heidelberg: CrossAsia-eBooks, 2021, 117–32. Open Access.

Karlin, Jason G., Patrick W. Galbraith and Shunsuke Nozawa, eds. *Japanese Media and Popular Culture. An Open-Access Digital Initiative of the University of Tokyo*, 2020.

Kim, Joon Yang. "South Korea and the Sub-Empire of Anime: Kinesthetics of Subcontracted Animation Production," *Mechademia*, 9 (2015), 90–103.

Kimi, Rito. *The History of Hentai Manga: An Expressionist Examination of Eromanga*. Portland, OR: FAKKU, 2021.

Kimura, Tomoya. *Tōei Dōga shiron: Keiei to sōzō no teiryū*. Tokyo: Nihon hyōron-sha, 2020.

Kimura, Tomoya. "Business and Production." In *Japanese Animation in Asia: Transnational Industry, Audiences, and Success*, edited by Marco Pellitteri & Wong Heung-wah. London: Routledge, 2021, 71–92.

Koulikov, Mikhail. *Online Bibliography of Anime and Manga Research* (since 2008). www.animemangastudies.com/bibliographies/

Koulikov, Mikhail. "A Field in Formation – A Citation Analysis of Japanese Popular Culture Studies," *Portal: Libraries and the Academy*, 20.2 (2020): 269–83.

Kukkonen, Karin. *Studying Comics and Graphic Novels*. Hoboken: Wiley, 2013.

Lamarre, Thomas. "Cartoon Film Theory: Imamura Taihei on Animation, Documentary, and Photography." In *Animating Film Theory*, edited by Karen Beckman. Durham: Duke University Press, 2014, 221–51.

Lamarre, Thomas. "Anime. Compositing and Switching: An Intermedial History of Japanese Anime." In *The Japanese Cinema Book*, edited by Hideaki Fujiki und Alastair Phillips. London: Bloomsbury, 2020, 310–24.

Lee, Laura. *Japanese Cinema between the Frames*. London: Palgrave Macmillan, 2017.

Lefèvre, Pascal. "Mise en scène and Framing: Visual Storytelling in Lone Wolf and Cub." In *Critical Approaches to Comics: Theories and Method*, edited by Randy Duncan and Matthew J. Smith. London: Routledge, 2011, 71–83.

Levitt, Deborah. *The Animatic Apparatus: Animation, Vitality, and the Futures of the Image*. Alresford: Zero/John Hunt Publishing, 2018.

Lunning, Frenchy. "Cosplay: A Surexistence of Multiple Modes of Fictional Existences," *Mechademia*, 15.1 (2022): 54–78.

Lunning, Frenchy. *Cosplay: The Fictional Mode of Existence*. Minneapolis: University of Minnesota Press, 2022.

Mazur, Dan, and Alexander Danner. "The International Graphic Novel." In *The Cambridge Companion to the Graphic Novel*, edited by Stephen E. Tabachnick. Cambridge: Cambridge University Press, 2017, 58–79.

Mikkonen, Kai. *The Narratology of Comic Art*. London: Routledge, 2017.

Miller, Ann. "Formalist Theory: Academics." In *The Secret Origins of Comics Studies*, edited by Matthew J. Smith and Randy Duncan. London: Routledge, 2017, 150–63.

Miyake, Toshio. "Towards Critical Occidentalism Studies: Re-inventing the 'West' and 'Japan' in Mangaesque Popular Cultures." In *Contemporary Japan: Challenges for a World Economic Power in Transition*, edited by Paolo Calvetti and Marcella Mariotti. Venezia: Edizioni Ca'Foscari, 2015, 93–116. Open Access.

Miyake, Toshio. "History as Sexualized Parody: Love and Sex Between Nations in Axis Powers Hetalia." In *Rewriting History in Manga: Stories for the Nation*, edited by Nissim Otmazgin and Rebecca Suter. New York: Palgrave Macmillan, 2016, 151–74.

Miyamoto, Hirohito. "Yureteyuku rinkaku: jidō yomimono tōseika niokeru kodomomuke monogatari manga no 'emonogatari'ka nitsuite," *Shirayuri Joshi Daigaku Jidō Bunka Kenkyū Sentā Ronbunshū*, 20 (2017): 1–30. Open Access.

Morikawa, Kaichiro. "Otaku/Geek," transl. Dennis Washburn, *Review of Japanese Culture and Society*, 25 (2013): 56–66.

Morishita, Tatsu. *Sutorī manga towa nani ka: Tezuka Osamu to sengo manga no "monogatari."* Tokyo: Seidosha, 2021.

Natsume, Fusanosuke. "Where is Tezuka? A Theory of Manga Expression," transl. Matthew Young, *Mechademia*, 8 (2013): 89–107.

Natsume, Fusanosuke. "Panel Configurations in Shōjo Manga," *U.S.-Japan Women's Journal: A Journal for the International Exchange of Gender Studies*, transl. Jon Holt and Teppei Fukuda 58 (2020): 58–74.

Natsume, Fusanosuke. "The Construction of Panels (Koma) in Manga," transl. Jon Holt and Teppei Fukuda. *ImageTexT: Interdisciplinary Comics Studies*, 12.2 (2020): 1–21. Open Access.

Natsume, Fusanosuke. "The Power of Onomatopoeia in Manga," transl. and introduced by Jon Holt and Teppei Fukuda. *Japanese Language and Literature*, 56. 1 (2022): 157–84. Open Access.

Nishimura, Tomohiro. *Nihon no animēshon wa ikani shite seiritsu shita no ka.* Tokyo: Shinwasha, 2018.

Onoda Power, Natsu. *God of Comics: Osamu Tezuka and the Creation of Post-World War II Manga.* Jackson: University Press of Mississippi, 2009.

Orbaugh, Sharalyn. "Manga and Anime." In *The Routledge Companion to Science Fiction*, edited by Mark Bould, Andrew M. Butler et al. London/New York: Routledge, 2009, 112–22.

Orbaugh, Sharalyn. "Compulsorily Queer: Coercion as a Political Tool in Queer Manga," *Orientaliska Studier*, 156 (2018): 176–89. Open Access.

Ōtsuka, Eiji. "Disarming Atom: Tezuka Osamu's Manga at War and Peace," transl. Thomas LaMarre. *Mechademia*, 3 (2008): 111–25.

Ōtsuka, Eiji. "World and Variation: The Reproduction and Consumption of Narrative," transl. Marc Steinberg. *Mechademia*, 5 (2010): 99–116.

Pruvost-Delaspre, Marie. *Aux Sources de l'Animation Japonaise: Le Studio Tōei Dōga (1956–1972).* Rennes: Presses Universitaires de Rennes, 2021.

Rendell, James, and Rayna Denison. "Special Edition Editorial: Introducing Studio Ghibli." *East Asian Journal of Popular Culture*, 4.1 (2018): 5–14.

Rivera Rusca, Renato. "The Changing Role of Manga and Anime Magazines in the Japanese Animation Industry." In *Manga Vision: Cultural and Communicative Perspectives*, edited by Sarah Pasfield-Neofitou and Cathy Sell. Clayton: Monash University Publishing, 2016, 52–69.

Robertson, Wes. "Orthography, Foreigners, and Fluency: Indexicality and Script Selection in Japanese Manga," *Japanese Studies*, 35.2 (2015): 205–22.

Roquet, Paul. "Solo Animation in Japan: Empathy for the Drawn Body." In *The Routledge Handbook of Japanese Cinema*, edited by Joan Bernardi and Shota Ogawa. New York: Routledge, 2020, 141–52.

Ruddell, Caroline. "From the 'Cinematic' to the 'Anime-ic': Issues of Movement in Anime," *Animation: An Interdisciplinary Journal*, 3.2 (2008): 113–28.

Ruh, Brian. *Stray Dog of Anime: The Films of Mamoru Oshii.* New York: Palgrave Macmillan, 2004.

Ruh, Brian. "Conceptualizing Anime and the Database Fantasyscape," *Mechademia*, 9 (2014): 164–75.

Sabin, Roger. "Barefoot Gen in the US and UK: Activist Comic, Graphic Novel, Manga." In *Reading Manga: Local and Global Perceptions of Japanese Comics*, edited by Jaqueline Berndt and Steffi Richter. Leipzig: Leipzig University Press, 2006, 39–58.

Sano, Akiko, and Hikari Hori, eds. *Sensō to Nihon anime: Momotarō umi no shinpei to wa nan datta no ka.* Tokyo: Seikyūsha, 2022.

Santiago Iglesias, and José Andrés. "The Anime Connection. Early Euro-Japanese Co-Productions and the Animesque: Form, Rhythm, Design," *Arts*, 7.4, 59 (2018): no pag.

Schmitz-Emans, Monika. "Graphic Narrative as World Literature." In *From Comic Strips to Graphic Novels: Contributions to the Theory and History of Graphic Narrative* (Narratologia series), edited by Daniel Stein and Jan-Noël Thon. Berlin: de Gruyter, 2013, 385–406.

Seaton, Philip, Akiko Sugawa-Shimada et al. *Contents Tourism in Japan: "Sacred Sites" of Popular Culture.* New York: Cambria Press, 2017.

Shamoon, Deborah. "Films on Paper: Cinematic Narrative in Gekiga." In *Mangatopia: Essays on Manga and Anime in the Modern World*, edited by Timothy Perper and Martha Cornog Santa Barbara: Libraries Unlimited, 2011, 21–36.

Shamoon, Deborah. "The Superflat Space of Japanese Anime." In *Asian Cinema and the Use of Space: Interdisciplinary Perspectives*, edited by Edna Lim and Lilian Chee. New York: Routledge, 2015, 93–108.

Shimizu, Isao, *Yokoi Fukujirō: sengo manga no toppu rannā.* Kyoto: Rinsen Shoten, 2007.

Shimizu, Isao, *Yonkoma manga: Hokusai kara 'moe' e.* Tokyo: Iwanami Shinsho, 2009.

Smith, Christopher. "The Text inside IUs: Text on Screen and the Intertexual Self in Bakemonogatari," *Word & Image*, 38.3 (2022): 254–64.

Smith, Christopher. "'Otoko no ko deshou?' Evangelion and Queer Masculinity," *The Electronic Journal of Contemporary Japanese Studies (EJCJS)*, 23.1 (2023): 1–11. Open Access.

Steinberg, Marc. "Inventing Intervals: The Digital Image in *Metropolis* and *Gankutsuō*," *Mechademia*, 7 (2012): 3–22.

Stewart, Ronald. "Post 3–11 Japanese Political Cartooning with a Satirical Bite: Non-Newspaper Cartoons and Their Potential," *Kritika Kultura*, 26 (2016): 179–221. Open Access.

Suan, Stevie. "Consuming Production: Anime's Layers of Transnationality and Dispersal of Agency as Seen in Shirobako and Sakuga-Fan Practices," *Arts*, 7.27 (2018): 1–19. Open Access.

Suan, Stevie. *Anime's Identity: Performativity and Form beyond Japan.* Minneapolis: University of Minnesota Press, 2021.

Sugawa-Shimada, Akiko. "Grotesque Cuteness of Shōjo Representations of Goth-Loli in Japanese Contemporary TV Anime." In *Japanese Animation*, edited by Masao Yokota. Jackson: University Press of Mississippi, 2013, 199–222.

Sugawa-Shimada, Akiko. "Playing with Militarism in/with Arpeggio and Kantai Collection: Effects of shōjo Images in War-related Contents Tourism in Japan," *Journal of War & Culture Studies*, 12:1 (2018): 53–66.

Sugawa-Shimada, Akiko. "Emerging '2.5-dimensional' Culture: Character-oriented Cultural Practices and 'Community of Preferences' as a New Fandom in Japan and Beyond," *Mechademia: Second Arc*, 12.2 (2020): 124–39.

Sugawa-Shimada, Akiko. "The 2.5-Dimensional Theatre as a Communication Site: Non-site-Specific Theatre Tourism." In *Contents Tourism and Pop Culture Fandom: Transnational Tourist Experiences*, edited by Takayoshi Yamamura and Philip Seaton. Bristol: Channel View Publications, 2020, 128–43.

Suter, Rebecca. "Japan/America, Man/Woman: Gender and Identity Politics in Adrian Tomine and Yoshihiro Tatsumi," *Paradoxa*, 22 (2010): 101–22.

Suzuki, Masao, ed. *Manga o "miru" to iu taiken: furēmu, kyarakutā, modan āto*. Tokyo: Suiseisha, 2014.

Suzuki, Shige (CJ). "Tatsumi Yoshihiro's Gekiga and the Global Sixties: Aspiring for an Alternative." In *Manga's Cultural Crossroads*, edited by Jaqueline Berndt and Bettina Kümmerling-Meibauer. London: Routledge, 2013, 50–64.

Suzuki, Shige (CJ). "*Yōkai* Monsters at Large: Mizuki Shigeru's Manga, Transmedia Practices, and (Lack of) Cultural Politics," *International Journal of Communication*, 13 (2019): 2199–15.

Suzuki, Shige (CJ). "Teaching Manga: A Medium-Specific Approach beyond Area Studies." In *Manga!: Visual Pop-Culture in Art Education*, edited by Masami Toku and Hiromi Tsuchiya Dollase. Viseu, Portugal: InSEA Publications, 2020, 208–17. Open Access.

Swale, Alistair. *Anime Aesthetics*. New York: Palgrave Macmillian, 2012.

Swale, Alistair. "Memory and Forgetting: Examining the Treatment of Traumatic Historical Memory in Grave of the Fireflies and The Wind Rises," *Japan Forum*, 29.4, (2017): 518–36.

Theisen, Nicholas A. "The 'Origins' of Manga, or the Problem of Manga Historiography," *International Journal of Comic Art*, 15.2 (2013): 546–58.

Theisen, Nicholas A. "Do You Read a Comics?." In *On the Edge of the Panel: Essays on Comics Criticism*, edited by Esther Claudio and Julio Cañero. Cambridge: Cambridge Scholars Publishing, 2015, 74–91.

Thomas, Jolyon Baraka. *Drawing on Tradition: Manga, Anime, and Religion in Contemporary Japan*. Honolulu: Hawai'i University Press, 2012.

Thomas, Jolyon Baraka. "Spirit/Medium: Critically Examining the Relationship between Animism and Animation." In *Spirits and Animism in Contemporary Japan: The Invisible Empire*, edited by Fabio Rambelli. London: Bloomsbury, 2019, 157–70.

Thompson, Kimberly D. "The Cross-Cultural Power of Yuri: Riyoko Ikeda's Queer Rhetorics of Place-Making in The Rose of Versailles," *Peitho Journal*, 19.2 (2017): 301–20. Open Access.

Unser-Schutz, Giancarla. "Language as the Visual: Exploring the Intersection of Linguistic and Visual Language in Manga," *Image[&]Narrative*, 12.1 (2011): 1–22. Open Access.

Unser-Schutz, Giancarla. "Redefining Shōjo and Shōnen Manga through Language Patterns." In *Shōjo across Media: Exploring "Girl" Practices in Contemporary Japan*, edited by Jaqueline Berndt, Kazumi Nagaike, and Fusami Ogi. Cham, Switzerland: Palgrave Macmillan, 2019, 49–82.

Ursini, Francesco-Alessio. "David Bowie's Influence on JoJo's Bizarre Adventure," *The Comics Grid: Journal of Comics Scholarship*, 7.1, 1 (2017): no pag.

Ursini, Francesco-Alessio. "Themes, Focalization and the Flow of Information: The Case of Shingeki no Kyojin," *The Comics Grid: Journal of Comics Scholarship*, 7.1, 2 (2017): 1–19. Open Access.

Ursini, Francesco-Alessio. "Social Control and Closed Worlds in Manga and Anime." In *Volume 5 Dialogues between Media*, edited by Paul Ferstl. Berlin, Boston: de Gruyter, 2021, 47–58. Open Access.

Warren-Crow, Heather. *Girlhood and the Plastic Image*. Hanover, New Hampshire: Dartmouth College Press, 2014.

Warren-Crow, Heather. "Vocational AestheticsVoice, Affect, and Energy in *Puella Magi Madoka Magica* (2011)," *Mechademia*, 13.1 (2021): 83–101.

Watanabe, Daisuke. "Shokkakusei kara miru manga to eizō no genzai: gamen no hen'yō o meguru shikiron." In *Manga/Manga/Manga: jinbungaku no shiten kara*, edited by Osamu Maekawa and Hiroshi Okumura. Kobe: Kobe Daigaku Shuppankai, 2020, 261–78.

Watz, Matteo. *Animétudes: Research on the Art and History of Animation*. https://animetudes.com/about-2/

Wei Lewis, Diane. "Shiage and Women's Flexible Labor in the Japanese Animation Industry," *Feminist Media Histories*, 4.1 (2018): 115–41.

Woo, Benjamin. "What Kind of Studies is Comics Studies?" In *The Oxford Handbook of Comic Book Studies*, edited by Frederik Luis Aldama. Oxford: Oxford University Press, 2019, 2–15.

Yamamoto, Tadahiro. "Two-Page Spreads and War: Battlefield Representations and Individual Expressions in *Norakuro*," *Dōjin Journal: An Academic Journal on Popular Cultures Established by the International Research Center for Japanese Studies*, 1 (2020): 1–13. Open Access.

Yonemura, Miyuki, and Akiko Sugawa. *Jiburi animēshon no bunkagaku: Takahata Isao, Miyazaki Hayao no hyōgen o saguru*. Tokyo: 7gatsusha, 2022.

Yonezawa, Yoshihiro. *Sengo gyagu manga-shi*. Tokyo: Chikuma shobō, 2009.

Yoshimi, Tomofumi. *Animēshon no sōzōryoku: moji tekusuto, eizō tekusuto no sōzōryoku no ōkan*. Tokyo: Kazama shobō, 2015.

Zahlten, Alexander. "*Doraemon* and *Your Name* in China: The complicated business of mediatized memory in East Asia," *Screen*, 60.2 (2019): 311–21.

Zahlten, Alexander. "Media Models of 'Amateur' Film and Manga." In *The Routledge Handbook of Japanese Cinema*, edited by Joanne Bernardi and Shota T. Ogawa. New York: Routledge, 2020, 153–69.

INDEX

Cambridge Companions to ...

AUTHORS

TOPICS

Printed in the USA
CPSIA information can be obtained
at www.ICGtesting.com
LVHW011656061224
798333LV00007B/131

* 9 7 8 1 0 0 9 0 0 9 9 8 0 *